Adventures Through the Bible

by Ivy M. Moody

revised by Dana Eynon

The pupil's workbook is included in this teacher's book.

STANDARD PUBLISHING
Cincinnati, Ohio 3234

CONTENTS

Library of Congress Catalog Card No. 79-91955

ISBN: 0-87239-378-X

Division of STANDEX INTERNATIONAL Corporation
Printed in U.S.A.

Part One

Adventures With Bible People

Boys and girls like adventure stories. But how many of them think of the Bible as a book of adventures? What could be more exciting than a sea opening up and allowing a whole nation of people to escape from their enemies; or the walls of a city crashing down after this nation marched around it and blew on their trumpets? Where could you read of more thrilling events than a man commanding the sun to stand still, or a man cast into a den of lions and not being harmed? These are just a few of the exciting adventures in this series. All the adventures are true, and happened to real people!

This series consists of thirteen stories of Bible people: eleven from the Old Testament, and two from the New Testament. The eleven Old Testament men are found in the list of "sixteen leading characters of the Old Testament," taken from *Training for Service: A Survey of the Bible:*

Adam	Moses*	Saul*	Isaiah
Noah*	Joshua*	David*	Jeremiah
Abraham*	Gideon*	Solomon	Daniel*
Joseph*	Samuel*	Elijah*	Nehemiah

*Lessons 1-11 of this series.

Seven of these eleven Old Testament "worthies" are mentioned by name, and one is referred to by an event, in Hebrews 11, the "Faith Chapter" of the Bible:

Noah	Joseph	(Joshua)	Samuel
Abraham	Moses	Gideon	David

A reference also is made in Hebrews 11 to the "prophets," and this would include Elijah and Daniel.

Knowledge of these key characters of the Old Testament will make possible for your pupils a deeper understanding of the Christian faith.

Lesson 12 centers on the key character of the entire Bible, Jesus Christ. Everything in the Old Testament points forward to Christ, and everything in the New Testament points back to Him. In subsequent lessons in Parts Two, Three, and Four of this volume, many teachings of Jesus will be considered. Lesson 12 presents just an outline of His life, but future lessons will deal with particular events and teachings of Jesus.

Lesson 13 presents the second-greatest character of the New Testament: the apostle Paul. Again, just a brief sketch of his life can be given in one lesson. In other sections of the book, other events from Paul's life will be included.

The lessons on the lives of these thirteen Bible people were chosen not only with the thought of adventure in mind, but with the emphasis on faith and obedience to God. Lessons from each life can be applied to the lives of both pupils and teachers.

When preparing the lessons, read not only the Scriptures given in each lesson, but read the background passages. Have a clear picture in mind of the incidents. Tell these stories in an interesting manner, so that the pupils will be able to visualize the action taking place in the narrative. Use the charts and other chalkboard presentations that are suggested in the lessons, particularly Lessons 7 and 11.

Present these lessons with enthusiasm. Point out that it takes courage to be a Christian.

Make a Flip Chart or Storybook

Here's an idea for a visual you can make to help connect the thirteen stories of this series. You will need fourteen sheets of colorful construction paper or posterboard. Punch holes in the sides for a storybook, or on top for a flip chart. Fasten the sheets with metal or plastic rings. On the cover sheet letter the title, "Adventures With Bible People." If at all possible, obtain Bible art pictures of the main characters in this series: Noah, Abraham, Joseph, Moses, Joshua, Gideon, Samuel, Saul, David, Elijah, Daniel, Jesus, and Paul. (Old visual packets, lesson books, take-home papers, or other sources could provide these pictures.) Paste the pictures in order, and letter the name of the Bible character in large black letters, using a felt-tipped pen.

Introduce each story with the flip chart or storybook. Use the pictures and the review questions to help pupils have an overview of the Bible's history. The message of the Scriptures will be more meaningful when they understand the sequence of events.

Lesson 1

Adventures With Noah

Genesis 5—9

Introduction to Lesson

Place the list below on the chalkboard. Have pupils look in Genesis 5 and find the names of ten Bible people, beginning with the first man who lived on earth.

1. A __ __ __
2. S __ __ __
3. E __ __ __
4. C __ __ __ __ __ __
5. M __ __ __ __ __ __ __ __ __ __ __
6. J __ __ __ __
7. E __ __ __ __
8. M __ __ __ __ __ __ __ __ __ __ __
9. L __ __ __ __ __
10. N __ __ __

The Bible Lesson

The Bible is filled with stories of people—real people—who lived on this earth thousands of years ago. The first people were Adam and Eve, and they had two sons: Cain and Abel. In a jealous rage one day, Cain killed Abel, and his punishment was to be a wanderer. Another son was born to Adam and Eve. From this son, Seth, we can trace the family all the way down to a man named Noah. (Point to the list on the chalkboard, and have students name the ten men.)

During the years from Adam to Noah, the people on earth became more and more sinful. Instead of living as God wanted them to live, nearly all of the people were continually thinking and doing evil things. God decided to destroy the earth with a great flood.

One man and his family were living the way God wanted them to live. One day God said to this man, "The earth is filled with sin and violence. I am going to destroy all the rest of the people. I want you to build a boat, exactly according to the directions I will give you, and you and your family will be saved from the great flood."

This was the beginning of Noah's great adventure! Noah followed all of God's directions very carefully. He made the boat, called an ark, of gopher wood. He made it the size God told him, three stories high. He put in the window and door, and made the rooms as God said. He covered the ark inside and out with a tar-like substance to make it waterproof.

No doubt the people who lived in the area near Noah wondered about this large boat that was being constructed far from any ocean, sea, or lake. They probably were even more puzzled when Noah began gathering the animals and food on board the ark, as God had commanded.

(Note: You may want to explain these facts to your students: The ark was **not** a small boat! It was 300 cubits long—about 450′, 50 cubits wide—75′, and 30 cubits high—45′. The ark would have held the same amount that 522 standard-size railroad stock cars would hold today. One stock car holds 240 sheep, so there was room for 125,280 sheep-size animals. God told Noah to take two of each unclean animal, and seven of each clean animal on board the ark. Since there are 17,600 species, this would make a total of 45,000 animals. There was plenty of room on the ark for the people, the animals, and the food supplies.)

Finally the day came when God told Noah and his family to go into the ark. God himself shut the door. Then the rains began! The ark began to float as the water kept rising. Rain fell for forty days and forty nights, until the highest mountaintops were covered. Still the ark continued to float. Noah, his wife, his three sons, and their wives, all the animals, and the food supplies were safe and dry.

But all the other people and all the other animals were covered by the flood and drowned. The waters stayed on the earth for 150 days. Then the ark came to rest on top of Mount Ararat. The waters started going down gradually, until after several months the ground was dry. God told Noah and his family to leave the ark. The animals also were brought out.

Imagine stepping out onto a fresh, clean earth, with all the wickedness gone! Noah built an altar and offered sacrifices to the Lord, to show how grateful he was that he and his family had been saved. The Lord promised that never again would a flood destroy the earth. God put the rainbow in the sky as a sign that He would keep His promise.

The Lesson Applied

Why was Noah, out of all the people on earth, chosen to be saved from the flood? Let's read these verses from God's Word:

Genesis 6:8 ("Noah found grace in the eyes of the Lord.")

Genesis 6:9 ("Noah was a just man and perfect in his generations, and Noah walked with God.")

Genesis 6:22 ("Thus did Noah according to all that God commanded him, so did he.")

Genesis 7:1 ("Thee have I seen righteous before me in this generation.")

In the midst of a wicked world, Noah did what was right. He obeyed God's commands.

Today we live in a world where there is much evil surrounding us. But we, like Noah, can do what is right, and obey God's commands.

Questions for Discussion: Where is it harder for you to be obedient to God's commands: at home, at school, at church, on the playground, at a friend's house?

If a group of your friends decided to do something that was wrong, what would you do?

The Lesson Quiz

1. Why did God destroy all living creatures—except for eight people and a few of each kind of animal?

   (Because sin and violence filled the earth.)
2. Why was Noah chosen to be saved?

   (Noah was righteous before God; he obeyed God's commands.)
3. Describe the ark that God commanded Noah to build.

   (300 x 50 x 30 cubits, made of gopher wood, three stories high, a window, door, rooms, covered inside and out with tar-like substance.)
4. Who were the eight people in the ark?

   (Noah, his wife, his three sons, their wives.)
5. How many animals went into the ark?

   (Two of each unclean, seven of each clean animal.)
6. How long did it rain?

   (Forty days and forty nights.)
7. How deep was the water on the earth?

   (It covered the highest mountaintops.)
8. Where did the ark come to rest?

   (On top of Mount Ararat.)
9. What did Noah do when he came from the ark to the dry ground?

   (He built an altar and offered sacrifices to God.)
10. What promise did God make, with the rainbow as a sign?

    (He would never again destroy the earth with a flood.)

Additional Lesson Activities

1. Noah in the New Testament

Find what is said about Noah in Matthew 24:37-39; Luke 17:26, 27; Hebrews 11:7; 1 Peter 3:20; 2 Peter 2:5.

2. A "Rainbow Wall Hanging"

Each pupil will need these materials: 2 dowel sticks, 6″ long, ⅛-¼″ in diameter; 1 sheet of heavy paper or piece of cloth, 5½ x 8½″; 7 pieces of yarn, each about 7″ long, in these colors: violet, indigo, blue, green, yellow, orange, red; piece of cord or string 12″ long; felt-tip pen; glue. On the top half of the sheet of paper or piece of cloth, glue the yarn pieces in the form of a rainbow. On the bottom half, letter the message, "God Keeps His Promises." Glue the dowel sticks to the top and bottom of the paper or cloth. Tie the cord to the ends of the top dowel stick to form a hanger.

Workbook Page

Page 3 of the pupil's Workbook contains two puzzles: "Noah's Logbook" and "God Keeps His Promises." Answers are on pages 62-64 of the Workbook.

Memory Verse: James 1:22

"But be ye doers of the word, and not hearers only, deceiving your own selves."

Lesson 2

Adventures With Abraham

Genesis 11—25

Introduction to Lesson

(Place this message and the Scripture references on the chalkboard. Let pupils find the answers.)

Unscramble these names of Abraham's relatives:

His father: R E T H A
His brothers: N O R A H, H A R N A
His wife: A I R A S
His nephew: O L T
(See Genesis 11:26, 30, 31.)

The Bible Lesson

After the great flood, Noah and his wife, and his sons (Ham, Shem, and Japheth) and their wives were the only people on earth. Children were born to Noah's sons, and, as years passed, there were many people on the earth again.

In Ur, a city of the Chaldees, lived a descendant of Shem named Terah. He and his son, Abram, his daughter-in-law, Sarai, and his grandson, Lot, had obeyed God's command and had traveled to Haran. There they lived until Terah died. Then God spoke to Abram and told him to take his wife and nephew to a new land, one that God would choose. This was a test of Abram's faith.

God made a wonderful promise to Abram: "I will make a great nation of your family, and I will bless you and make your name great. All families of the earth will be blessed because of you." Abram took Sarai and Lot, and gathered up all of his flocks and herds and servants. They journeyed toward the land of Canaan.

The Lord spoke to Abram again, and said that he would give this land to Abram's descendants. Abram built an altar to the Lord, and then continued his journey.

Finally Abram settled in Canaan. Lot and his family chose to live in the city of Sodom, on the plain of Jordan. One day a messenger came to Abram, and said, "I have just escaped from an attack by several kings on our city of Sodom. Your nephew, his family, and everything he owns have been taken captive!"

Abram wasted no time. He took 318 of his servants, gave them weapons, and chased the enemy armies to the city of Dan. During the night, Abram and his servants battled them and were victorious. They brought back Lot and all the other people who had been captured, and all of their possessions. The king of Sodom was grateful and wanted Abram to keep the goods and just return the people. But Abram refused to take a reward. Later, the Lord came in a vision to Abram and said, "Fear not, Abram: I am thy shield, and thy exceeding great reward."

God changed Abram's name to Abraham, and Sarai's name to Sarah. He promised that a son would be born to them. Then the Lord told Abraham that He was going to destroy Sodom and another city, Gomorrah, because of their sin. Abraham asked the Lord, "Will You destroy the good people along with the bad? Suppose there are fifty good people in the city. Will You spare it?" The Lord said that He would spare the city for fifty righteous people.

Then Abraham asked if God would spare Sodom if there were forty-five, then forty, then thirty, then twenty, then ten. The Lord said He would not destroy Sodom if ten righteous people could be found. But there were not ten righteous people in that city!

Once again Lot and his family had to be rescued from danger, this time by messengers from the Lord. Then the Lord rained fire and brimstone out of Heaven upon those two wicked cities.

Abraham got up early in the morning, and went to the place where he had talked to the Lord. As he looked toward the cities, all he could see was smoke. The two cities were completely destroyed. God keeps His promises.

Abraham was a very wealthy man. He had many herds of cattle, flocks of sheep, and much silver and gold. But one thing made Abraham very sad. God had promised that he would be the father of a great nation, but no child had been born to him and Sarah. Many years had gone by and now they were old. Then God sent them word that a son would be born to them the next year! He was to be called Isaac.

God keeps His promises, and just as He had said, a son was born to Abraham and Sarah. Another test of Abraham's faith came when Isaac was a young boy. God asked him to give him up! (Read aloud Genesis 22:1-19.) Because Abraham believed God, he was obedient. He passed the test that God gave him.

When Isaac grew up, Abraham wanted him to find a wife among his own people. He sent a trusted servant back to Haran. The servant found Rebekah and brought her to Isaac. They were married, and twin sons, Jacob and Esau, were born to them.

The same promise that God made to Abraham was made to Isaac, and then to Jacob: "All the families of the earth will be blessed by your family." Jacob's sons became the fathers of the twelve tribes of Israel, and from one of those tribes, Judah, the Savior came!

The Lesson Applied

Abraham's life was filled with adventure for the Lord, from the time God called him at the age of seventy-five, until he died at the age of 175. Abraham lived a life of faith, trusting God to lead him. (Read Hebrews 11:8-10, 17-19.) Each event in his life was a test of his faith. Events in your life can test your faith, too! Do you have faith to let God lead your life? Remember, "Without faith it is impossible to please him."

Questions for Discussion: Why was Abraham chosen to be the "father of a great nation"? What was Abraham's greatest test of faith? How can we prepare while we're young for tests of faith in the future?

The Lesson Quiz

1. Where was Abram when God called him and told him to go to a new land?
   (First in Ur, then in Haran.)
2. What family members went with Abram to Canaan?
   (Sarai and Lot.)
3. What promise did God make to Abram?
   (He would be the father of a great nation, receive a special land, and be a blessing to all nations.)
4. How did Abram show his concern for Lot?
   (He rescued him when enemies captured him, and asked the Lord to spare his city.)
5. What new names were Abram and Sarai given?
   (Abraham and Sarah.)
6. What name did they give to their son?
   (Isaac.)
7. How did God test Abraham's faith?
   (Asked him to leave his home and go to a new land; asked him to sacrifice his only son.)
8. Where did Abraham find a wife for Isaac?
   (In Haran, where his people lived.)
9. What was the name of Isaac's wife?
   (Rebekah.)
10. What were the names of the twin sons born to Isaac and Rebekah?
    (Jacob and Esau.)

Additional Lesson Activities

1. Map of Abraham's Journey

Let pupils draw a very simple map showing Ur, Haran, and Canaan. Draw a line showing Abraham's journey.

2. The "Faith Chapter" Research

Let pupils read Hebrews 11 and find the names of the "heroes of the faith." Let them note especially the verses about Abraham.

Workbook Page

"People and Places," a crossword puzzle on page 4, reviews Abraham's life. The exercise, "Abraham's Diary," is designed to encourage pupils to put the Bible's facts in their own words.

Memory Verse: Hebrews 11:6

"But without faith it is impossible to please him: for he that cometh to God must believe that he is, and that he is a rewarder of them that diligently seek him."

Lesson 3

Adventures With Joseph

Genesis 37; 39—46

Introduction to Lesson

(Put the following assignment on the chalkboard and let pupils complete it.)

Find the names of Jacob's twelve sons in Genesis 35:23-26:

1. R _ _ _ _ N	7. J _ _ _ _ H
2. S _ _ _ _ N	8. B _ _ _ _ _ _ _ N
3. L _ _ I	9. D _ N
4. J _ _ _ H	10. N _ _ _ _ _ _ I
5. I _ _ _ _ _ _ _ R	11. G _ D
6. Z _ _ _ _ _ _ N	12. A _ _ _ R

The Bible Lesson

Suppose you had ten older brothers and every one of them was jealous of you! You would have a very unhappy home life, to be sure. And you would understand how Joseph felt.

Joseph lived in the land of Canaan, with his father Jacob, and his eleven brothers. Benjamin was the youngest boy in the family.

Joseph was his father's favorite child. Jacob gave Joseph an ornamented, long-sleeved, ankle-length coat. Favorite sons often were identified by such special garments. The brothers hated Joseph all the more because he had received the coat. Worse still, Joseph had dreams that were special. In one of these dreams there were sheaves in a field that bowed down to another sheaf. When Joseph told his brothers the dream, they said, "Do you think that means we will bow down to you?" Just the thought of bowing to him made them angry all the more.

One day Jacob said to Joseph, "Your brothers are taking care of the sheep at Shechem. I want you to go and see how they are getting along." Joseph put on his new coat and started out to find his brothers. When they saw him coming, they said, "Look who is coming to see us—our brother, the dreamer! Let's kill him and put him in a pit." But Reuben, one of the brothers said, "Let's not kill him. Let's just put him in the pit." So when Joseph arrived, they took off his new coat and threw him into the pit.

A while later some merchants came by with their caravan. One of the brothers said, "Let's sell Joseph, and then we will be rid of him forever." They took him out of the pit and sold him for twenty pieces of silver. They put goat's blood on Joseph's coat and took it home to their father. They told him wild beasts had killed Joseph.

In the meantime the caravan reached Egypt, and there Joseph was sold to be a slave in the house of Potiphar, an officer of Pharaoh, the ruler of Egypt. Soon Joseph was made overseer of Potiphar's house, and he managed things very well. But because Joseph refused to do something wrong, he was falsely accused and was thrown into prison.

One day Pharaoh had two dreams. In the first he saw seven thin cows eat up seven fat cows. In the second dream he saw seven thin ears of corn devour seven fat ears. He was troubled and called for all the wise scholars and magicians of the kingdom, but none could tell him what the dreams meant.

Finally, the king's cupbearer, who had once been in prison, remembered Joseph and told Pharaoh about him. Joseph was brought before the ruler, who told again the dreams that were troubling him.

"There are going to be seven years when many crops will be grown," Joseph explained. "Then there will be seven years of famine." Pharaoh believed Joseph and decided to plan for the years ahead. He gave Joseph the job of storing food during the seven years of plenty. In this job, Joseph had great authority, second only to the king.

All too soon the seven years of plenty were over and the famine began. Joseph's family in Canaan began running out of food. When Jacob heard that grain could be bought in Egypt, he sent his ten oldest sons to buy some.

As soon as Joseph saw his brothers, he knew them right away, but they did not know him. Joseph decided to test them. He called them spies and put them in prison for three days. "I will let you have grain," he said, "but you must promise to bring your youngest brother, Benjamin, so I will know the things you have said are true." Secretly, he put the money for the grain back into their bags.

Jacob did not want to let Benjamin return to Egypt with the brothers, but the famine grew worse and they were out of food.

When they reached Egypt, Joseph invited them to dinner and seated them according to their ages. How surprised they were! Joseph then had a silver cup put in Benjamin's bag of grain. When the brothers were on their way home, Joseph sent a servant to find the cup and order them all back. "I shall make Benjamin my slave for stealing that cup," Joseph said.

Judah came near and said, "Please do not keep him. Our father would be very sad. Keep me as your slave instead."

Joseph knew that his brothers had repented of the things they had done to him and he told them who he was. What a reunion they had! The brothers were happy that Joseph held no grudges.

Joseph asked them to go home and get their father and their families. "Come down to Egypt to live," he said, and they did. They settled in the area called Goshen.

The Lesson Applied

Joseph could have been bitter against his brothers because of their evil deed. Instead he forgave them, and told them that God caused good to come from the evil they did. (See Genesis 45:4-8; 50:19, 20.)

It is one thing to mumble, "I forgive you," when someone asks for forgiveness. But real forgiveness is something far more than a polite expression.

Jesus says that we shouldn't wait until the one who has done wrong comes to us. We should go to him!

Questions for Discussion: What about the expression often heard, "I'll forgive him, but I'll never forget it"? How does God forgive us?

The Lesson Quiz

1. How many brothers did Joseph have?
   (Eleven.)
2. What was the youngest brother's name?
   (Benjamin.)
3. What did Joseph's father give him?
   (A special coat, the kind given to favorite sons.)
4. What did Joseph's brothers call him?
   (A dreamer.)
5. Where did the brothers put Joseph?
   (In a pit.)
6. For how much did they sell him?
   (Twenty pieces of silver.)
7. Who bought him from the Ishmaelites?
   (Potiphar, an officer in Pharaoh's army.)
8. What did Joseph finally become?
   (A ruler, second only to the king.)
9. Why did Joseph's brothers come to Egypt?
   (To buy grain.)
10. Did Joseph forgive his brothers?
    (Yes. He invited them to come to Egypt to live.)

Additional Lesson Activities

1. Memory Verse Mix-up

Using Romans 8:28, make two sets of words. Put each word on a separate strip of paper. Letter one set in red and one in blue. Divide the class into two groups. Put all the strips of paper upside down on a table. Let the two teams find their colors, and then put the verse in order. See which team can complete the verse first. Be sure to discuss the meaning of the verse, and how it applies to Joseph's life. Decide how it applies to our lives today.

2. Map Study

Find the land of Goshen on the map of Bible lands. This is the section of Egypt in which Jacob and his sons settled. Why was this area chosen? (See Genesis 46:28-34.)

Workbook Page

"Joseph's Journal" on page 5 will help pupils see how God was with Joseph and brought good out of evil. The acrostic, "Work the Puzzle," reviews facts from Joseph's story.

Memory Verse: Romans 8:28

"And we know that all things work together for good to them that love God, to them who are the called according to his purpose."

Lesson 4

Adventures With Moses

Exodus 14—20; 32; 35—40

Introduction to Lesson

(Let pupils find the names of these people in Moses' early life, before he led the Israelites from Egypt. Put the assignment on the chalkboard.)

1. The king of Egypt (Exodus 1:22).
2. The tribe from which Moses came (Exodus 2:1).
3. Moses' father, mother, brother, and sister (Numbers 26:59).
4. Moses' wife (Exodus 2:21).
5. Moses' son (Exodus 2:22).
6. Moses' father-in-law (Exodus 3:1).

The Bible Lesson

The family of Jacob lived in Egypt many years, and they had become a great nation. Then a new ruler made slaves of them. When they asked God to help them, God chose Moses to lead them out of Egypt to the land He had promised to Abraham, Isaac, Jacob, and their children after them. God had to send many plagues before the Pharaoh let them go.

When the Israelites reached the Red Sea, the Egyptian king sent his army to bring them back. But God parted the Red Sea and His people crossed on dry land. When the Egyptians followed, He caused the water to come together again.

As the last of their Egyptian enemies disappeared under the waters of the Red Sea, the children of Israel must have stood there in amazement. Then, led by Moses, they lifted up their voices in a great song of praise to the living God who had so wonderfully rescued them. Afterward, they turned their faces in the direction of their new home, Canaan.

Many things were to happen to them before they would reach the end of their journey. The first trouble was that of thirst. They began to lose faith in God, thinking they were surely going to die. But God had not forsaken His people. He told Moses to put a branch from a certain tree into the bitter water, and when he did so it became sweet. Later on, when there was no water at all, God caused water to flow out of a rock.

The next trouble came when the Israelites ran out of food. Again they complained and again God had patience with them. That night while the people were asleep God performed another miracle. When the Israelites awoke, the ground was covered with small round seeds that tasted something like wafers made with honey. This seedlike food the Israelites called "manna," which means, "What is it?" God also sent hundreds of small birds called quail which the people caught and ate with the manna. Every day thereafter, as long as the people were in the desert (forty years), God sent this food for them to eat. There was just one exception to this rule—God did not give manna on the Sabbath days. The people had to gather twice as much as usual on the sixth day of each week so they would have food for the Sabbath day.

After three months of traveling, this great company of people finally came to a high mountain called Sinai. God told Moses that the people were to make camp in this desert area. Since the Israelites had grown to be a great nation of people, God knew they would need laws to follow.

He called Moses up on the mountain. With a great earthquake shaking the ground, and with thunder and lightning crashing over the mountaintop, God wrote laws on tablets of stone. He told Moses to take them down and read them to the people. Part of these laws were called the Ten Commandments. When Moses read them to the people, they said, "All that God has said we will do."

When Moses went back on up the mountain to talk with God, the people began to complain once again. "Moses has been up in that mountain for forty days," they said, "and we don't know what has happened to him. Maybe he isn't coming back." Then the people did something very sinful. They gathered up all their golden rings and jewelry, and made a golden calf so that they could worship it!

Soon after this Moses came down from the mountain with the tablets of stone. When he saw the people dancing around the idol, he became very angry. He dashed the stone tablets to the ground and broke them into pieces. Then he made the people grind up the idol into powder, put the powder in water, and drink it.

Moses then had to make another trip up the mountain to receive another set of the laws from God. With these laws God gave plans for the building of a place of worship, called a tabernacle. This was like a tent. It was made in such a way that in just a few hours it could be taken down, packed up neatly, and carried by the people as they continued their journey through the desert.

When the Israelites came closer to the promised land of Canaan, Moses sent twelve spies, one from each tribe, to look over the land. Only two of them, Joshua and Caleb, said the land could be taken. The rest were afraid because the people were strong and their cities well fortified.

For this lack of faith, the Israelites were punished by spending forty years wandering in the wilderness. These years were filled with adventures, many of which were not pleasant.

The Lesson Applied

Moses faithfully carried out the work that God had chosen him to do. (Read Hebrews 11:23-29.) Moses believed God's promises, and his actions showed his faith.

If the Israelites had had more faith, they would have been more patient, knowing that God would take care of them. By that time they should have known that God would keep all of His promises. He would lead them, feed them, and protect them. Instead they doubted and complained, and God had to punish them.

Do you ever sit down at the table and complain about the food saying, "I don't like this," or "I don't want any of that," or "Why can't I have something different?" We should be very thankful for whatever is set before us, remembering that every good gift comes from God. Suppose that God suddenly should cause the sun to stop shining or say that there would be no more rain. Nothing would grow! Then we would wish we had some of the things we thought we did not like so well.

Questions for Discussion: Did the Israelites have more reason to doubt God than we? Why or why not?

The Lesson Quiz

1. Who led God's people out of Egypt?
   (Moses.)
2. How did they cross the Red Sea?
   (God parted the waters and they crossed on dry land.)
3. What complaints did the people begin to make?
   (About lack of water and food.)
4. How did God feed the Israelites while they were wandering through the wilderness?
   (He sent them manna and quails to eat.)
5. How did they get water to drink?
   (God sweetened the bitter water, and, where there was no water, He caused it to flow out of a rock.)
6. What great thing happened on Mount Sinai?
   (God gave Moses the law written on tablets of stone.)
7. What did the people do while Moses was up on the mountain?
   (They made a golden calf and worshiped it.)
8. What was the name of the place of worship the people had while they were in the desert?
   (Tabernacle.)
9. How long did the Israelites wander?
   (Forty years.)
10. Why did God cause them to wander?
    (Because of their lack of faith in Him.)

Additional Lesson Activities

1. Journey of the Exodus

On a map of Egypt and Canaan, trace the journey of the children of Israel. Follow this route: Rameses, Succoth, Etham, Marah, Elim, Rephidim, Mount Sinai, Kadesh-barnea, Wilderness, Ezion-gaber, Elath, Mount Hor, Mount Nebo.

2. Ten Commandments

Let pupils copy the Ten Commandments from Exodus 20:1-17 on pieces of gray construction paper, cut in the shape of the stone tablets.

Workbook Page

Page 6 contains "Moses' Memoirs" and "Matching Questions."

Memory Verse: Philippians 4:19

"But my God shall supply all your need according to his riches in glory by Christ Jesus."

Lesson 5

Adventures With Joshua

Joshua 1:1—10:14

Introduction to Lesson

Have a review quiz, using the ten questions from each of the four previous lessons. Let some of the pupils take turns asking the questions, or divide into teams. The captain of team one asks the questions for team two.

The Bible Lesson

Although the Israelites were now in sight of their new home across the Jordan River, they still had a number of thrilling adventures ahead of them. First of all a great sadness came into their lives. Moses, who had led them so faithfully all these years, was taken away from them. God called him up a high mountain, named Nebo, from which point he could see all over the land of Canaan. In Deuteronomy 34 we are told that Moses died, and that God himself buried him up on the mountain.

The Israelites had to have a new leader. God had chosen the man, and Moses had trained him. This man's name was Joshua. He was a brave and good soldier who trusted God.

Then came the first of their new adventures. Joshua lined up all the people on the banks of the Jordan River, and at his command the priests, carrying the ark of the covenant, went forward into the river. As their feet touched the water, it parted and made a dry path for them. All the people followed until they were on the other side of the river. At last they had reached their new home!

But other adventures followed soon afterward. This land of Canaan had been given to Abraham, Isaac, and Jacob many, many years before—long before Jacob had gone down to Egypt to live. But heathen people, called Canaanites, lived in the land and called it their own. The Israelites had to conquer these people in order to get the land back.

The first city that had to be captured was Jericho. It was a large city, completely surrounded by high, thick walls and strong heavy gates. No doubt the Israelites were a little discouraged when they saw how well this city was protected. But God had plans for capturing the city, and He told those plans to Joshua.

All the people of Israel were to march around the city once every day for six days. The people inside the city must have been very curious about this great multitude that marched around the city and then went back to their camp. Perhaps they were fearful, too. According to God's plan, the Israelites were to do something different on the seventh day. Instead of marching around the city once, they marched around it seven times. On the seventh time around, some shouted with all their might and others blew on trumpets. The great walls of the city began to tremble and shake, and finally came crashing down. The Israelites were able to capture the city.

In capturing the city, however, a man by the name of Achan disobeyed God. The Israelites had been forbidden by God to take anything for themselves from the city. Achan did not obey this command. He took some gold, some silver, and some clothing and hid them in his tent.

Soon after the capture of Jericho, Joshua sent a part of his army to capture another and smaller city named Ai. But instead of being victorious, the Israelites were beaten and driven back to their camp. Joshua could not understand why God had not helped them win the battle, so he prayed to God about it. God told him that the reason his army had been defeated was because one of the Israelites had disobeyed orders and had stolen certain things from the city of Jericho.

The next day Joshua called the people before him and told them why they had been defeated at Ai. Then God showed Joshua who the guilty man was. Soldiers were sent to Achan's tent, and there they found the stolen goods. Achan's punishment was to be stoned to death. Joshua then sent his army again to the city of Ai. This time God was with them. They captured the city without any trouble.

Another thrilling adventure happened soon after this. The people of the city of Gibeon became very worried when they saw the Israelites capturing the country. They talked with Joshua and tricked him into making peace with them, so that he could not take their city. This caused the kings of five other cities to attack Gibeon. When Joshua heard what was happening, he marched his armies to rescue Gibeon. In order that he might have enough time to defeat his enemies, Joshua commanded the sun to stand still for several hours. Of course, it was God who really caused the day to be longer, so that Joshua could win the battle.

Many other battles were fought, and exciting things happened under the leadership of Joshua. When almost all this land had been conquered, it was divided among the twelve tribes of Israel. Just before Joshua died, at the age of 110, he reminded the people to serve the Lord faithfully. When he called them together he said, "Choose you this day whom you will serve. As for me and my house, we will serve the Lord!"

The Lesson Applied

Joshua was a brave and trusting follower of God. He was a strong leader and required that his people obey God's rules. Not all of the people listened to Joshua. One man's disobedience caused the Israelites to be defeated in a battle.

Perhaps you sometimes wonder why there are so many rules that you have to obey, and why God has rules for us to follow. These rules or laws are not given to make us unhappy but they are given for our good. When we disobey these rules, we not only hurt ourselves, but many times we hurt other people. Let us be good soldiers of Christ and obey all His orders!

Questions for Discussion: If we disobey, does it always hurt someone else? What would happen if there were no more laws in our land?

The Lesson Quiz

1. Did Moses lead God's people into the promised land?
   (No, he died before they entered Canaan.)
2. Where did God bury Moses?
   (Mount Nebo.)
3. What new leader took Moses' place?
   (Joshua.)
4. What happened when the Israelites started to cross the Jordan River?
   (The waters parted and they went over on dry ground.)
5. What was the first city of Canaan captured by the Israelites?
   (Jericho.)
6. How was the city captured?
   (The Israelites marched around once a day for six days, and seven times on the seventh day. Then they shouted, and blew trumpets, and the walls came down.)
7. Why were the Israelites defeated the first time they tried to capture the city of Ai?
   (A man named Achan had disobeyed God. He had stolen some things from the city of Jericho.)
8. What city made peace with Joshua?
   (Gibeon.)
9. How did Joshua get extra hours in the day to win a battle?
   (He commanded the sun to stand still.)
10. After the Israelites conquered the land, how was it divided?
    (Among the twelve tribes of Israel, with each tribe receiving a certain territory.)

Additional Lesson Activities

1. The Witness Stone

Explain that when Joshua, near the end of his days, called the people together, he urged them to serve the Lord. When the people agreed, Joshua took a great stone and set it up under an oak tree by the tabernacle. The stone was to be a witness.

Provide stones and black felt-tipped pens. Let pupils letter the words of the people: "The Lord our God will we serve, and his voice will we obey" (Joshua 24:24).

2. The Twelve Tribes

Let pupils look up the names of the twelve tribes and find their territories on a map. Explain that Joseph's two sons were heads of tribes, and that Levi's tribe (priests) received only cities.

Workbook Page

Page 7 contains "Choose the Right Words" and "Joshua's Records." Check the answers on pages 62-64 of the Workbook.

Memory Verse: 2 Timothy 2:3

"Thou therefore endure hardness, as a good soldier of Jesus Christ."

Lesson 6

Adventures With Gideon

Judges 6—8

Introduction to Lesson

Interviews

(Let five pupils who are familiar with the first five Bible stories pretend to be Noah, Abraham, Joseph, Moses, and Joshua. One pupil can be the interviewer. The following questions may be used with each Bible character.)

1. What events took place in your life because you obeyed God?
2. What time in your life required the most faith?
3. What can you tell us about the promises that God makes?

The Bible Lesson

When the Israelites came into Canaan to possess it, God told them they were to drive all of the Canaanites out of the land. God had a reason for wanting this done. He knew that if any of those heathen people remained in the land, the Israelites would begin mixing with them and worshiping their idols. And that is exactly what happened. When they did this, God would allow some of their enemies to capture and rule them. When they repented and cried to God for help, God would send men, called judges, who would deliver them from their enemies.

Among the enemies of Israel were the Midianites. For seven years these enemies made life miserable for the Israelites. Because the Midianites stole their food, they almost starved. Then the Israelites realized they had sinned against God, and they were being punished for their sins. They prayed to God, and He heard their prayers.

God sent an angel to a young man, whose name was Gideon, and the angel told him that God had chosen him to deliver the Israelites out of the hand of the Midianites. At first, Gideon said that he was not able to do such a great thing. But when he knew that God was with him and would give him strength and wisdom, he started out to do what God wanted him to do.

Gideon had built an altar to the Lord after the angel left him. That same night the Lord told Gideon to take a bullock and tear down the altar to the heathen god Baal. Joash, Gideon's father, had built the altar, but Gideon obeyed the Lord's command. He took ten servants with him and destroyed the altar during the night. He was afraid to do it during the day because he feared his father and the other men of the city. Gideon then built an altar to the Lord in the same place, and offered the bullock as a sacrifice, as God had commanded.

The next morning when the people saw that Baal's altar was cast down, they asked angrily, "Who has done this?"

"Gideon, the son of Joash, is the one!" came the answer.

The men of the city said to Joash, "Bring out your son! He must die because he tore down Baal's altar."

Joash answered, "If Baal is a god, let him plead for himself!" From that day on, Gideon was known also by the name of Jerubbaal, because he had thrown down Baal's altar.

When the Midianites heard what Gideon had done, they gathered their armies together and made ready to attack the Israelites. Gideon also called the armies of Israel together. They numbered 32,000 men. But God spoke to Gideon and told him there were too many men in his army. God knew that when they won the battle, the Israelites would think they had won because of their own strength, and would not give Him the glory. Gideon told the soldiers that if any of them were afraid to go into battle they should drop out of the army. One by one 22,000 went back to their tents. God said this was still too many, so 9,700 were taken out, leaving only 300 men to fight against an army of thousands!

Gideon had a plan. That night he divided his little army into three groups of one hundred each. A trumpet, a water pitcher, and a torch were given to each man. Then Gideon's men surrounded their enemies—one group going to the left, another group going to the right, and the third group going in back of the Midianites, who were asleep in their camp. At a signal every soldier broke his pitcher, waved his flaming torch over his head, and blew his trumpet. When the

Midianites awoke, heard the noise, and saw the torches all around them, they thought there were thousands of Israelites attacking them. They began to run! The Israelites pursued them and drove them out of their land.

After more battles in which Gideon was victorious, the men of Israel wanted him to be their king. They said to him, "Be the ruler over us, then your son, and your son's son."

But Gideon said to them, "I will not rule over you, neither shall my son rule over you. The Lord shall rule over you."

Because of Gideon's leadership, the enemies of Israel were defeated, and the land had peace for forty years, until Gideon's death.

The Lesson Applied

God knows that people are tempted to boast about things they accomplish. That is why He would not let Gideon take his entire army into battle. When the Israelites were victorious with only 300 men, they knew it was really God who had won the battle.

In the New Testament we read, "Blessed are the meek: for they shall inherit the earth" (Matthew 5:5). A meek person is one who does not boast about the things he does. When we work for Christ, we should do that work well, and we should be pleased with what we do. But we should not go around boasting about what good workers we are. We should always remember that unless God gives us health and strength and minds we could not do any of these things for Him.

Questions for Discussion: Is it easy to have the kind of faith Gideon showed? Would you have been afraid if you had been Gideon or one of his men? Is it easy to have the attitude of meekness that Gideon had? In what ways did he show it? How can we show meekness?

The Lesson Quiz

1. What were the leaders of the Israelites called when the people settled in the land of Canaan?

(Judges.)

2. What judge did God choose to overcome the Midianites?

(Gideon, the son of Joash.)

3. What was the first thing God told Gideon to do?

(Break down the altar of Baal, and build an altar to God.)

4. What new name was Gideon given, after he broke down Baal's altar?

(Jerubbaal.)

5. How many soldiers did Gideon take to battle the Midianites?

(300.)

6. How did Gideon's small army fool the enemy?

(The men were divided into three groups. Each man had a pitcher, torch, and trumpet. While the Midianites slept, the Israelites surrounded them, breaking the pitchers, waving the torches, and blowing the trumpets.)

7. What did the Midianites do?

(They thought a great army was coming down on them, and they ran. The Israelites pursued.)

8. What did the people of Israel ask of Gideon after the Midianites were defeated?

(To be their ruler.)

9. What did Gideon reply?

("The Lord shall rule over you.")

10. How many years of peace did the Israelites have while Gideon lived?

(Forty years.)

Additional Lesson Activities

1. Scripture Hunt

Call out these Scripture references on the subjects of pride, humility, and meekness. The pupil who finds the verse first stands and reads it aloud.

1. Proverbs 11:2
2. 1 John 2:16
3. Proverbs 8:13
4. Daniel 4:37
5. Proverbs 13:10
6. Proverbs 16:18
7. Psalm 69:32
8. Matthew 18:4
9. Ephesians 4:2
10. James 4:10

2. Find the Judges

Find the names of other judges who led the people of Israel. Look in the book of Judges.

Workbook Page

On page 8 you'll find "Gideon's Account" and "Acrostic Puzzle."

Memory Verse: Ephesians 6:10

"Finally, my brethren, be strong in the Lord, and in the power of his might."

Lesson 7

Adventures With Samuel

1 Samuel 1—7

NAMES	FAITH	OBEDIENCE	COURAGE	HUMILITY	FORGIVENESS
1. Noah					
2. Abraham					
3. Joseph					
4. Moses					
5. Joshua					
6. Gideon					

Introduction to Lesson

(Place the above chart and assignment on the chalkboard. Let pupils fill in the check marks.)

Assignment: From what you have learned about these Bible leaders, check the good characteristics they showed in their lives. Tell how they showed these traits.

The Bible Lesson

When Joshua led the children of Israel into the promised land of Canaan, many of the enemy tribes were driven out. However, there still were some left when the Israelites moved in and divided up the territory. Those who were left caused Israel a lot of trouble. One group, the Midianites, finally were forced out by Gideon, a judge of Israel for forty years. After Gideon died, eight more judges ruled, from Abimelech who judged three years, to Samson who judged twenty years. While Samson was judge, the Philistines were the greatest enemies of Israel. God gave Samson great strength, and he was victorious over the Philistines many times. After Samson's death, there was no leader for a time.

God really was the ruler of Israel, but the people did not follow Him faithfully. Every person did what he thought was right, instead of obeying the laws God had given them.

Finally a man named Eli served as a judge and also as the priest of Israel. When he was old, a very young boy named Samuel was brought to the tabernacle to be his helper. Samuel listened carefully to God, and delivered His messages, no matter how unpleasant. As Samuel grew up, the Lord was with him. The whole nation, from the city of Dan in the north to Beer-sheba in the south, knew that Samuel was to be a prophet of the Lord. After Eli's death, Samuel became the judge of Israel. He traveled a circuit of about 200 miles, to the cities of Bethel, Gilgal, and Mizpeh, and then back to his home in Ramah.

During Samuel's days the Philistines were troubling the Israelites again. In one battle the Philistines carried off the ark of the covenant. The ark was very important to Israel—it contained the stones on which the Ten Commandments were written, the rod that Moses' brother, Aaron, had carried, and some of the "manna" that the Lord had provided for the Israelites in the wilderness.

The ark caused problems for the Philistines wherever it was taken, bringing destruction and death. They decided to return it, and carried it to a place where the Israelites could pick it up. The ark was taken to the house of a certain man and left there for twenty years. The people of Israel were sad because the ark was not back where it belonged, in the tabernacle.

Samuel called the people together and spoke to them. "If you will return to the Lord, and put away your false gods, and serve only the Lord, He will deliver you from the Philistines." The people listened to Samuel. They stopped worshiping the idols, and served the Lord only.

Samuel said to them, "Gather all the people in Mizpeh, and I will pray to the Lord for you." When the Philistines heard that the Israelites were gathering, their leaders went up, too.

The Israelites begged Samuel to pray for them. "Ask Him to save us from the Philistines!" they cried.

Samuel offered a burnt offering to the Lord,

and then he prayed for Israel. The Lord heard him, and sent a great thunder on the Philistines, and they were defeated. The army of Israel chased them and killed them. Samuel took a stone and set it up as a reminder of the victory. He called the name of it "Ebenezer," meaning, "Here the Lord helped us."

The Philistines never came again into the land of Israel all the days of Samuel. The cities that the Philistines had taken away were given back to Israel.

Samuel continued to judge Israel all the rest of his days. He helped the nation during a difficult time, and faithfully served the Lord. He was the last of the fifteen judges who ruled in Israel. But Samuel's work was not yet finished. God had chosen him to anoint the first two kings of Israel!

The Lesson Applied

Even as a child, Samuel listened to the Lord's voice and obeyed Him. As he grew up, the people listened to him as he gave God's messages. When the people were troubled, they went to Samuel and said, "Pray for us!"

Perhaps you have thought, "It doesn't matter what I do when I'm young. When I grow up I'll pay more attention to God's Word." But it does matter what you do now! In the Old Testament we read: "Even a child is known by his doings, whether his work be pure, and whether it be right" (Proverbs 20:11).

If you obey God now, you will grow strong in the Lord. You may become a great leader for God when you are a grown-up. People will know that you are faithful to God by your daily life. They will ask you to pray for them and lead them.

Questions for Discussion: How can you hear the Word of the Lord today? How will people know if you are growing strong in the Lord?

The Lesson Quiz

1. What elderly judge and priest did Samuel help as a young child?
   (Eli.)
2. What enemy nation was troubling the people of Israel at this time?
   (The Philistines.)
3. What did the Philistines take from Israel?
   (The ark of the covenant.)
4. Why did the Philistines want to get rid of the ark?
   (It caused death and destruction wherever it was taken.)
5. When the ark was returned to Israel, how long was it kept in a certain man's house, rather than in the tabernacle?
   (Twenty years.)
6. What did Samuel tell the people they must do to be delivered from the Philistines?
   (Put away all idols and worship only God.)
7. What happened when Samuel prayed and offered a burnt sacrifice?
   (God sent a great thunder on the Philistines, and they were defeated.)
8. What did Samuel call the stones that he set up as a reminder of this victory?
   (Ebenezer, meaning "Here the Lord helped us.")
9. How long did the Philistines stay away from Israel?
   (All the days of Samuel.)
10. To what cities did Samuel travel as a judge?
    (Bethel, Gilgal, and Mizpeh.)

Additional Lesson Activities

1. Map Study

On a map of Bible lands, find the following cities: Shiloh, Dan, Beer-sheba, Bethel, Gilgal, Mizpeh, Ramah.

2. The Example of Samuel's Life

Let pupils read 1 Samuel 12:1-5, and tell the things that showed his good character and example.

Workbook Page

The "Crossword Puzzle" on page 9 reviews the facts from Samuel's life. For "Samuel's Story," pupils are to write the Scripture passage in their own words. Encourage creativity! Suggest that some may wish to write a playlet about this event. Class members may enjoy presenting the story from Samuel's childhood for a younger group at church.

Memory Verse: 2 Peter 1:21

"For the prophecy came not in old time by the will of man: but holy men of God spake as they were moved by the Holy Ghost."

Lesson 8

Adventures With Saul

1 Samuel 8—15

Introduction to Lesson

The people of Israel said they wanted a king to rule over them. Samuel told them what would happen if they had a king. Have students read 1 Samuel 8:11-18 and make a list on the chalkboard of all the things a king would require.

Their sons would be taken for these duties:

Their daughters would be taken for these duties:

Their servants would be:

Their animals would be:

Their fields, vineyards, and oliveyards would be given to:

The Bible Lesson

Samuel, the last of the judges of Israel, was getting old. He appointed his sons to be judges, but the people were not pleased. Samuel's sons did not follow the teachings of God as their father did. The elders of Israel came to Samuel and said, "You are getting old, and your sons do not follow your example. We want a king to rule over us, like the other nations have."

Samuel was very unhappy because of their request, and he prayed to the Lord. The Lord answered, "Samuel, the people are not rejecting you, they are rejecting Me. They have forgotten Me and have served other gods. Now, I want you to listen to them, but tell them exactly what will happen if they are ruled by a king."

Samuel told the people all that the Lord had said. "These are the things that will happen," Samuel said. (Review the information gathered in the section "Introduction to Lesson.")

Even though Samuel told them these things, the people said, "We want a king! We want to be like all the other nations!"

Samuel prayed to the Lord again, and told Him what the people said. The Lord answered, "Let them have a king!"

In the tribe of Benjamin there was a mighty man of power named Kish. He had a son named Saul—tall, handsome, a very special young man. Samuel was told by the Lord to anoint him king. At first Saul was reluctant. "I'm from the tribe of Benjamin, the smallest tribe. My family is not the most important in the tribe. Why have I been chosen for this great task?"

Samuel assured Saul that he was the Lord's choice, and anointed him king of Israel. Some time later, Samuel called all the people together, and proclaimed Saul as their king. All the people shouted, "God save the king!"

Samuel solemnly told all the people, "If you will fear the Lord, and serve Him, and obey His voice, and not rebel against His commandments, the Lord will be with you and your king. But if you do not obey the Lord, He will turn against you."

At first King Saul obeyed the commandments of the Lord. But after ruling for two years, he began to change. Before he was chosen king, he was a humble man. Now he began to boast about his victories in battle. "Let the people hear that Saul was victorious over the Philistines!" he told the heralds to announce as they blew their trumpets throughout the land.

Next, King Saul took over the duties of the priest. Instead of waiting until Samuel arrived to offer the burnt offering before the battle with the Philistines, Saul did it himself. When Samuel came, Saul excused himself saying, "I waited seven days, but you didn't keep the appointment, and the Philistines are gathering."

"You have done a foolish thing," Samuel told Saul. "You have not kept the commandment of God. Because of this, your sons will not rule as kings. Another man will be chosen to rule."

Many battles followed, with Moab, Edom, the Philistines, and other enemy nations. One such group was the Amalekites. God sent Samuel to King Saul with this message: "Go and destroy the Amalekites. Don't save even an animal alive!"

King Saul went to battle against this enemy as God commanded. But he took the king prisoner and saved the best of the sheep and other animals.

God spoke to Samuel and told him what Saul

had done. Very sadly, the next morning, Samuel went to see Saul. "I have obeyed the command of the Lord!" reported Saul.

Samuel said, "Then why do I hear the sounds of sheep and cattle?"

King Saul quickly placed the blame on others. "The people saved out the best animals to sacrifice them to the Lord," he said.

Samuel said to Saul, "When you did not think you were important, God made you the head of the tribes of Israel. Now you have disobeyed Him. It is better to obey than to offer sacrifices. You have been rebellious and stubborn. Because you have rejected God's Word, He has rejected you from being king."

Then a sad event took place. "The Spirit of the Lord departed from Saul, and an evil spirit from the Lord troubled him" (1 Samuel 16:14). Jealousy, anger, and revenge possessed him, and Saul's forty-year reign ended when he took his own life with a sword, rather than be taken captive by the Philistines. But long before Saul's death, God already had chosen the one who was to be the next king.

The Lesson Applied

Saul started out as a humble young man, one who did not boast and one who obeyed God's commands. But as he got more powerful, he forgot about the Lord and His commands. He began doing what he wanted to do. Finally he even lied to God's prophet and blamed others for his disobedience. Instead of being "little in his own sight," he became very important in his own sight. This can happen to us!

Questions for Discussion: What lessons can we learn from Saul's life? How can we keep from being boastful, disobedient, and untruthful?

The Lesson Quiz

1. What kind of a ruler did the people of Israel want, instead of a judge?
   (A king, like the nations around them.)
2. Who was chosen by the Lord as Israel's first king?
   (Saul, son of Kish.)
3. From what tribe did Saul come?
   (Benjamin, the smallest tribe.)
4. What kind of a person was Saul when he became king?
   (Humble and obedient.)
5. How did Saul begin to change in his behavior?
   (He began to boast and to disobey God's commands.)
6. What enemy nation was Saul sent to destroy?
   (The Amalekites.)
7. How did he disobey God's command?
   (He saved the king and the best of the animals.)
8. What did Samuel say when Saul told him the people had saved the animals for sacrifice?
   ("To obey is better than sacrifice.")
9. What punishment was given to Saul?
   (His sons would not rule Israel.)
10. How did Saul's life end?
    (He took his own life with a sword, rather than be taken by the enemy.)

Additional Lesson Activities

1. Character Traits

Put these words on strips of cardboard: RESPECTFUL, HUMBLE, OBEDIENT, BOASTFUL, TRUTHFUL, DISOBEDIENT, LYING, PROUD, STUBBORN, JEALOUS, REBELLIOUS, ANGRY.

On the chalkboard letter these headings:

AT THE BEGINNING OF SAUL'S REIGN, HE WAS. . . .

AT THE END OF SAUL'S REIGN, HE WAS. . . .

Have pupils attach the character traits to the chalkboard with tape or Plasti-Tak.

2. Make Mottoes

Let pupils copy the memory verse, 1 Peter 5:6, on 5 x 7 pieces of lightweight cardboard. Provide different colors of felt-tipped pens and other drawing materials.

Workbook Page

Two puzzles on page 10 review the Bible facts: "Saul's Family History" and "Find the MiSSing Letters." (Work all puzzles before class. Check your answers with those on pages 62-64 of the Workbook.)

Memory Verse: 1 Peter 5:6

"Humble yourselves therefore under the mighty hand of God, that he may exalt you in due time."

Lesson 9

Adventures With David

1 Samuel 16—19; 2 Samuel 1; 2; 5:1-10

Introduction to Lesson

Who Am I? Quiz

Call out each clue. As soon as a pupil thinks he knows the answer, he stands. After all three clues have been given, ask the first pupil who stood to give the answer. If he misses, ask the second, etc.

1. My brothers were jealous of me.
   I became a great ruler.
   I was my father's favorite son.
   (Joseph)
2. God chose me to be a leader.
   I led a large group of people.
   I received the Commandments on two stone tablets.
   (Moses)
3. God chose me to lead His people after Moses died.
   I was a soldier.
   I helped my people conquer the land of promise.
   (Joshua)
4. I was a farmer and a soldier.
   I had a small army.
   We drove the Philistines from our land with trumpets, torches, and pitchers.
   (Gideon)
5. God called me when I was a young child.
   I was the last judge of Israel.
   I anointed Saul, the first king of Israel.
   (Samuel)

The Bible Lesson

The life of David, the shepherd boy who became a king, is full of adventures from the time he was anointed by Samuel until the end of his long life. Few men have lived through so many thrilling adventures.

When Saul, the first king of Israel, disobeyed God, God told Samuel to go to Bethlehem to the home of Jesse, a man from the tribe of Judah. There Samuel was to anoint the new king. From among Jesse's eight sons, David, the youngest, was chosen as the future king.

David knew how to play the harp and sing. When King Saul became ill with a strange sickness, a servant suggested that David be called to the palace to play for the king. King Saul was pleased with David and his music.

One of David's best-known adventures is the story of his battle with the giant, Goliath. (If you have time, review this event from 1 Samuel 17:4-51.) Because he was so brave, David was made an officer in King Saul's army. David helped Saul to win other battles with the Philistines.

But when the people began to show their love for David, King Saul became very jealous of him. One day, when David was playing his harp before the king, the king threw his spear at David, but he missed him (1 Samuel 18:10, 11). When David had to flee for his life, he was helped by Jonathan, the king's own son. Jonathan and David had become good friends and had grown to love each other dearly (1 Samuel 18:1-4).

Saul sent messengers to watch David's house one night. They were to kill him in the morning. David's wife, Michal, who was the daughter of King Saul, knew about the plot and told David. Michal helped David escape by letting him down through a window. Then she took a pillow, laid it on the bed, and covered it with a cloth to make it look as though someone was asleep in the bed. Saul's messengers came into the house the next morning, because Saul ordered them to bring David to him to be killed. They found the pillow in the bed, but David was gone (1 Samuel 19:11-18).

King Saul called together his armies and went after David. David and the men who were with him fled from one place to another. Once David could have killed Saul, when Saul came into a cave where David was hiding, but David did not wish to harm the king whom God had anointed (1 Samuel 24:1-11).

Another time David took the king's spear and water jug while he was asleep, to show the king that he had the opportunity to kill him but did not do it. King Saul hated David even more.

One day, as the armies of Saul were fighting against the Philistines, Saul was wounded. To keep from being captured and killed by the enemy, Saul killed himself by falling on his own sword.

Sometime later David became king over all the land of Israel. David ruled in the city of Hebron for seven and a half years. Jerusalem was held by people called the Jebusites. In this fortified city the inhabitants thought there was no way that David and his men could conquer them. But David overcame the stronghold, and made it the capital of his nation. He called it the "city of David." Later, David brought the ark of the Lord to Jerusalem, and placed it in the tabernacle.

The Bible tells us that David "grew great, and the Lord God of hosts was with him" (2 Samuel 5:10). David was king of Israel for forty years. Although he did some things that were wrong, he was sorry and God forgave him.

One thing David wanted to do very much was to build a temple for God. But God would not allow him to do it because he had been a soldier, a man of blood. However, David made the plans and began to gather some of the materials. When his son, Solomon, became king, he built the beautiful temple.

David wrote many beautiful songs that we find in the Bible. We call them psalms.

The Lesson Applied

When Samuel went to find the new king, God said, "Man looketh on the outward appearance, but the Lord looketh on the heart." Another time David was called "a man after mine (God's) own heart."

David made mistakes, but he was sorry and asked God to forgive him. One of his psalms shows this: "For I acknowledge my transgressions: and my sin is ever before me. Against thee, thee only, have I sinned . . . Create in me a clean heart, O God" (Psalm 51:3, 4, 10).

When God looks at you, does He see a heart that is pure, or does He see one that is filled with all kinds of sin? God was able to use David to accomplish a great work because David loved God with all his heart. We can see how much greater he was than Saul, whose heart was filled with jealousy and hate. Wouldn't it be much better to be a David than a Saul?

Questions for Discussion: Why do you suppose God chose David as king? What were some of the differences between Saul and David as far as outward appearance? What were some of the differences between Saul and David in the ways that matter with God—the heart?

The Lesson Quiz

1. Who was David's father?
   (Jesse, of the tribe of Judah.)
2. Who anointed David to be king of Israel?
   (Samuel.)
3. For what king did David play the harp?
   (Saul.)
4. Why was Saul jealous of David?
   (David had done many brave things, and the people loved and praised him.)
5. What son of Saul became David's close friend?
   (Jonathan.)
6. Why did David have to run away?
   (Saul tried repeatedly to kill him.)
7. When did David become king?
   (After Saul killed himself.)
8. What city did David conquer and make his capital?
   (Jerusalem, the "city of David.")
9. Why didn't God allow David to build the temple?
   (He had been a soldier, a man of blood.)
10. How long did David rule Israel?
    (Forty years.)

Additional Lesson Activities

1. A King's Kindness

Read how David showed kindness to a grandson of King Saul in 2 Samuel 9.

2. Praise and Prayer

Look through the book of Psalms, and find all those called "A Psalm of David," or "A Prayer of David." Choose three or four of them and read the ways that David praised the Lord, and prayed for His help.

Workbook Page

"Choose the Names" on page 11 reviews some of King David's history. "David's Psalms" encourages students to express themselves on Psalm 23. You will want to provide three or four different translations of the Bible for this exercise.

Memory Verse: 1 John 1:9

"If we confess our sins, he is faithful and just to forgive us our sins, and to cleanse us from all unrighteousness."

Lesson 10

Adventures With Elijah

1 Kings 17—22; 2 Kings 1, 2

Introduction to Lesson

To review the history of God's people from the creation to the time of the kings, use the questions under "The Lesson Quiz" for the past nine lessons. Divide the students into two teams for the quiz.

The Bible Lesson

The first three kings of Israel, Saul, David, and Solomon, each ruled for forty years. After King Solomon, the nation divided into a northern and southern kingdom. There followed many kings who ruled God's chosen people. A few kings were good, but most of them were bad. One of the worst of these was Ahab. He was married to a wicked woman named Jezebel, who worshiped idols. She led Ahab and many of the Israelites to worship idols, too.

God chose good men to speak to the people and give His message. We call these men "prophets." One of the bravest of these prophets was Elijah. He not only preached to the people, but he told the king himself that he was doing wrong. Because of the king's sins and the sins of the people, God was not going to let any rain fall for three years. This meant that there would be a famine in the land.

When King Ahab heard the message of the prophet, he became very angry and wanted to kill Elijah. God told Elijah to escape to the brook called Cherith, near the Jordan. There he could drink water from the brook, but he had nothing to eat. God supplied food for Elijah by sending ravens with pieces of food in their beaks. They came down low enough for Elijah to reach out and take the food.

Finally the brook dried up; but God had not forgotten Elijah. He called to him and said, "Leave the brook and go to the home of a certain widow. There you will find food." When Elijah reached the widow's home, he found that she and her son were almost starving because of the famine. They had only enough meal and oil to make a small cake. When that was gone, there would be nothing left for them to eat. Elijah asked the woman to make the cake and give it to him. This seemed to be a very strange request, but the woman made the cake and gave it to Elijah. He told her to go and make another cake for herself and her son. She knew she had used all the meal and oil, but when she looked into the barrel and cruse she found enough meal and oil to make another cake. A miracle had happened! Until it rained, the meal and oil never were used up!

At the end of the three years God sent Elijah back to King Ahab. "Gather all of the Israelites together on Mount Carmel, and bring the four hundred and fifty false prophets of Baal," Elijah told the king. Baal was the name of the idol that many of the people worshiped.

When all the people had gathered at Mount Carmel, Elijah told the false prophets he wanted them to build an altar to Baal, put the wood and sacrifice on it, and pray to their god to send down fire and burn up their sacrifice. Elijah said that he would do the same thing, but that he would pray to the God of Heaven. "This will prove which one is the true God," said Elijah.

The prophets of Baal built their altar, placed the sacrifice upon it, and then began to pray to their god. But nothing happened. Elijah began to taunt them and said, "Your god must be asleep, or perhaps he has gone on a journey. You had better pray louder." So they shouted louder, and danced around the altar, cutting themselves with knives until the blood gushed from their bodies. They prayed until evening, but still nothing happened.

Elijah called the people around him and began building his altar of stones. When it was finished, he placed the wood on the altar, and then the sacrifice. "Now bring four barrels of water and pour it on the sacrifice," he commanded. He had them do this three times, until the sacrifice and wood were soaked, and the trench around the altar was full of water. Very quietly Elijah looked up to Heaven and said, "O Lord, hear my prayer so that all Israel may know that you are God." Then fire fell from Heaven and burned up the sacrifice, the wood, the stones, and dried up all the water! Nothing was left.

When the people saw this, they fell on their faces and worshiped God, realizing that the gods of wood and stone that they had been worshiping had no power.

Later God sent rain again on the land, and the famine ended. Only the true God has such power!

Many other adventures took place in the life of Elijah as he traveled through the land, giving God's message to the people. At last it was time for him to leave the earth and go to Heaven. Even this was a thrilling adventure, for God sent a fiery chariot from Heaven, and a whirlwind caught up Elijah and took him away!

The Lesson Applied

There were many times in the life of Elijah when he felt that he was the only one who stood with God. The people seemed so wicked and the king and queen were so wicked, that Elijah was sad and dejected. But God knew that there were other people in Israel who loved Him and would not worship false gods. And Elijah found the faith and courage to go ahead with the work that God had given him.

Sometimes we feel that we are alone. We see people doing sinful things, and we forget that there are still people willing to serve God. But suppose you were the only one trying to do right. God can show the world great things with just one person who has the courage to stand up for Him. Just as God needed Elijah, He needs you.

Questions for Discussion: Would you be willing to stand for God if you were the only Christian left in the world? If you were the only Christian in your class at school? If you were the only Christian in your family?

The Lesson Quiz

1. What do we call the men whom God chose to give His messages to the people of Israel?
   (Prophets.)
2. What prophet lived in the days of Ahab, the king?
   (Elijah.)
3. What did Elijah tell the king God was going to do to punish the people for their sins?
   (He was going to keep rain from falling for three years.)
4. How was Elijah fed by the brook Cherith?
   (God sent ravens with food.)
5. Where did Elijah go when he left the brook?
   (To the home of a poor widow and her son.)
6. What happened to the oil and the meal in the widow's house?
   (Until it rained, the oil and meal were never used up.)
7. Where did Elijah challenge the false prophets of Baal?
   (On Mount Carmel.)
8. What happened when the false prophets prayed to their god to send fire down on their sacrifice?
   (Nothing happened!)
9. What happened when Elijah prayed?
   (God sent fire down and burned the sacrifice, the altar stones, the wood, and all the water.)
10. How did Elijah go to Heaven?
    (God sent a fiery chariot, and Elijah went up by a whirlwind into Heaven.)

Additional Lesson Activities

1. Act Out the Stories

Divide students into two groups. Have each group choose one of the stories of Elijah and act it out: Elijah at the home of the poor widow

The contest on Mount Carmel between Elijah and the prophets of Baal

2. Association Quiz

Write this list of objects on the chalkboard. Students are to name the person associated with the object. (Answers are in parentheses.)

1. Coat (Joseph)
2. Sling (David)
3. Trumpets, pitchers (Gideon)
4. Stone tablets (Moses)
5. Stone (Samuel)
6. Stone altar (Elijah)

Workbook Page

Page 12 contains "Elijah's Problem" and "Fill in the Blanks." Both puzzles review events in the life of the prophet Elijah.

Memory Verse: James 5:16

"Confess your faults one to another, and pray one for another, that ye may be healed. The effectual fervent prayer of a righteous man availeth much."

Lesson 11

Adventures With Daniel

Daniel 1—6

Introduction to Lesson

Let pupils use encyclopedias and Bible dictionaries to look up information about the ancient land of Babylon.

The Bible Lesson

God sent many messengers like Elijah to warn His people to stop worshiping idols and worship only God. But the people of the northern kingdom, Israel, and the southern kingdom, Judah, did not listen. Finally the punishment that God promised did come, and both kingdoms were captured by enemy armies. The southern kingdom was invaded by Nebuchadnezzar, king of Babylon. He destroyed the temple and burned the city of Jerusalem. Many people were taken to Babylon as captives.

Among the children taken to Babylon by King Nebuchadnezzar were a boy named Daniel and three of his friends. These boys were healthy and handsome and had good minds. The king wanted to train them for work in his palace. He ordered that they be fed with his finest dainties and he gave them the best wine to drink. But the four boys decided that they would not eat the king's rich food nor drink his wine. "We will eat vegetables and drink water," they said to the king's servant.

When the servant objected, the boys asked that they be allowed to make a ten-day test. At the end of the ten days they were much healthier than the other boys.

Daniel became a great man in Babylon because he was wise. God had given him the power to tell the meanings of the king's dreams.

When Belshazzar, the king's son, became the next ruler, he was more wicked than his father, King Nebuchadnezzar. One night he had a feast and invited a thousand of the great men in the kingdom. He brought out all the golden vessels his father had taken from the beautiful temple in Jerusalem. The people at the feast drank wine from these golden vessels, and praised their idols.

At that very moment the fingers of a man's hand appeared on the wall and began to write. The king was very much afraid, and he called in all his magicians to tell him what the writing meant. None of them could read the message.

Then the queen suggested that Daniel be called. This was the writing on the wall: Mene, Mene, Tekel, Upharsin. When Daniel saw it, he said, "This is what it means: Your kingdom will be destroyed. God is going to give it to the Medes and Persians."

That very night King Belshazzar was killed by the armies of the Medes and Persians. Darius became king of Babylon.

King Darius was very fond of Daniel, and this made the lords of the kingdom jealous. They decided to plot against him. They made a law that said if anyone asked anything of either God or man, other than the king, he would be thrown into a den of lions. This law was to last for thirty days. The king signed the law, and it could not be changed.

These men knew that Daniel prayed every day to God, so they watched to see if he would disobey the king's law. Daniel prayed each day to God, no matter what the king had decreed. The men hurried to tell the king that Daniel had prayed to God. The king was sad because he liked Daniel, but he could not change the law. So Daniel was thrown into a den of lions. A large stone was placed over the door and the door was sealed.

The unhappy king did not sleep well. When morning came, he hurried to the lions' den. He called, "Daniel, Daniel! Did your God save you?"

"Yes," answered Daniel. "He sent His angels to shut the mouths of the lions." Daniel was taken from the den, and the men who had accused him were punished.

The Lesson Applied

Daniel is the kind of person who gives us an example of courage. Never once did he fail God in the many years he lived in Babylon. It may be easy to live a good life when everyone around us is good. But to stand up for God when others are against God demands bravery.

Being brave does not always mean not being afraid. But it does mean doing the right thing even though we are afraid. God blessed Daniel and took care of him in times of danger. He will never fail us.

Questions for Discussion: Do you think that prayer made Daniel brave? Do you think the person who stands for right is admired by those who live evil lives?

The Lesson Quiz

1. What king invaded the southern kingdom of Judah and took captives?
   (Nebuchadnezzar of Babylon.)
2. What young man and his three friends were taken to Babylon?
   (Daniel.)
3. What order of the king did Daniel and his friends refuse to obey?
   (To eat the king's rich food and drink wine.)
4. How did the four young men compare with the others, after ten days of eating vegetables and drinking water?
   (They were much healthier than the others.)
5. What wicked thing did King Belshazzar do when he gave a great feast?
   (He used the golden vessels taken from God's temple in Jerusalem, drank wine from them, and praised idols.)
6. What unusual event happened while they were having the feast?
   (The fingers of a man's hand appeared and wrote on the wall.)
7. Who told the king what the writing meant?
   (Daniel, with God's help.)
8. What law did the next king, Darius, make concerning prayer?
   (People could pray only to the king for thirty days.)
9. What was Daniel's punishment for praying to God?
   (He was thrown into a den of lions.)
10. What happened to Daniel in the lions' den?
   (He was saved, because God sent angels to shut the lions' mouths.)

Additional Lesson Activities

1. Prayer Reminders

Let students copy this verse on 3 x 5 cards: "Evening, and morning, and at noon, will I pray" (Psalm 55:17).

2. Learn Songs

Let students learn a song about Daniel, such as "Brave Daniel in the Lions' Den," or "Dare to Be a Daniel."

3. Review Chart

Place the chart below on the chalkboard, and let students review the lessons about the eleven Old Testament characters.

Workbook Page

"Find the Answers" on page 13 reviews facts from Daniel's story. "Daniel's Prayer Diary" will help students realize that God answers prayer. You may wish to encourage your students to start their own prayer diaries.

NAMES	FAITH	OBEDIENCE	COURAGE	HUMILITY	FORGIVENESS
1. Noah					
2. Abraham					
3. Joseph					
4. Moses					
5. Joshua					
6. Gideon					
7. Samuel					
8. Saul					
9. David					
10. Elijah					
11. Daniel					

Memory Verse: 1 Peter 3:12

"For the eyes of the Lord are over the righteous, and his ears are open unto their prayers: but the face of the Lord is against them that do evil."

Lesson 12

Adventures With Jesus

Matthew, Mark, Luke, John

Introduction to Lesson

Let pupils find these places on the map of Bible lands: Bethlehem, Egypt, Nazareth, Jordan River, Sea of Galilee, Jerusalem.

The Bible Lesson

From the very beginning of the world, God had promised that He would send a Savior. He was to come through the family of Abraham. All the Bible people whose adventures we have followed since Abraham were descended from him! From the journey to the promised land, to Egypt, back to Canaan, we have seen how God led His people. We have met some of the leaders of those people, and we have learned lessons from them. But God's people did not always follow His commands, and they did not always pay attention to the leaders He sent to them. Finally the time came for God to send the Savior to the world, to bring salvation and to show people how God wanted them to live. The Savior was to be God's only Son, Jesus.

For hundreds of years the Jewish people had been waiting for the coming of Christ—their Messiah as He was called. At last, on that quiet, starlit night, as shepherds watched over their sheep, a wonderful thing happened in the little town of Bethlehem. Jesus had come down from Heaven and had been born as a baby—the Son of God. An angel appeared to the shepherds, telling them the Savior had been born. They hurried to the stable in Bethlehem to worship the new king (Luke 2:1-20). Wise-men came from the east, guided by a star, to bring gifts to the Savior (Matthew 2:1-6).

The Wise-men told King Herod in Jerusalem that they were looking for the newborn King of the Jews. Being a wicked man, Herod wanted to get rid of Jesus. He feared that Jesus might grow up to be king in his place. Not knowing where to find Jesus, he ordered his soldiers to go out and kill all the boy babies under two years of age. But God was watching over His Son. He spoke to Joseph in a dream and told him to take Jesus and His mother, Mary, to Egypt. The little family left Bethlehem and went to Egypt to live (Matthew 2:7-15).

When Herod died, God again spoke to Joseph and told him Herod was dead. Joseph, Mary, and Jesus went back to their own country to live. They went to Joseph's home in Nazareth, where Jesus lived until He was a grown man (Matthew 2:19-23).

When Jesus was thirty years old, He left His home in Nazareth to start the work He came into this world to do—to teach people about the love of God, how they might have their sins forgiven, and how they should live in order to be pleasing to Him. The first thing Jesus did was to go to the river Jordan. There He was baptized by John the Baptist (Matthew 3:13-17), after which God led Him into the desert where He spent forty days praying and fasting. It was then that Satan appeared to Jesus and tried to turn Him from His work, but Christ came through that temptation victoriously (Matthew 4:1-11).

Jesus chose twelve men from among His disciples to be His special helpers. They traveled with Him and He taught them (Matthew 10:2-4).

Then came adventures with Christ when He healed the sick (Luke 13:10-17; John 4:46-54); opened the eyes of the blind (Mark 10:46-52); unstopped the ears of the deaf (Mark 7:32-37); healed the cripples (John 5:1-16); fed the multitude (John 6:1-14); and raised the dead (Luke 7:11-16; John 11:32-44).

There were also sad adventures in the life of Christ, such as the time when He went back to His hometown of Nazareth. The people would not accept Him. They dragged Him up to the top of a high hill, intending to throw Him over; but He disappeared out of their midst (Luke 4:16-32). There was the time when many of His followers turned back and did not follow Him any more (John 6:66-69). The saddest of those times came when His enemies sent soldiers to arrest Him, and His own disciples fled, leaving Him alone with His captors (Mark 14:26-50).

Jesus was put on trial; He was spit upon and beaten. Finally He was forced to carry His own cross through the streets, which were lined with shouting, mocking people. Then, on the hill called Calvary, He was crucified for the sins of the world. At the moment He died the sky became dark, there was a great earthquake, and the curtain in the temple was ripped from top to bottom. Great fear came upon all the people. One of the Roman soldiers, on guard at the cross, exclaimed, "Truly this man was the Son of God!" (Mark 15:1-47).

But out of this very dark picture came the great adventure of resurrection morning! An angel of God came down from Heaven and rolled away the stone that sealed the tomb where Christ had been buried. Friends coming to anoint the body with spices found the tomb empty. Christ had risen from the dead! (Mark 16:1-11).

The next forty days were crowded with adventures. Christ appeared to His followers on many occasions. He walked along the road with two of them (Luke 24:13-35); He had breakfast on the seashore with others (John 21:1-14); and on one occasion He appeared to His followers in a locked room where they were hiding for fear of the Jews (John 20:19, 20). Then at last, on the Mount of Olives, surrounded by His eleven faithful disciples, Jesus said good-bye to them. He commissioned them to go into all the world and preach the gospel to every creature (Mark 16:15, 16). Jesus then went back to live with His Father in Heaven (Luke 24:50, 51).

The Lesson Applied

We can learn so many things from the life of Christ. Jesus set the greatest example of all—that of a perfect life.

The most important thing to remember is that Christ, the Son of God, died for our sins. If we believe on Him and follow Him, we have the promise of eternal life (John 3:16).

But being a follower of Christ is not always easy. There are temptations to do wrong. Jesus did not promise us that we would not be tempted or discouraged. He did not promise money, or other kinds of wealth. He promised eternal life with Him in Heaven.

Questions for Discussion: Why does God love us so much? Since He loves, why does He punish?

The Lesson Quiz

1. Where was Jesus born?
   (In Bethlehem of Judea.)
2. How did the child Jesus escape death by the order of King Herod?
   (God warned Joseph in a dream to take Mary and Jesus to Egypt.)
3. Where did Jesus live after the family returned from Egypt?
   (In Nazareth of Galilee.)
4. How old was Jesus when He started to do His work on earth?
   (About thirty years old.)
5. After Jesus was baptized by John in the Jordan River, what happened to Him in the wilderness?
   (He was tempted by the devil, but He never gave in to temptation.)
6. Name five kinds of miracles that Jesus did.
   (Healed the sick, opened the eyes of the blind, unstopped the ears of the deaf, fed the multitude, raised the dead.)
7. What did the disciples do when Jesus was arrested?
   (They ran away and left Jesus with His enemies.)
8. How did Jesus die?
   (He was crucified.)
9. What happened on the third day after Jesus was crucified?
   (He rose from the dead.)
10. After His resurrection, how long was Jesus on earth before He went back to Heaven?
   (Forty days.)

Additional Lesson Activities

1. Mural

Let students make a mural of the life of Christ. Tape a piece of shelf paper, about six feet long, to the wall. Provide crayons or felt-tipped pens. The mural may be divided into these sections: Birth, Baptism, Temptation, Ministry (healing, preaching), Crucifixion, Resurrection, Ascension.

2. Bookmarks

Let students make Bible bookmarks with words of Jesus lettered on them. Choose from these verses: Mark 1:17; Luke 9:23; John 11:25, 26.

Workbook Page

"Jesus: The Gospel Accounts," on page 14, may be used as a written exercise. You will need to provide paper. "Matching Quiz: The Words of Jesus" reviews important teachings of Jesus from Matthew's Gospel.

Memory Verse: Hebrews 13:8

"Jesus Christ the same yesterday, and today, and for ever."

Lesson 13

Adventures With Paul

Acts 8:1-4; 9:1-31; 13—28

Introduction to Lesson

Let students find these names or places:

1. The places where the apostles were to be witnesses (Acts 1:8).
2. The names of the eleven apostles (Acts 1:13).
3. The name of the missing apostle (Acts 1:16).
4. The name of the man chosen to take the place of the missing apostle (Acts 1:26).
5. The name of another apostle, chosen later (1 Corinthians 1:1).

The Bible Lesson

As Jesus disappeared into Heaven forty days after He arose from the grave, the apostles stood looking up in amazement, scarcely believing what they had seen. Two angels appeared who said, "Why do you stand here looking up into Heaven? This same Jesus, whom you have seen going into Heaven, will come back again in the same way that He left the earth!"

Then the disciples remembered that Jesus had told them these things while He was with them. They also remembered that He had told them to wait in the city of Jerusalem until He sent them power from God. They went into the city and waited. On the Day of Pentecost, the fiftieth day after Jesus' crucifixion, as they were all together, the Holy Spirit came upon them. He began to guide them in the work they were to do for Christ.

After this, the apostles went everywhere preaching about Jesus. Many people believed in Jesus as the Son of God and accepted Him as their Savior. However, this did not please the Jewish rulers. They did not want the people to believe in Jesus, for they knew this would take away their power over the people. They began to persecute the Christians (Acts 8:1-4).

At the time of this persecution there lived a man by the name of Saul. He had a good education, he was well-known, and he believed in God. But because he did not believe that Jesus was God's Son, he began to fight against the Christians. He had many of them arrested, and he was present when Stephen was stoned to death.

One day when Saul was on his way to Damascus to arrest more Christians, Jesus appeared to him. Saul realized that Jesus was the Lord and asked Jesus what he should do. Jesus told him to go into the city and someone there would tell him what to do.

The brightness of the light when Jesus had appeared to him had blinded Saul. The men who were with him had to lead him into the city, where he remained without sight for three days. Jesus spoke to a Christian by the name of Ananias, and told him to go to Saul. Saul received his sight again, and Ananias told him, "Arise, and be baptized, and wash away thy sins."

Saul, whose name was changed to Paul (Acts 13:9), remained with the Christians in Damascus for several days. Before he left Damascus he was preaching to the Jews, trying to prove to them that Jesus was the Christ, the Son of God!

Barnabas had gone to Antioch to preach, and when he found that he needed help, he went to get Paul. After a while God asked the church at Antioch to send Paul and Barnabas out as missionaries.

Paul made three missionary journeys, and he visited many lands and cities. No matter where he was, if he was able to get the people to listen to him, he would preach about Christ. Paul started many churches.

When Paul returned to Jerusalem after his third missionary journey, some of the wicked Jews who had been following him and causing so much trouble, stirred up more trouble by telling lies about him. Paul was arrested. He was taken before the chief captain, then to the governor, and finally to King Agrippa. After listening to Paul, Agrippa decided he was innocent. However, because Paul had said he wanted to go before Caesar, ruler over all the Roman empire, Agrippa could not release him. Paul, with a number of other prisoners, was turned over to a centurion named Julius. He placed them aboard a ship at Caesarea and the voyage to Rome was begun (Acts 27:1, 2).

All went well until a storm came down upon them. Day after day the wind blew and the sea became more and more rough. When the voyage continued this way for many days, the sailors became frightened and would not eat. Paul called them to him and said, "God spoke to me last night and told me that the ship would be wrecked but that no one would be drowned."

After fourteen days and nights of this terrible storm, they finally sighted land. They allowed the ship to be driven as near the shore as possible. At last they had to let down the anchors because the waves were so high and the wind was blowing so hard. They were afraid the ship would be broken into pieces on the rocks. As it was growing dark, they decided to stay there all night.

At last daylight came. They took up the anchors, hoisted up the mainsail, and let the wind drive them toward a river in the island they were approaching. But the front of the boat stuck in the sand, and the back part was soon broken up by the heavy waves. When the soldiers saw that they would have to leave the ship in order to save their lives, they suggested that all the prisoners be killed. Julius, the centurion, was anxious to save Paul, and he would not let the soldiers do this. He commanded that all those who could swim should go first. The rest reached the shore safely by floating on boards and broken pieces of the ship.

They stayed on the island of Melita for about three months. When all danger of storms was over, they all went aboard a ship that had been anchored at the island all winter. They continued their journey to Rome.

In Rome Paul was imprisoned twice, and finally put to death. From prison Paul wrote many wonderful letters to the churches that he had started when he was on his missionary journeys. He also preached to those who came to visit him (Acts 28:30, 31).

The Lesson Applied

Paul's ministry lasted about thirty-five years. He won multitudes to Christ, established churches, and wrote letters to help people live the way God wanted them to live. He obeyed Christ's command to take the gospel to the world.

Being ready to serve Christ any place in the world is something we must be willing to do, even though it means leaving our homes, our friends, and our comforts.

Questions for Discussion: Why was Paul a great missionary? Can every Christian be a missionary?

The Lesson Quiz

1. Why was Saul (Paul) on his way to Damascus?

   (To arrest more Christians.)

2. Why did Paul have to be led into the city?

   (The bright light that appeared when Jesus spoke to him blinded him.)

3. What Christian man did Jesus send to Paul?

   (Ananias.)

4. What did Ananias tell Paul to do?

   ("Arise, and be baptized, and wash away thy sins.")

5. In what city was the church that sent Paul and Barnabas as missionaries?

   (Antioch.)

6. How many missionary journeys did Paul make?

   (Three.)

7. What happened when he returned from the last of these journeys?

   (He was arrested.)

8. What happened to the ship in which Paul was being taken as a prisoner to Rome?

   (The ship was wrecked in a storm off the island of Melita.)

9. How many of the passengers and prisoners were saved from drowning?

   (They all were saved.)

10. What did Paul do while he was in prison in Rome?

    (He preached to those who came to visit him, and he wrote letters to the churches he had started.)

Additional Lesson Activities

1. Journeys

Trace Paul's three missionary journeys on a map of Bible lands.

2. Letters From Prison

Let students read these letters Paul wrote while he was in prison in Rome: Ephesians, Philippians, Colossians, Philemon.

Workbook Page

Page 15 contains "Paul's Voyage" and "Paul's Letters."

Memory Verse: Philippians 4:13

"I can do all things through Christ which strengtheneth me."

Part Two

Adventures in Christian Living

After studying the "Adventures of Bible People," and learning from the lives of those who obeyed God's Word, your pupils will be ready for a series of lessons on Christian living. Living a Christian life can be a great adventure!

In each of these lessons you will find examples from both the Old and New Testaments. All the lesson themes, such as worship, prayer, giving, choosing friends, telling the truth, are found in both Testaments. The Old Testament Scriptures help us understand what God commanded before Jesus came. The New Testament Scriptures give us the example and teachings of Jesus, God's Son, and His disciples.

In some of the lessons there are as many as four Bible stories. If your pupils are familiar with most of the Bible stories, you may wish to divide the class into groups and give each group a Scripture reference. Let the pupils share the stories with each other. Or, you may wish to choose fewer story examples and expand them. Adequate background Scriptures are given. Read them carefully and add more details to the stories.

However you present the lessons in this series, you will find that the entire study shows the unity of God's Word.

What Do Your Pupils Need?

A series of lessons on "Christian living" may be assumed by some to mean that all the pupils must already be Christians in order to profit from the study.

Pupils who have accepted Christ as their Savior will learn what Jesus expects of them in their daily lives. Pupils who have not yet made their decisions will learn the ideal way that Christians should live, if they truly are following Jesus' example and teachings.

You will want to get acquainted with each pupil and learn his or her spiritual condition. You may want to have a special emphasis in the beginning of this study to explain God's plan of salvation. Share these Scriptures and others that tell what God and Jesus have done for us, and what we are expected to do:

John 3:16	Acts 16:30, 31
Romans 3:23, 24	1 John 4:15
Acts 2:38	1 Corinthians 15:3, 4
Acts 17:30	Romans 6:4-6

Keep a prayer notebook during this series of lessons, and put the name of each pupil on a page. Add the pupil's age, grade in school, and any information that is helpful in praying for the particular needs of that pupil. When a pupil becomes a Christian, or shows signs of spiritual growth, record it in your notebook. Refer to your notes as you plan your lessons. Your teaching will be more effective when you meet the needs of your pupils.

Memory Verses

The thirteen memory verses selected for this series will be valuable to your pupils in their Christian lives. If they will commit these verses to memory, they can recall them during times of temptation. They will know what God's Word commands. For example, when a pupil is tempted to argue or fight, he can remember "Live peaceably with all men."

Work out some visual ideas to connect the themes and the memory verses. Perhaps 3 x 5 cards with one word from each verse could be used:

FRIENDS	- John 15:13
PRAY	- 1 Thessalonians 5:17
TRUTH	- Ephesians 4:25

Another idea is to let pupils draw pictures to illustrate the meanings of the verses. These pictures could be used as flash cards to review the memory verses.

Special Features in the Pupil's Workbook

You might want to teach your pupils the song, "Living for Jesus Daily," which was an old VBS song. Use it as your theme song for this series of lessons.

Page 16 tells of the great adventure that is yet to come: Christ's return! Encourage your pupils to read the Scriptures included on the page.

Page 17 contains three projects for your pupils: "My Memory Verse Scroll," "Old and New Game," and "Start a Spiritual Notebook." These projects will help your pupils grow in knowledge as they review their Bible lessons.

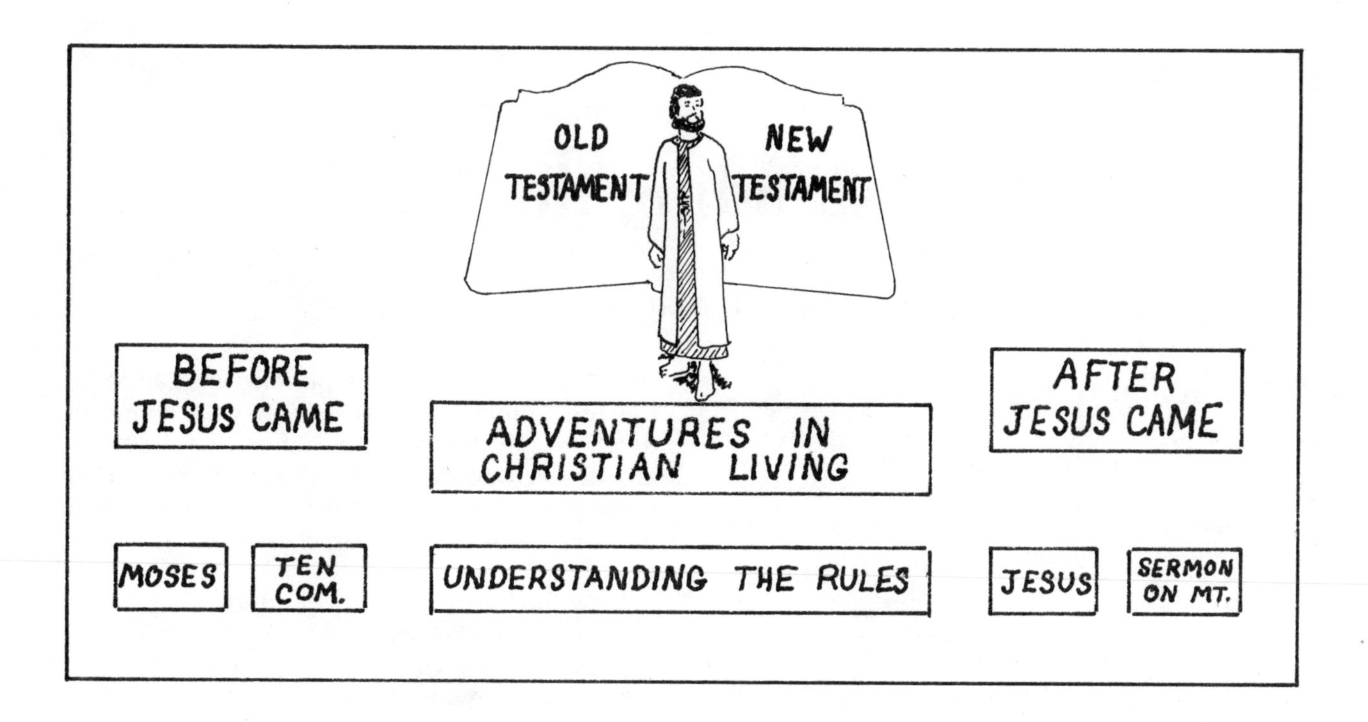

Bulletin Board Idea

If you have access to a bulletin board, chalkboard, or large wall area, prepare the following items to display as shown in the illustration.

1. Large figure of Jesus in the middle of an open Bible, to place in the center at the top of the display. On the left side of the Bible print "Old Testament," on the right side print "New Testament."
2. Large sign for center lettered "Adventures in Christian Living."
3. Two smaller signs for either side: "Before Jesus Came" and "After Jesus Came."
4. A sign for each lesson title on a strip of paper or poster board, the same width as the center sign.
5. Several 3 x 5 cards to place beneath the Old Testament and New Testament sections. On these you may use the names of the Bible people in the lessons, Scripture references, or a combination of both.

The general signs should remain in place for all thirteen lessons. The lesson titles and 3 x 5 cards will be changed each week.

This bulletin board display will be a visual aid that will tie the lessons together and serve to emphasize the teachings from God's Word.

Extra Suggestions for the Display

1. If you use a chalkboard for your display, use colored chalk to make the presentation more attractive.
2. Use 3 x 5 cards in different colors.
3. If you letter your signs on white poster board, use different colors of felt-tipped pens for the messages.
4. Make a background of colorful crepe paper or construction paper for the bulletin board.
5. Add newspaper clippings that illustrate the lessons. For example, when you are studying the lesson, "Learning Self-Control," find current stories that show what happens when a person loses control of himself and brings harm to someone else. Make the lessons you teach relevant to pupils' lives.
6. Be sure to change the lesson strips and 3 x 5 cards each week. Let pupils help you put up and take down the display materials.
7. If you have a collection of Bible art pictures from visual aids packets or other Sunday-school material, add the pictures to the display. For example, with lesson six, "Reading God's Word," you could display a picture of young King Josiah and a picture of young Timothy.
8. Save the lesson title strips and the 3 x 5 cards from each lesson. Use them for reviews and learning games and activities.
9. Let pupils draw pictures for the lesson displays.
10. Be creative—think of other ideas to make your bulletin board display an effective tool during this series of lessons.

Lesson 1

Understanding the Rules

Exodus 20:1-17; Deuteronomy 5:7-21; Matthew 5, 6, 7; 22:34-40; Luke 6:20-49

Introduction to Lesson

Let each pupil choose one of the twenty-two divisions of Psalm 119 (each division contains eight verses), and count how many times these words appear in the section:

law	precepts
testimonies	statutes
commandments	judgments

(Explain that all of these words refer to laws or commands of God.)

The Bible Lesson

(Hold up a box game that boys and girls like to play. Ask the following questions.) How many of you have played this game? How would you explain this game to someone who never had played it? Suppose that person wanted to play it some other way? (Open box and display the rules printed inside the box lid.) In order to play this game the way the author intended, you have to go by the rules.

God made us, and He made the rules that we should follow! If we live according to His rules, we'll have happy lives.

(Display the bulletin board visual idea that is suggested on page 31. Add this week's lesson title and name or Scripture cards.) In each lesson of "Adventures in Christian Living," we'll talk about Scriptures and stories from the Old Testament and from the New Testament. The Old Testament Scriptures are given to us as examples to help us understand what God commanded before Jesus came. The New Testament gives us examples and teachings of Jesus, God's Son. We are to follow Jesus' teachings.

Before Jesus came . . .

In the Old Testament we learn that God chose a special nation to be His people. Through this nation, Israel, God was going to bring a great blessing to all the people of the world: a Savior. To help the children of Israel live the right way, and prepare for the Savior's coming, God gave Moses some rules to give to the people. We call them the Ten Commandments, and they are found in two books of the Old Testament: Exodus 20:1-17 and Deuteronomy 5:7-21. (Have students find these passages and look at the verses. Mention the commands—briefly paraphrased here—as follows.)

1. Do not worship any other gods.
2. Do not make any idols.
3. Do not take God's name in vain.
4. Keep the Sabbath Day holy.
5. Honor your father and mother.
6. Do not kill.
7. Do not commit adultery.
8. Do not steal.
9. Do not tell falsehoods (lies) about someone.
10. Do not covet (want) what belongs to someone else.

These ten laws, along with other rules in the books of Exodus, Leviticus, and Deuteronomy, guided God's people for hundreds of years.

After Jesus came . . .

Finally the time came for God to bring that great blessing to the world through the nation He had chosen. Jesus, God's Son, came from Heaven to be the Savior of the world. When Jesus was on earth, He taught God's Word and He showed by His life how God wanted people to live. Jesus said, "Don't think that I am come to destroy the law, but to fulfill it." To fulfill the law, Jesus had to obey every law completely, and He did.

Jesus said that the first and great commandment in the law is to love God with all your heart, mind, and soul. The second commandment is to love your neighbor as yourself.

Let's look at some of the teachings of Jesus from the "Sermon on the Mount," found in two New Testament books: Matthew and Luke.

Jesus said:

Don't even be angry with your brother without a cause (Matthew 5:22).

Bless them that curse you (Luke 6:28).

Love your enemies (Matthew 5:44).

You can't serve God and mammon (money) (Matthew 6:24).

Seek first the kingdom of God (Matthew 6:33).

Forgive and you shall be forgiven (Luke 6:37).

Don't lay up treasures for yourself on earth; lay up treasures in Heaven (Matthew 6:19, 20).

Don't judge others (Matthew 7:1).

Do unto others as you would have others do unto you (Matthew 7:12).

These are only a few of the many teachings of Jesus. These are some of the "rules" or "guidelines" by which Christians are to live.

The Lesson Applied

The rules God gave the nation of Israel were right for them. The rules God has given us, through Jesus, are right for us.

No one ever had kept all of God's laws perfectly until Jesus came! Jesus lived a sinless life, and He sacrificed His life on the cross, making it possible for us to be forgiven of our sins. After we accept Jesus as our Savior, we must try to live by His teachings. He will help us overcome temptations and guide us all through our lives. The Christian life is an adventure. Each day can be an exciting challenge to do what Jesus wants us to do!

Questions for Discussion: Which command is harder for you to obey: "Do not murder anyone" or "Love your enemies"? "Do not tell falsehoods about your neighbor" or "Love your neighbor as yourself"? "Do not steal" or "Do unto others as you would have others do unto you"?

The Lesson Quiz

1. What special nation did God choose as His people?

(Israel.)

2. What rules did God give them?

(The Ten Commandments.)

3. In what Bible books are the Ten Commandments?

(Exodus and Deuteronomy.)

4. What great blessing for the whole world came from the nation of Israel?

(The Savior, Jesus, God's Son.)

5. What did Jesus say about the law that God had given to the children of Israel?

(He said He came to fulfill it, not destroy it.)

6. What did Jesus mean by "fulfilling" the law?

(He meant that He would keep it perfectly—something no one else ever had done.)

7. How did Jesus let people know how God wanted them to live?

(By His life and teachings.)

8. In what Bible books are Jesus' teachings from the "Sermon on the Mount"?

(Matthew and Luke.)

9. What did Jesus say was the first and great commandment in the law?

(To love God with all your heart, mind, and soul.)

10. What is the second commandment?

(To love your neighbor as yourself.)

Additional Lesson Activities

1. Compare the Old and the New

Let pupils compare the Ten Commandments with Jesus' teachings in Matthew 5—7. For example, the old law said, "Thou shalt not kill." Jesus said, "Don't even be angry with your brother without a cause." Let pupils use concordances and other reference books.

2. The Golden Rule

Let pupils make up short stories explaining the meaning of Jesus' teaching in Matthew 7:12, called the "Golden Rule." They may take turns reading their stories aloud.

3. Rules to Live By

Let pupils choose eight or ten commands of Jesus and paraphrase them. Then let each pupil select several and copy them on a 3 x 5 card. Suggest that they put the card where they will see it every day, and really try to put these teachings into practice.

Workbook Page

On page 18 of the Pupil's Workbook, you'll find a puzzle, "Bible Verse Crossword," that reviews the Scriptures from Matthew. Check your answers on pages 62-64 of the Workbook. A blank scroll will be found at the bottom of each workbook page of this series. Encourage pupils to copy the memory verse in this space provided.

Memory Verse: John 14:15

Lesson 2

Following Jesus' Example

Matthew 5:8; 19:19; Luke 2:52; 1 Corinthians 6:19; James 1:5; 1 John 3:22

Introduction to Lesson

Let pupils tell briefly everything they can remember about Jesus' life: His birth, boyhood, baptism, ministry, death, resurrection, ascension. Stress the fact that Jesus experienced what we experience: hunger, pain, fatigue, sorrow, temptation. Yet He never disobeyed a single command God had given, and He never failed to do a single thing that God had commanded.

The Bible Lesson

Before Jesus came . . .

From the beginning, when God created the first people, there have been men and women who have tried to live according to His commands. Some of the leaders we learned about during our study of "Adventures of Bible People" are examples, such as: Noah, who was obedient; Abraham, who had faith; Joseph, who showed forgiveness; Gideon, who was humble; and Daniel, who was courageous.

But none of these leaders was perfect. There was one who was to come who would be a perfect example in every way: Jesus Christ, the Son of God.

After Jesus came . . .

The Bible does not tell us about the boyhood of Jesus after He was a small child and the family returned to Nazareth. Only one event is mentioned: a trip that Jesus made to Jerusalem when He was twelve years old, to attend the Passover. Jesus is about thirty years old when the Bible takes up His life story again. The time between the years of twelve and thirty are described by this verse of Scripture: "And Jesus increased in wisdom and stature, and in favor with God and man" (Luke 2:52).

Jesus not only taught God's message, but He lived exactly the way He taught. We must follow Jesus' perfect example.

Jesus Grew in Wisdom

"Growing in wisdom" means to grow mentally—to learn more each day. We must learn from God's Word, and from Christians who are older and wiser than we are. We must choose carefully what we read and what people we listen to. Our minds are fed by what we see and hear. Christians should not feed their minds with evil words and pictures. Jesus said, "Blessed are the pure in heart: for they shall see God" (Matthew 5:8). The person who is growing in wisdom will want to have clean and pure thoughts.

(Read aloud James 1:5.)

Jesus Grew in Stature

"Growing in stature" means to grow physically. Every young person wants to grow tall and strong and healthy. In order to do this we must keep our bodies clean—not only the outside but the inside as well. We must never take anything into our bodies that will harm them. We must get plenty of sleep and eat good wholesome food. Exercise in the out-of-doors, hikes to view God's handiwork, and games that teach good sportsmanship are all valuable to our physical growth. The Bible says that our bodies are the temple of the Holy Spirit. We will want to keep our bodies pure places in which God's Spirit can live.

(Read aloud 1 Corinthians 6:19.)

Jesus Grew in Favor With God

"Growing in favor with God" is to grow spiritually. To live a life that truly is pleasing to God, we must give Him our lives. But that is only the beginning. We cannot continue to be pleasing to God unless we live according to Jesus' teachings.

To live in favor with God, we must reverence His name. One of the commands God gave to Israel was, "Thou shalt not take the name of the Lord thy God in vain." We must not use the name of God as a swear word, or use it lightly. In the prayer Jesus taught His disciples, He said, "Our Father . . . Hallowed (holy) be thy name." To be pleasing to God we must be reverent, we must praise Him, and we must serve Him.

(Read aloud 1 John 3:22.)

Jesus Grew in Favor With Man

To "grow in favor with man" is to grow socially. We must learn to get along with other people. This includes using good manners, and thinking of the other person's needs as well as your own.

Getting along with others does not always mean being the most popular person. Sometimes young people, in order to be popular, will do things that they know they should not do. If you have to do wrong things in order to keep your friends, then you have the wrong friends and you should look for new ones.

To live in favor with man, you must be obedient to the laws of your city and country, and set a Christian example to people in your community.

(Read aloud Matthew 19:19.)

The Lesson Applied

Many times people who are not Christians look at those who are Christians to see how they act. If Christians truly follow Jesus' example, people will see the difference and may want to become Christians themselves.

Wherever you are, live a clean and pure life. Prove you are a Christian by the things you do and say. A Christian can enjoy life and also have the respect of the people around him. Best of all, he is pleasing to God.

Questions for Discussion: Is it possible to please everyone? How can we make up our minds whether a thing is right or wrong?

The Lesson Quiz

1. Why is Jesus' life the best example of all?

(Jesus lived a perfect life—something no one else has done.)

2. In what four ways did Jesus grow?

(Wisdom, stature, in favor with God, in favor with man.)

3. What does "growing in wisdom" mean?

(To grow mentally, to learn more each day—especially learning from God's Word.)

4. What does "growing in stature" mean?

(To grow physically—to grow taller, stronger.)

5. Whose "temple" is the body?

(The temple of the Holy Spirit.)

6. What is meant by "growing in favor with God"?

(Growing spiritually, living in a way that is pleasing to God.)

7. What are some things we should do to be pleasing to God?

(Give reverence to His name, praise Him, and serve Him.)

8. What is meant by "growing in favor with man"?

(Growing socially—getting along with others.)

9. What did Jesus say about the way we should treat our neighbors?

("Thou shalt love thy neighbor as thyself.")

10. How can other people tell if we are Christians?

(By the things we do and say—living a clean and pure life.)

Additional Lesson Activities

1. Wall Mottoes

Let pupils make simple wall mottoes by lettering the memory verse, Luke 2:52, on 7 x 10 pieces of lightweight cardboard, with colorful felt-tipped pens. Attach yarn hangers. Pupils may choose one of the other Scriptures from the lesson: Matthew 5:8; 1 Corinthians 6:19; Matthew 19:19.

2. More Ways to Grow

Let pupils look up Galatians 5:22, 23 and list the nine ways that Christians should grow. Encourage pupils to watch for ways they can increase in love, joy, peace, etc.

Workbook Page

For the "Scripture Crossword," page 19, let each pupil open his or her Bible to one of the six verses. To find the answers in the puzzle let pupils share the verses with each other. Note: The modern spellings of "neighbor" and "favor" are used.

Memory Verse: Luke 2:52

Lesson 3

Worshiping God

Genesis 8:20-22; Exodus 36—38, 40; 1 Kings 5—8; 2 Chronicles 3—7; Luke 4:16-20; Acts 2:41-47; 13:14-16; Colossians 4:15

Introduction to Lesson

Let pupils discuss what takes place in a worship service. Provide a church bulletin that contains the order of worship, or simply list on the chalkboard the various activities that make up the worship hour. Ask if the people in the congregation are there just to observe, or are they supposed to participate. How can people participate in these parts of a service:

singing	sermon
prayers	meditation
offering	Scripture reading
Communion	fellowship

The Bible Lesson

Worshiping God isn't something we do just once a week in a special building. We can praise God and pray to Him wherever we are all week long. God's Word tells us, however, that we are not to neglect meeting together (Hebrews 10:25). There are times when we are to join with others to worship the Lord.

Before Jesus came . . .

To learn how people worshiped God in the beginning, we go back to the first book in the Bible.

The Altar

The first way people worshiped God was by building an altar of stones, according to God's directions. On the altar they offered sacrifices of their very best animals. As the smoke from the sacrifices would rise up from the burning offerings, the people would pray to God, asking Him to forgive them of their sins, and thanking Him for blessings.

The first thing Noah did after the great flood was to build an altar and offer a sacrifice, thanking God for saving him and his family. (Read aloud Genesis 8:20-22.)

The Tabernacle

When the people of Israel were on their way to the promised land, God gave Moses the Ten Commandments. One command was "Remember the sabbath day, to keep it holy." God also gave Moses directions for building a tabernacle. This was a place for worship, and it was made like a tent. It could be taken down and carried when the people were traveling. When the Israelites finally reached the promised land, they continued to worship God in the tabernacle for many years. (Read aloud Exodus 40:34-38.)

The Temple

Israel became a great and wealthy nation. When David became king, he wanted to build a beautiful place to worship God at Jerusalem. God would not permit David to do this, because he had been a "man of war." David made the plans, but his son, Solomon, built the temple. Everything was done according to God's directions. When the temple was dedicated to the worship of God, Solomon offered great sacrifices on the altar. (Read aloud 2 Chronicles 5:1-6.) The temple was used for worship by the Israelites until it was destroyed by enemy armies.

Synagogues

When the temple was in ruins during the time of captivity, the Jews began building synagogues in each community. These buildings were used for worship on the Sabbath Day, and for Bible study and school during the week. A council of elders, known as "rulers of the synagogue" directed the services. Others helped take care of the buildings and served as schoolteachers.

After Jesus came . . .

We read in the New Testament that Jesus worshiped in the temple that had been rebuilt. He also went to the synagogue on the Sabbath. Sometimes He sat and listened to the leaders of the synagogues. Other times He taught the people. (Read aloud Luke 4:16-21.)

The Church

After Jesus went back to Heaven, the church that He promised was started in Jerusalem on the Day of Pentecost. No special meeting place was built. The church is not a building, it is people: Jesus' followers who meet together for worship on the first day of the week. In the early days the Christians met in homes. (Read aloud Acts 2:41-47.)

The Lesson Applied

God's chosen people, the Jews, first gathered at an altar. Later they worshiped at the tabernacle, then in the temple, and finally in synagogues on the Sabbath Day.

Today God's chosen people are called Christians, and they meet on the first day of the week in many different kinds of places. Some churches have large, beautiful buildings, and other churches meet in store buildings, schools, shelters, open fields, or under large trees. It doesn't matter whether we meet in an adobe hut, in a large building in a big city, or under a tree in a tropical land. Wherever we are, we must worship God from our hearts. Jesus said that we are to worship God in spirit and in truth.

Questions for Discussion: What are some ways that we worship God? What happens to us when we miss times of worshiping with other Christians? Why does our behavior matter when we're worshiping the Lord?

The Lesson Quiz

1. What was the first thing Noah did when he came out of the ark?
(He built an altar and worshiped God.)
2. What kind of a place of worship did the Israelites have while they were in the wilderness?
(A tabernacle—tent.)
3. On what day of the week did the Jews worship?
(The Sabbath or seventh day.)
4. What place of worship did King Solomon build?
(The temple in Jerusalem.)
5. When the temple was destroyed, what places of worship did the Jews build?
(Synagogues.)
6. For what other meetings were the synagogues used?
(Bible study and school during the week.)
7. Where did Jesus go to worship?
(To the temple in Jerusalem, and to synagogues in other towns.)
8. When and where did the church begin?
(After Jesus went back to Heaven, on the Day of Pentecost in Jerusalem.)
9. What is the church?
(Christians—followers of Christ.)
10. On what day do Christians meet?
(The first day of the week.)

Additional Lesson Activities

1. Bookmarks

Let pupils prepare bookmarks, using strips of light-colored construction paper, 2 x 5. On their bookmarks they may write the Scripture phrase that is found in three Old Testament passages: Psalm 29:2; 96:9; 1 Chronicles 16:29. (Let pupils find the answer: "Worship the Lord in the beauty of holiness.") Provide felt-tipped pens for the Scripture verse. Cover the bookmarks with clear self-adhesive paper.

2. Hymn Hunt

Provide hymnals and let pupils find hymns about worshiping God.

Workbook Page

On page 20 of the Workbook, you will find a variety of activities. If you have a photo of your church building, perhaps you could have copies made for your pupils. If your church bulletin or newsletter has a photo of the church that could be cut out and pasted in the space provided.

Memory Verse: John 4:24

Lesson 4

Sharing in the Lord's Work

Exodus 35, 36; 2 Chronicles 24:1-14; Luke 21:1-4; Acts 4:32-37

Introduction to Lesson

Let pupils list on the chalkboard all the things at church for which money is needed. Guide the discussion in helping the students understand the congregation's financial needs. Perhaps the church treasurer could be a guest and answer questions concerning church finances.

The Bible Lesson

Before Jesus came . . .

The Israelites Build the Tabernacle

Long before Jesus came, God had work for His people to do. When the Israelites had been led out of Egypt and were on their way to Canaan, God told Moses the kind of a place of worship that He wanted the people to build. Moses asked the people to bring gifts of all kinds to provide materials: gold, silver, brass, fine linen, cloth of goats' hair, rams' skins, wood, oil, spices, incense, and precious stones. Moses also asked people who had special skills, such as working with wood, stones, and metals, or weaving and embroidering, to volunteer to work in building the tabernacle. The people brought such generous offerings that Moses had to tell them to stop! They had all they needed for the work! (Read aloud Exodus 36:5-7).

King Joash Repairs the Temple

Many years after this, King Solomon built a beautiful temple to take the place of the tabernacle. Many of the kings who came after Solomon were wicked men and they led the people away from God. They began to worship idols. Because of this, they forgot to take care of the wonderful temple. Finally, a young man by the name of Joash became king. The first thing he did was to start working for God. He had a chest placed at the gate of the temple and asked the people to bring offerings and put them in the chest. The people repented of their sins and were glad to bring their offerings to show God they were sorry for the things they had been doing. So much money came in that the chest had to be emptied many times. Then Joash took the money and repaired the temple. He made it as beautiful as it had been before. There was enough left over to have some beautiful vessels made to go in the temple. (Read aloud 2 Chronicles 24:8-11.)

After Jesus came . . .

The Widow's Mite

After Jesus came, He taught many lessons about how God expects us to share what we have. Jesus told parables about selfish people such as the rich farmer. He gave warnings to people who thought of nothing but what they would eat and what they would wear.

One day when Jesus was in the temple, He saw some rich men putting money in the offering box. They were making a great show, pretending to give generously. A poor widow came by, and put in two mites—a very small amount of money. Jesus turned to His disciples and said, "This woman has put in more than all the rich men. They gave a small amount of their wealth, but she gave all she had." (Read aloud Luke 21:1-4.)

Barnabas Shares With Others

In the early days of the church, the Christians shared their possessions with each other. Many of those who owned lands or houses sold them, and brought the money to the apostles. The apostles then distributed the money to those in need. One of the Christians who shared in this way was Barnabas. He owned some land, which he sold, and brought the money to the apostles. Barnabas later became a missionary and traveled with the apostle Paul. (Read aloud Acts 4:36, 37.)

The Lesson Applied

We have looked at two examples of giving from the Old Testament, before Jesus came, and two examples from the New Testament, after Jesus came. All four Scriptures tell how the people gave willingly to help with the Lord's work.

In God's Word we read that God loves a cheerful giver. Let's follow the example of these cheerful givers. We may not be able to give much money now, because we're not working and earning our living. But we can give up some treats, or save some out of our allowance or money we earn delivering papers, raking leaves, mowing grass, shoveling snow. We can share what we have to help with the Lord's work. We also can give our time, our talents, and our abilities in service for the Lord.

Questions for Discussion: How much of our money should we give to God? How can we give our time to Him? Our talents and abilities? How would the Lord's work get done if no one gave time, talent, or money?

7. According to Jesus, how did the widow's gift compare with the money given by the wealthy men?

(Jesus said the widow gave more than all the wealthy men, because she gave all she had.)

8. How did the early Christians share with each other?

(Those who had lands or houses sold them, and brought the money to the apostles to be distributed.)

9. What disciple sold his land and brought the money to the apostles?

(Barnabas.)

10. What kind of a giver does God love?

(A cheerful giver.)

The Lesson Quiz

1. What did Moses ask the people to give to help build the tabernacle?

(Their possessions—gold, cloth, wood, etc.—and their skills.)

2. What unusual command did Moses make when the offering was being collected?

(The people had given so much that no more was needed. Moses told them to stop giving!)

3. What young king began plans to repair the temple in Jerusalem?

(Joash.)

4. How was the money collected?

(A chest was placed beside the gate of the temple, and the people brought their offerings. The chest was emptied each day.)

5. After the repairs were paid for, what was done with the money that was left?

(Some beautiful vessels were made for temple use.)

6. While Jesus was in the temple, how much money did the widow place in the offering box?

(Two mites—a very small amount of money.)

Additional Lesson Activities

1. Scriptures About Money and Possessions

Let pupils look up these Scriptures about money and possessions: 1 Timothy 6:10; Mark 10:17-22. What should be the Christian's attitude toward money and possessions?

2. Choose a Project

Let pupils choose a project in which they will share their time, talents, or possessions to help the church in some special way. This could include working in the churchyard, cleaning and beautifying a room, washing windows, etc. Any project should be cleared with those in charge of the building and grounds.

Workbook Page

Page 21 of the Workbook contains two puzzles: "Finish the Story" and "Can You Picture This?" Check the answers on pages 62-64 of the Workbook. Continue to encourage pupils to copy their memory verses on the scrolls.

Memory Verse: 2 Corinthians 9:7

Lesson 5

Praying Every Day

1 Samuel 1—3; Nehemiah 1, 2, 4, 6; Matthew 6:9-13; Luke 18:10-14

Introduction to Lesson

What is prayer? (Put these Scriptures and parts of prayer on the chalkboard. Let pupils find the Scriptures and read them, and then match each verse with one part of prayer.)

1. Psalm 103:1	a. giving thanks
2. Psalm 107:1	b. asking forgiveness
3. Psalm 25:18	c. confessing sin
4. Psalm 70:1	d. asking for help
5. Psalm 51:4	e. praising God

(Answers: 1, e; 2, a; 3, b; 4, d; 5, c.)

The Bible Lesson

Before Jesus came . . .

Prayer is mentioned in Genesis, the first book of the Bible. From the beginning people have prayed to God, praising Him, thanking Him, confessing their sins, asking forgiveness, and asking for help. Let's look at some of the prayers in the Old Testament.

Hannah Prays for a Son

During the time when judges ruled God's people, a woman named Hannah lived in Ramah, near Mount Ephraim. Hannah's husband, Elkanah, loved her very much, and he provided well for her. But Hannah was unhappy because she did not have a child. Every year Elkanah and Hannah went up to Shiloh to worship the Lord. One year Hannah went to the house of the Lord and prayed very earnestly that she would have a son. She cried as she prayed. She promised the Lord that if He gave her a son, she would give him back to serve Him. Eli, the priest, told Hannah that God would answer her prayer, and she went home a very happy woman. God kept His promise and sent her a son. He was named Samuel. Hannah kept her promise to God, and when Samuel was old enough to leave home, she took him back to the house of the Lord. Hannah prayed again, this time thanking and praising the Lord: "There is none holy as the Lord!" The Lord blessed Hannah with several more children.

Nehemiah Prays for His People

Many years later, after God's people had been taken as captives to other lands, a Jewish man named Nehemiah was a cupbearer to the king in Persia. He learned that the city of Jerusalem was in need of being rebuilt—the walls were broken down, the gates had been burned, and the people living there needed help. Nehemiah was so sad to hear of this trouble in Jerusalem that he cried and fasted, and prayed to God. He confessed the sins of himself and his people, and he asked the Lord for help.

The king sent him back to Jerusalem to help rebuild the city walls. When Nehemiah arrived, he told the people that God would be with them. The people said, "Let us rise up and build!" The walls were built in fifty-two days, because the people "had a mind to work." God answered Nehemiah's prayers.

After Jesus came . . .

Jesus, God's Son, spent a lot of time in prayer. He also taught many lessons about prayer to His followers. Let's look at some of Jesus' teachings in the New Testament.

The Prayer Jesus Taught

Jesus' disciples saw Him praying to God. They knew that Jesus lived very close to His Father. They wished they could live closer to God, and they wanted to know more about prayer. One day they said to Jesus, "Lord, teach us to pray." Jesus gave them this prayer, sometimes called "The Lord's Prayer." (Read aloud Matthew 6:9-13.) It is a model prayer for us. We may pray it, but it is not the only prayer we can pray. However, our own prayers should contain the ideas given in this prayer.

Two Kinds of Prayer

Jesus not only taught us some of the things we should say to God, but He taught how we should pray. To explain this He told a story or parable. He said that two men went to the temple to pray. One was a Pharisee, a religious leader of the Jews. The other was a publican, a despised tax collector. When the Pharisee prayed to God, he said, "I am thankful that I am not wicked like other men. I do not do wrong like that publican. I give my money and I fast twice a week."

The publican was praying, too. He was so ashamed that he would not even lift his head as he prayed, "God have mercy on me for I am a sinner."

Then Jesus said that God heard the prayer of the publican because he was humble before God and sorry for his sins. God will bless those who pray to Him in a humble way.

The Lesson Applied

We can see by studying God's Word that prayer always has been important for God's people. The Jews, God's chosen people before Jesus came, prayed regularly. The Christians, God's chosen people after Jesus came, also are to pray regularly. How often should we pray? (Read 1 Thessalonians 5:17.) We can pray at work and at play, at home and at school, out loud or silently. To pray without ceasing means that we live so close to God that we can talk to Him anytime, anywhere. Some of the times we should pray each day are before we go to sleep, when we get up, and when we eat. But these should not be the only times we pray.

Questions for Discussion: Will God answer all of our prayers? What is the difference between "saying" a prayer and "praying" a prayer?

The Lesson Quiz

1. What did Hannah ask of the Lord?
(She wanted to have a son.)
2. What promise did she make to the Lord?
(She would give her son back to the Lord, to serve Him.)
3. What was the name of the son born to Hannah and Elkanah?
(Samuel.)
4. What did Nehemiah ask of the Lord?
(To go back to Jerusalem and help rebuild the city walls.)
5. How did God answer Nehemiah's prayer?
(The king of Persia sent Nehemiah back to Jerusalem with permission to rebuild the walls.)
6. What did Jesus' disciples ask Him about prayer?
(They said, "Lord, teach us to pray.")
7. By what names is this prayer known?
(The Lord's Prayer, or the model prayer.)
8. What story or parable did Jesus tell about the way to pray?
(The parable of the Pharisee and the publican.)
9. Which prayer did God hear?
(The prayer of the publican, "God be merciful to me a sinner.")
10. Why was this prayer accepted?
(The publican was humble before God, and sorry for his sins.)

Additional Lesson Activities

1. Praying in Jesus' Name
Let pupils read John 14:13, 14 and learn why we pray "in Jesus' name."
2. Write a Prayer
Let pupils study carefully the prayer that Jesus taught His disciples, and then write prayers of their own, using Jesus' prayer as a model.
3. Prayer Booklets
Let pupils make small booklets with construction-paper covers and plain white pages inside. Cut 8½ x 11 sheets in half and fold to 4¼ x 5½. On the covers pupils may draw praying hands or add a praying hands seal. On each page let them put the name of someone for whom they will pray each day: parents, friends, teachers, minister, missionaries.

Workbook Page

Page 22 of the Workbook contains three activities. If time is short, divide the class into three groups, and have each group do one of the activities. Then let each group share its answers with the rest of the class. The first section, "When Jesus Prayed," also may be used as a Bible drill.

Memory Verse: 1 Thessalonians 5:17

Lesson 6

Reading God's Word

2 Kings 22:8—23:25; Acts 16:1-3; 2 Timothy 1:5; 2:15; 3:15

Introduction to Lesson

Every Christian should know where to find certain "Key" Bible passages quickly. Some of these are listed below. Use the key pattern on this page and make ten copies for each pupil. Let them cut out the keys and put the following Bible references on them. They may use a piece of string or ribbon for a key chain and string the keys together.

1. Ten Commandments (Exodus 20:1-17)
2. The Beatitudes (Matthew 5:1-11)
3. The Lord's Prayer (Matthew 6:9-13)
4. The Golden Rule (Matthew 7:12)
5. The Great Commission (Mark 16:15, 16)
6. The Golden Text (John 3:16)
7. Faith Chapter (Hebrews 11)
8. Love Chapter (1 Corinthians 13)
9. Resurrection Chapter (1 Corinthians 15)
10. Comfort Chapter (John 14)

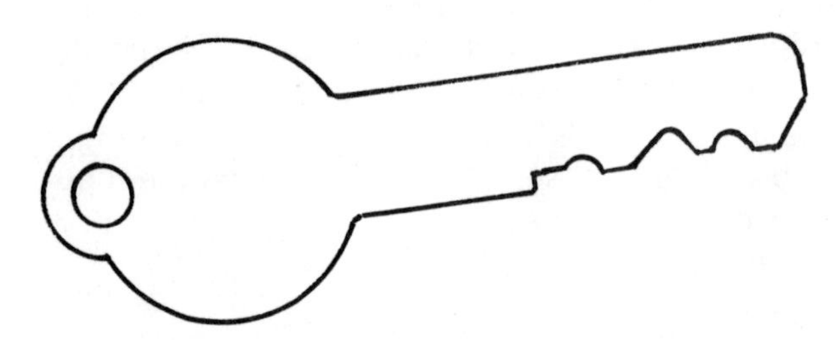

The Bible Lesson

Before the Bible was written, God spoke to the people and told them what they should do. Today God speaks to us through His Word. We should read the Bible every day. By reading God's Word we find out the things that God wants us to do.

Before Jesus came . . .

If we do not read the Bible, we might become like the people who lived at the time of King Josiah.

God's Book Found

Josiah became king of Israel when he was only eight years old! During his life he tried to do the things that were pleasing to God. After he had been king for many years, King Josiah decided to repair the temple. While this work was being done, a book was found in the temple. The king's scribe, Shaphan, took it to the king. When the book was read to the king, he became very worried, for this book was the law that God had given to Moses many years before. The king and his people had not been doing many of the things that God had commanded. The king then sent for all the people of his kingdom, and he read to them the things that were written in the book. "I am going to keep God's law all my life," the king promised. The people promised that they would also. And then Josiah commanded the priests to pray to God and ask Him to forgive them for not obeying God's law.

Josiah did not know God's complete law until the book was found. When he learned what God had commanded, he wanted to obey!

After Jesus came . . .

The New Testament is our guide today. It has not been lost and we can read it whenever we want to. If we do not read it, we will not know what God wants us to do, and we may be disobeying God in many ways. In the New Testament we learn about a young man who studied God's Word.

A Young Man and the Scriptures

In the town of Lystra there lived a young man whose name was Timothy. Timothy's mother, Eunice, was a Jewess, but his father was a Greek. Timothy's family included his grandmother, Lois. Although the Bible does not tell us much about his father, it does tell us that his mother and grandmother taught him the Scriptures. They must have taught him the law of God and told him stories about Abraham, Joseph, David, and Daniel. They may have told him about Jesus, the Son of God. When Timothy became a disciple, he worked for Jesus in Lystra.

One day, when the apostle Paul came to the city of Lystra on a missionary journey, he heard good reports about Timothy's faith and his good work for Christ. Paul was glad to hear this, and he asked Timothy to travel with him on his missionary journeys.

Later Timothy became a minister for Christ. When Paul was in prison, he wrote two letters to Timothy, encouraging him to be a faithful minister of the gospel. Paul wrote, "Since you were a child you have known the holy Scriptures, which are able to make you wise unto salvation through faith which is in Christ Jesus." Paul also told Timothy, "Study to show yourself approved unto God, a workman that doesn't need to be ashamed, rightly dividing the word of truth."

The Lesson Applied

The words that Paul wrote to Timothy are important for us, too. We are not only to read the Bible, but we are also to study it.

When we are hungry, we eat food for our physical bodies. When we read our Bibles, we are getting food for our souls, our spiritual bodies. Just as we eat often, so should we read our Bibles often. If we do, and if we try to live as it teaches, we will be workmen that do not need to be ashamed.

Questions for Discussion: How can we be sure we know the right meaning of certain Scriptures? Is it all right to ask God to help us to understand His Word?

The Lesson Quiz

1. How old was Josiah when he became king?
(He was eight years old.)

2. After he had been king for many years, what did he ask workmen to do?
(Repair God's temple.)

3. What was found in the temple?
(A book containing God's law.)

4. What did Josiah do?
(He called all the people together and read God's law to them. He promised God that he would keep His law.)

5. What did the people say?
(They promised to keep God's law, too.)

6. Where did Timothy live?
(In Lystra.)

7. What did his mother and grandmother teach him?
(The Scriptures.)

8. What did Paul hear about Timothy when he came to Lystra?
(Good reports of Timothy's faith and good works.)

9. What did Paul ask Timothy to do?
(Travel with him on his missionary journeys.)

10. How did Paul communicate with Timothy when he (Paul) was in prison?
(He wrote two letters to Timothy, to encourage him to be a faithful minister of the gospel.)

Additional Lesson Activities

1. Daily Bible Readings

Encourage pupils to begin daily Bible reading if they haven't done so. Suggest that they choose a definite time and place each day for reading. They may start with just a few verses, and then work up to a chapter or more a day. Keeping a chart and checking it each day would be helpful.

2. Bible Quiz: Do You Know?

Let pupils answer these questions, using their Bibles if necessary.

How many books are in the Bible?
How many books are in the Old Testament?
What book tells about the creation?
How many psalms are there?
How many books in the New Testament?
Which books in the New Testament tell the life of Jesus?
In what book would you find the history of the church?
What is the last book of the New Testament?
(Answers: 66, 39, Genesis, 150, 27, Matthew, Mark, Luke, John, Acts, Revelation.)

Workbook Page

"What Paul Said," on page 23 of the Workbook, is quoted from the King James Version of the Bible. Explain that Timothy and Timotheus are the same person. Encourage pupils to read what Paul said to Timothy, as well as what he said about him. Point out Paul's two letters to Timothy in the New Testament. The puzzle, "Scripture Acrostic," includes the memory verse for this lesson.

Memory Verse: 2 Timothy 3:16

Lesson 7

Learning Obedience

2 Samuel 15—18; Book of Esther; Luke 2:41-52

Introduction to Lesson

Let pupils compare these Scriptures:
Exodus 20:12
Ephesians 6:1-3
Colossians 3:20
Discuss the fifth Commandment. Why does God want children to obey their parents?

The Bible Lesson

Sometimes we do not like to hear the word "obey" because we do not always like to do as we are told. We forget sometimes that God made rules so that we would be happy.

In the Bible we find many stories that teach us how important it is to be obedient to rules.

Before Jesus came . . .

One of the Ten Commandments says: "Honor thy father and thy mother: that thy days may be long upon the land." The Bible also gives us some examples of good and bad sons and daughters.

A Disobedient Son

Absalom was a son of King David, and he was disobedient. His father loved him and was always good to him; but Absalom was not satisfied—he wanted to be king. He went out among the people and for a time he did many kind things for them.

Before long the people began to love him even more than they loved his father, the king. This is what Absalom wanted them to do. He then began to make them dislike his father. Finally he got together an army to fight against his own father. Absalom wanted to drive his father from his palace so he could be king. However, King David heard about it and sent out his own armies to fight against Absalom. The king's army was successful and drove the enemy away. As Absalom was running away on his mule, the mule ran under a tree and Absalom was caught in the branches by his long hair. He was killed by one of the king's soldiers who came by. King David felt very sad to think that his own son had turned against him. He mourned for his son for many days.

An Obedient Daughter

In the capital city of Persia there lived some Jews who had been taken as captives from Jerusalem. One man, Mordecai, had a beautiful cousin named Esther. Her parents were dead, so Mordecai brought her up as his own daughter. She was obedient to her cousin, just as though he were her father. The king, Ahasuerus, sent out a decree that a new queen was to be chosen. Esther was one of the young maidens selected to go before the king. She followed Mordecai's instructions carefully, not telling anyone that she was from the Jewish people. The king chose Esther for his queen.

When a wicked man named Haman plotted to kill all the Jews in the kingdom, again Esther followed Mordecai's advice. She was able to save all her people from death by exposing Haman's evil plan.

Because Esther had honored and obeyed the man who was like a father to her, she received many blessings from God. Her life was a blessing to many others, too.

After Jesus came . . .

Jesus Was Obedient

When Jesus was twelve years old, He went with His parents to Jerusalem to the feast of Passover. After the week-long celebration, the crowds of people began returning to their homes. Jesus' parents were traveling with many of their relatives. The group had started back to Nazareth, not knowing that Jesus had stayed behind in Jerusalem. At the end of a day's journey, Mary and Joseph looked for Jesus among their relatives and friends, but He was not there. They walked back to Jerusalem. After three days they found Him in the temple. He was sitting in the middle of a group of very wise men, listening to them and asking questions. All who heard Him were astonished at His knowledge. When Mary and Joseph saw Him they were amazed. His mother said to Him, "Son, why have you treated us this way? Your father and I have been looking for you."

Jesus answered, "Did you not know that I had to be in my Father's house?" Mary and Joseph did not understand what Jesus meant. He was talking about God, His Father. But even though He was God's Son, He honored and respected His earthly parents, and He returned to Nazareth with them. There, the Bible tells us, He "was subject unto them." This means that He was obedient to them.

The Lesson Applied

As children learn to obey their parents, they realize that there are reasons behind the rules at home. Godly parents want only the best for their children; they want to guide them in living the right way.

Children who learn to be obedient at home also learn to be obedient to others in authority, such as teachers and law enforcement officers. They become good citizens. This is all part of God's plan.

But most important of all, children who learn to obey will do what Jesus wants them to do! They will know what God commands in His Word, and they will be obedient. God promises happiness when we live by Jesus' commands.

The Lesson Quiz

1. Whose son was Absalom?

(The son of King David.)

2. How did he show disobedience to his father?

(He wanted to be king and plotted against David.)

3. What happened to him?

(He was killed.)

4. Who was Esther's father?

(She was an orphan, and her cousin, Mordecai, was like a father to her.)

5. How did Esther become a queen?

(She was chosen from all the beautiful young maidens brought before the king.)

6. Because Esther was an obedient daughter, what great service was she able to do for her people?

(She was able to expose the wicked Haman's plot and save the Jews from death.)

7. Who were Jesus' earthly parents when He came from Heaven to earth?

(Mary and Joseph.)

8. Where did Jesus go with His parents when He was twelve years old?

(To Jerusalem for the Passover.)

9. Where did Mary and Joseph find Jesus after discovering on the way home He was missing?

(In the temple, talking to the wisest men of the land.)

10. How do we know that Jesus was obedient to His parents?

(He returned to Nazareth and was "subject unto them"—meaning He was obedient.)

Additional Lesson Activities

1. Discussion Groups: Land Without Laws?

Let pupils discuss what it would be like to live in a land without laws. Divide them into groups and assign each one a question, such as: What would your family life be like if your parents made no rules?

What would your school be like if there were no rules?

What would your city be like if there were no laws?

Groups may put their thoughts on the chalkboard or on sheets of paper. Allow a few minutes for group meetings. Then let each group report to the class. Discuss the importance of having rules and laws. Stress finally the importance of God's laws, given through His Son, Jesus.

2. For Advanced Students: Romans 13

Let pupils read Romans 13 and discover what Paul says about obeying laws. Find the answers to these questions:

Who are the "higher powers"?

Which five of the Ten Commandments are mentioned?

What is the "fulfilling" of the law?

Workbook Page

Page 24 of the Workbook contains two puzzles and a list of questions under "Are You Obedient?" Encourage pupils to answer these four questions truthfully. Check the puzzle answers on pages 62-64.

Memory Verse: John 13:17

Lesson 8

Choosing Friends

Genesis 13:1-13; 19:1-29; 1 Samuel 18:1-4; 19:1-24; Luke 10:38-42; John 11:1-46; Acts 18:1-4, 18-28

Introduction to Lesson

On the chalkboard write this question: "What kind of a person should a good friend be?" Let pupils suggest or list the qualities that they consider important in a friend. Discuss each qualification. Ask them if they know someone who fits all of these qualifications. Also, ask if they have these qualities themselves.

The Bible Lesson

Every person should be very careful to pick out the right kinds of friends. If you choose friends who say and do things that are not right, you soon may be doing and saying those same things. The people with whom you spend time will be influences in your life. It is much better to have just a few friends who are good, than a lot of friends who are bad.

Before Jesus came . . .

Lot Chooses the Wrong Companions

Abraham's nephew, Lot, made the mistake of choosing the wrong kinds of companions. Lot and Abraham decided to live in different parts of the country so there would be enough land for their flocks and herds. Lot chose the part of the country in which there were two large cities, Sodom and Gomorrah. These cities were full of wicked people who did not worship God. Perhaps Lot thought that living among evil people would not make any difference to him. He moved into Sodom and even began to sit with other men of the city at the gate. The city was getting more wicked, and God decided to destroy it. He sent two angels to warn Lot to leave the city. Lot's sons-in-law did not take the warning seriously, and refused to leave. The angels took Lot, his two daughters, and his wife, and told them to leave. The angels said, "Do not look back!" But Lot's wife looked back at the city as they were leaving. Because she disobeyed God's command, she turned into a pillar of salt. Much trouble came to Lot and his family because he chose evil people as his companions. He learned that it did make a difference.

A King's Son Chooses a Friend

When the people of Israel wanted a king, God told Samuel to anoint Saul. At first Saul was a good king. Then he began to disobey God. God sent Samuel to Bethlehem to the home of Jesse. There Samuel anointed the young shepherd boy, David, to be the next king.

David was a young man, and many years would go by before he would be crowned as king. However, David was brought to King Saul's palace. Saul had a strange illness that made him very moody. David played his harp for King Saul, and the music helped Saul to feel better.

At the palace David met Jonathan, the king's son. Jonathan was a fine young man—brave, loving, and unselfish. David and Jonathan soon became close friends. They pledged themselves to be friends forever. To show that he meant to keep his promise of friendship, Jonathan gave David his princely robe, his sword, his bow, and his belt or girdle.

In a battle with the Philistines, King Saul was wounded. To avoid being killed by an enemy, Saul killed himself. His son, Jonathan, was killed in the same battle. David mourned for his friend and sang a song about him (2 Samuel 1:19-27). David never forgot Jonathan. When he was crowned king, David asked if anyone from the family was still alive. He was told that a crippled son of Jonathan's was living. David brought the son to his palace and took care of him the rest of his life (2 Samuel 9).

After Jesus came . . .

Jesus' Friends in Bethany

In the village of Bethany, not far from Jerusalem, lived a man named Lazarus and his sisters, Mary and Martha. Jesus often visited in their home when He was teaching and preaching in the area around Jerusalem. Jesus loved them very much, and they became close friends. They provided food and shelter for Him, and He taught them God's Word.

One day Jesus received a message that Lazarus

was very sick. When He reached Bethany, He was too late. Lazarus had died four days earlier. Mary and Martha each said to Jesus, "Lord, if You had been here, my brother would not have died!"

Jesus went to the tomb where Lazarus had been buried, and He prayed to God. Then Jesus spoke, "Lazarus, come forth!" Lazarus came out of the tomb, still wrapped in the cloth that had been bound around him. Jesus had brought him back to life and restored him to his sisters!

The week before Jesus was crucified He was eating in the home of Simon the leper in Bethany. Mary anointed Jesus' feet with very precious ointment. This was the last time Jesus visited His friends in Bethany.

Paul's Friends in Corinth

On a missionary journey, Paul went to Corinth. There he met a man named Aquila and his wife Priscilla. They had lived in Rome, but because the emperor had made all the Jews leave Rome, they had moved to Corinth. Paul had two things in common with them—they were Christians and tentmakers. Paul had learned the trade of tentmaking, because it was customary for every Jewish boy to learn a trade. Paul lived with Aquila and Priscilla, helping them make tents. He preached the gospel whenever he could.

The Lesson Applied

God's Word has much to say about choosing friends and companions. God does not want us to make friends with those who get into trouble and do wicked things. Lot chose to associate with evil people, and they brought a lot of trouble to his life. (Read Proverbs 13:20.)

A true friend loves you whether you are rich or poor. He will stick by you when you have problems. He will love you and help you when you are in need. Jonathan and David are examples of such friends. (Read Proverbs 17:17.)

Friends are important. We need them! But we must choose the right kinds of friends and be the right kinds of friends to others.

The best friend we can have is Jesus! He will never let us down.

Questions for Discussion: Is it wise to choose friends who do not go to church? Should a friend be faithful to you when you are unkind or selfish?

The Lesson Quiz

1. What foolish choice did Lot make?
(He decided to live in a city where the people were very wicked.)

2. What happened to Lot's family when God destroyed the wicked cities?
(Only Lot and his two daughters escaped.)

3. What prince and shepherd pledged to be friends forever?
(Jonathan and David.)

4. After Jonathan's death, how did David show friendship to his family?
(David learned that Jonathan's crippled son was still living. David brought the son to the palace to live for the rest of his life.)

5. What brother and two sisters were close friends of Jesus?
(Lazarus, Mary, and Martha.)

6. In what ways did Jesus and His friends in Bethany share with each other?
(Lazarus, Mary, and Martha provided a place for Jesus to stay when He visited, and Jesus taught them God's Word.)

7. How did Jesus help Mary and Martha when Lazarus died?
(Jesus brought Lazarus back to life.)

8. Who befriended Paul in the city of Corinth?
(Aquila and Priscilla.)

9. What did Paul have in common with them?
(They were Christians and tentmakers.)

10. How did they share with each other?
(Aquila and Priscilla provided a home for Paul while he was in Corinth, and Paul helped them make tents. They heard him preach the gospel.)

Additional Lesson Activities

1. A Friendly Note
Provide notepaper and envelopes. Let pupils write friendly notes to those who are ill or shut in, or those who have been absent from class.

2. Friendship Charts
Let pupils make charts showing the good qualities a friend should have.

Workbook Page

"Make the Right Choices," on page 25 of the Workbook, reviews the Scripture about Lot. "Match These Scriptures About Friends" is taken from verses in Proverbs.

Memory Verse: John 15:13

Lesson 9

Getting Along With Others

1 Samuel 25:2-42; 2 Kings 4:8-37; Luke 10:30-37; Acts 9:36-43

Introduction to Lesson

Old Testament—New Testament Quiz

Teachings from both the Old Testament and the New Testament have been presented in each of the first eight lessons of this series. Call out the names or titles of the following people and let pupils identify them as to Old or New Testament.

1. Moses
2. Jesus
3. Solomon
4. David
5. Noah
6. Barnabas
7. The Pharisee
8. King Josiah
9. Timothy
10. Paul
11. Absalom
12. Esther
13. Mordecai
14. Mary and Joseph
15. Lot
16. Jonathan
17. Lazarus
18. The Publican

(Answers: Old Testament: 1, 3, 4, 5, 8, 11, 12, 13, 15, 16; New Testament: 2, 6, 7, 9, 10, 14, 17, 18.)

The Bible Lesson

Getting along with others is not always easy. If we are Christians, we try our best to avoid trouble with those around us. Two good rules for the Christian are: Be kind and be a peacemaker. In our lesson we will see examples of these virtues.

Before Jesus came . . .

In the Old Testament there are examples of people who were kind, and people who were peacemakers.

Abigail, the Peacemaker

One day, David, who was to become king of Israel, was traveling with his soldiers in the wilderness of Paran. He and his men were hungry, and David heard that a wealthy man named Nabal was having his sheep sheared nearby. David sent ten soldiers to ask Nabal if some food could be sent for him and his men. Nabal was a very evil, selfish man, and he refused to give any of his meat, bread, or water to them. David and his men were angry.

Nabal's wife, Abigail, was a good, kind woman. When she heard what her husband had done, she hurriedly set out with food for the soldiers: two hundred loaves of bread, something to drink, five sheep roasted, corn, a hundred clusters of raisins, and two hundred cakes of figs. Abigail's kindness and generosity made peace between David's soldiers and Nabal and his men.

A Husband and Wife Were Kind to Elisha

The prophet Elisha traveled through Israel giving God's messages. In one of the cities through which Elisha often passed, there lived a good man and his wife. They did a very kind thing for the prophet. They added a room to their house and furnished it with a bed, table, chair, and candlestick. The next time Elisha came to their city, they took him into their house and showed him the room. They told him it was to be his room whenever he was in that city.

This couple had a son. One day he became sick and died very suddenly. The mother thought of Elisha. She saddled a donkey and started out. Soon she came to the city where Elisha was staying. When she told him of her trouble, he immediately returned with her. When he saw the boy lying there in the bed, Elisha shut the door and prayed to God. God heard the prophet's prayer and brought the son back to life.

After Jesus came . . .

Jesus taught that people should learn to get along with others. He said, "Blessed are the peacemakers: for they shall be called the children of God" (Matthew 5:9). Jesus also talked about the importance of showing kindness to others.

The Parable of the Good Samaritan

A Jewish leader asked Jesus, "Who is my neighbor?" He knew that God commanded that we are to love our neighbors as we love ourselves. To explain, Jesus told a parable about a man who had been robbed and beaten and left on the road half dead. Two men came by—religious leaders—but they passed by without helping him. A Samaritan came by. Jews and Samaritans did not associate with each other, but the Samaritan stopped, put medicine on the man's wounds, put him on his own donkey, and took him to an inn. The next day he gave the owner of the inn some money to take care of the man. The Samaritan was a "neighbor" to the wounded man.

The Kindness of Dorcas

After Jesus rose from the dead and went back to Heaven to be with God, His disciples went everywhere preaching about Him and telling the people how they should live. One day, while Peter was preaching in Lydda, a messenger came and told him that a disciple named Dorcas had just died. Her friends wanted Peter to come quickly to Joppa. When he arrived, he found the house full of people who were weeping. They began to tell Peter what a wonderful woman Dorcas had been, and how kind she was to everyone. They showed Peter some of the clothes she had made and given to them. Then Peter went into the room where Dorcas was lying. After he had prayed to God, he took Dorcas by the hand and told her to get up. Through God's power Dorcas lived again.

The Lesson Applied

Two ways you can let people know you are a Christian: Be a peacemaker and be kind to others. Jesus is the greatest example of both kindness and peaceful attitudes. Being kind to others doesn't mean you are kind only to friends. Be kind to those you don't know very well, and to those who are younger or older than you are. Do not tease in a cruel way. Be thoughtful. You can get along with most people if you really try—if you live and act like a Christian.

Questions for Discussion: Is it possible to get along with everyone? Does "getting along with others" mean we should always do as they say?

The Lesson Quiz

1. What woman acted as a peacemaker between her husband and David?
(Abigail, wife of Nabal.)

2. What kindness did Abigail show to David and his men?
(She provided a generous amount of food.)

3. What kind deed was done for Elisha by a husband and wife?
(They built and furnished a special room where he could stay when he visited their city.)

4. What kindness did Elisha show to them later?
(When their son died, Elisha came immediately and prayed to God. God gave him power to bring the son back to life.)

5. What parable did Jesus tell to teach that we should be kind to others in need?
(The parable of the good Samaritan.)

6. In the story, who was a "neighbor"?
(A Samaritan.)

7. Why was it unusual for a Samaritan to help a Jew?
(The Jews and Samaritans did not associate with each other.)

8. While Peter was preaching in Lydda, what news did a messenger bring?
(A faithful disciple named Dorcas had died.)

9. For what kindnesses was Dorcas known?
(She had made clothing for needy people.)

10. What did God give Peter the power to do?
(Bring Dorcas back to life.)

Additional Lesson Activities

1. Class Project: Showing Kindness
Let pupils choose a project to show that they care about others: collecting good used clothing for a mission, putting on a program at a home for the elderly, visiting a shut-in, etc.

2. Peacemaker's Pledge
Let pupils decide that they will be peacemakers and keep track of opportunities they have to make peace. Encourage them to keep notebooks for the next month. In them they record times they have averted arguments or avoided fights at school, at home—with brothers and sisters—or on the playground. Let them discuss the kinds of situations where arguments occur, and how they can be peacemakers.

Workbook Page

Page 26 of the Workbook contains a puzzle, "Unscramble and Match," and two exercises taken from Scripture verses.

Memory Verse: Romans 12:18

Lesson 10

Learning Self-Control

Genesis 4:1-15; Exodus 2:11-22; Matthew 4:1-11; Luke 9:51-56

Introduction to Lesson

Good or Bad Examples?

Some of the Bible people we have learned about were good examples, and some were bad. Call out these names from lessons 1-9. Let pupils tell if they were good or bad examples, and why.

1. Dorcas
2. Abigail
3. The Samaritan
4. Barnabas
5. Absalom
6. King Josiah
7. Lot
8. Jonathan
9. Esther
10. Aquila and Priscilla

The Bible Lesson

One of the worst things a person can have is a bad temper. People who always are getting angry often make themselves ill because of it. A bad-tempered person never has as many friends as the good-natured person. A person who keeps losing his temper is likely to get into trouble.

Before Jesus came . . .

Here are two examples of people who lost their temper. They're found in the Old Testament books of Genesis and Exodus.

Cain Loses His Temper

Cain and Abel were brothers, the sons of Adam and Eve. One day Abel, who was a shepherd, brought a lamb from his flock to offer as a sacrifice to God. Cain, who was a farmer, brought some of the crops he had grown. Abel's offering was accepted and God was pleased with him. Cain's offering was not pleasing to God—perhaps Cain's attitude was not right. When Cain saw that God was pleased with his brother's offering and not his, he became jealous and killed Abel. Cain lost his temper and became guilty of murder.

Moses Loses His Temper

Moses also learned that it does not pay to lose your temper. You remember how Moses' mother had placed him in a little basket on the river when he was a baby? The princess found him and took him as her son. Moses grew up in the palace of the Pharaoh. However, Moses knew he was an Israelite and not an Egyptian. His mother, who had been hired by the princess to take care of him as a child, had taught him about his own people. The Israelites were slaves and were being treated cruelly by the Egyptians.

When Moses went out to the place where the Israelites were working, he became very angry when he saw the Egyptians beat them if they did not work fast enough. One day when Moses saw an Egyptian beating an Israelite, he became so angry that he killed the Egyptian and buried him in the sand. Although Moses had a reason for being angry, he should have learned how to control his temper. He could have stopped the Egyptian from beating the Israelite without killing him. When the word got out about Moses' deed, he had to leave the country in order to save his own life.

After Jesus came . . .

The Temptation of Jesus

There is more to self-control than controlling your temper. Jesus showed us a perfect example when He was tempted by Satan. After Jesus was baptized by John the Baptist, the Spirit of God led Him into the wilderness. He had been there forty days without food when Satan came to Him, tempting Him. Knowing Jesus was hungry, the devil said, "Why don't you turn these stones into bread?"

Jesus answered, "Man shall not live by bread alone." He refused to do what Satan suggested, even though He must have been very hungry.

Then Satan took Him to the top of the temple. "You are God's Son," he said. "Why don't you jump down? God will not let you get hurt, and the people will think you are a great hero." But Jesus told him that it is not right to tempt God.

Then Satan took Him to the top of a high mountain. There he showed Jesus all the kingdoms of the world. "If you will bow down and worship me, I will give you all of these," Satan said. But Jesus refused and told him that only God is to be worshiped.

No matter how much Jesus was tempted, He did not lose His self-control. Each time Jesus answered Satan by quoting from God's Word.

Two Disciples Lose Their Tempers

There were many times in the life of Jesus when He taught that we should control our tempers. One of these times was when Jesus and His disciples were traveling through a village of Samaria. The people of that village would not receive Jesus. James and John became so angry that they asked Jesus if He would let them call down fire from Heaven to destroy these people! But Jesus said that they should not get angry and wish for harm to come even to their enemies. Jesus had come to save lives, not take them. Because James and John lost their tempers easily, they were sometimes called "sons of thunder."

The Lesson Applied

Can you face things that happen and keep your self-control? Or do you lose your temper and say and do things that are not pleasing to God? Jesus was able to keep control over His desires. He refused to give in to Satan's temptations.

Self-control is not easy. It takes much prayer and faith and courage, and sometimes years of trying before one develops it. Jesus will help us if we ask Him. God's Word helps us, too, as we read it each day.

Questions for Discussion: Is it ever right to get angry? Is self-control a habit?

The Lesson Quiz

1. Why was Cain jealous of his brother, Abel?

(Abel's offering was accepted by God and Cain's was not.)

2. What did Cain's jealousy lead to?

(Murder—Cain killed his brother.)

3. What caused Moses to become angry?

(He saw an Egyptian beating an Israelite slave.)

4. What did Moses do?

(He killed the Egyptian and buried him in the sand.)

5. What did Moses do when he realized that others knew about his killing the Egyptian?

(He had to leave the country in order to save his own life.)

6. How did Jesus show self-control when Satan tempted Him?

(Jesus refused to give in to the temptations.)

7. How did Jesus answer each of Satan's temptations?

(By quoting God's Word.)

8. What caused James and John to become so angry?

(People in a village of Samaria would not receive Jesus and His disciples.)

9. What did James and John want to do?

(To call down fire from Heaven and destroy the people.)

10. What did Jesus say to these "sons of thunder"?

(Jesus said that He did not come to destroy men's lives but to save them.)

Additional Lesson Activities

1. Discussion Questions: How to Show Self-Control

Let pupils as a group, or in small groups, discuss the following situations:

a. When someone picks a quarrel with you.
b. When someone makes fun of you for going to church.
c. When you could avoid punishment by telling a lie.
d. When you feel like gossiping.
e. When someone wins a game you're playing, and you want to win.

2. Scripture Hunt

Let pupils look up these verses on the subject of "anger."

Proverbs 15:1	Proverbs 29:22
Proverbs 14:17	Ecclesiastes 7:9
Proverbs 22:24	Matthew 5:22

Workbook Page

"Find Out," on page 27 of the Workbook, reviews some of the Scriptures from the lesson. "Look Up These Scriptures" repeats the verses suggested in No. 2 of "Additional Lesson Activities." The puzzle, "The Printer's Mistake," is the helpful verse on overcoming temptation, James 1:12.

Memory Verse: Ephesians 4:26

Lesson 11

Telling the Truth

1 Kings 22:1-28; 2 Kings 5:1-27; Mark 6:17-32; Acts 5:1-11

Introduction to Lesson

Let pupils suggest different words that are used for "lies." (Fibs, white lies, falsehoods, exaggerations, half-truths, etc.) Discuss why these different terms are used, and whether or not there is any difference in the meanings.

Let pupils read aloud and discuss these Scriptures: Exodus 20:16; Leviticus 19:11; Proverbs 14:5; Psalm 63:11.

The Bible Lesson

Telling lies is a very bad habit. But lying is worse than a bad habit—it is a sin! (Those who tell lies continually are included in a list of sinners who will not be allowed to enter Heaven. Read Revelation 21:8). Jesus wants us always to tell the truth. The Bible gives us several stories about the importance of telling the truth, even when it isn't the most popular thing to do.

Before Jesus came . . .

Here are two examples, one bad and one good, from the Old Testament.

A Prophet Who Would Not Lie

While Ahab was king of Israel, there was a prophet of God named Micaiah. Micaiah knew how wicked Ahab and his wife, Jezebel, were.

Ahab decided to join the king of Judah in a battle, that together they might take a city from the king of Syria. The king of Judah said, "Let us find out if God is with us. Let us ask the prophets." They called four hundred prophets together, and all of them said, "Yes, God will be with you."

But the king of Judah was not satisfied. "Are there no more prophets in Israel?" he asked. "Yes," said king Ahab, "but I hate him. He never says anything good about me." However, Micaiah was called. The messenger who was sent to his home said, "Speak only good things to the king."

But Micaiah answered, "I will speak the truth!" When he stood before the kings, he did just that. He told them that God would be against them so that they would not be able to take the city, and that Ahab would be killed. For speaking the truth as God gave it to him, Micaiah was cast into prison. Not long afterward the things that Micaiah had spoken came true.

Gehazi Lies to Naaman

In the land of Syria lived a great general by the name of Naaman. He was in charge of a large army. But Naaman had the dread disease of leprosy.

A young Hebrew girl, who had been taken away from Israel as a captive, was a servant in Naaman's house. Naaman's wife was good to the young girl. The servant told her mistress that if Naaman would go to the land of Canaan, he would find a prophet of God named Elisha who could heal him.

Naaman went to the place where the prophet lived and was healed. He was so happy that he offered many gifts to Elisha. Elisha would not take any of them.

Elisha had a servant named Gehazi. When he heard his master refuse to accept the gifts from Naaman, he decided to get some of them for himself. He ran after Naaman. When he caught up with him, he said, "My master has changed his mind, and he would like to have the gifts." Naaman gladly gave them to Gehazi to take back to Elisha. Then Gehazi took the things to his own home and hid them. Elisha, being a prophet of God, knew what Gehazi had done. As a punishment, Gehazi became sick with the same disease, leprosy, from which Naaman had been healed!

After Jesus came . . .

The New Testament gives examples of those who lied, and those who bravely told the truth.

John Tells the Truth

John the Baptist was a messenger sent from God to prepare people to listen to Jesus. He fearlessly told the truth to the crowds that came out to the wilderness to hear him. John gave God's messages to rich and poor, rulers and slaves, soldiers and tax collectors. One day John bravely told King Herod that it was against God's law for him to take his brother's wife. Because John told the truth, he was put in prison. Herod's wife plotted to get even with John for what he had said about her and her husband. Through her daughter she asked that John be killed. John was beheaded, and the disciples came and buried him.

A Husband and Wife Who Lied

In Jerusalem, during the days soon after the church began, many of the Christians shared their money with those who were in need. Some who had houses and lands sold them and brought the money to the apostles. A husband and wife, named Ananias and Sapphira, sold their land. Ananias brought part of the money to the apostles. He pretended to bring all of it. Peter told Ananias that he had lied to the Holy Spirit, and immediately Ananias fell dead. Later Sapphira came in and told the same lie. She, too, fell dead. Their punishment was not for keeping back part of the money—it was theirs to keep or share. Their punishment was for telling a lie. God wants His followers to always tell the truth.

The Lesson Applied

Some people tell lies in order to get out of trouble. This usually gets them in more trouble, for sooner or later they get caught. Other people tell lies to make their friends think they are rich or important. Still others tell lies in order to get other people in trouble. Lying, in God's sight, is a sin just like stealing or killing.

Jesus had much to say about telling the truth. He always told the truth, even when it made Him unpopular. Sometimes it takes courage to tell the truth. God is pleased when we choose to be truthful.

Questions for Discussion: Is it all right to lie if it will keep someone out of trouble? Why is a lie dangerous? Why does one lie usually lead to another?

The Lesson Quiz

1. What did the four hundred prophets say would happen when the kings of Judah and Israel planned to go to war against Syria?

(They said what the kings wanted to hear, that God would be with them.)

2. When the prophet Micaiah was asked, what did he say?

(He said that God would not be with them, and that King Ahab would be killed.)

3. What happened to Micaiah when he told the truth?

(He was put into prison.)

4. When the prophet Elisha refused money and gifts for his part in healing Naaman, what did his servant, Gehazi, do?

(He told a lie, saying that his master had changed his mind. He wanted the gifts for himself.)

5. What was Gehazi's punishment?

(He became sick with the same disease from which Naaman had been cured—leprosy.)

6. To whom did John the Baptist bravely tell the truth and accuse of breaking God's command?

(King Herod, who had taken his brother's wife.)

7. What happened to John?

(He was put in prison and later beheaded.)

8. What husband and wife in Jerusalem agreed to tell a lie to the apostles?

(Ananias and Sapphira.)

9. What was their lie?

(They sold their property, decided to keep back part of the price, but pretended to give it all.)

10. What was their punishment?

(Both fell dead.)

Additional Lesson Activities

1. Make a List: Why Christians Tell the Truth

Provide paper and pencils. Let pupils list reasons why Christians should tell the truth always.

2. Act Out the Stories

Divide the students into four groups. Let each group act out one of the four stories:

A Prophet Who Would Not Lie (1 Kings 22:1-28)
Gehazi Lies to Naaman (2 Kings 5:1-27)
John Tells the Truth (Mark 6:17-32)
A Husband and Wife Who Lied (Acts 5:1-11)

Workbook Page

"Words of Truth" Crossword, on page 28 of the Workbook, stresses New Testament Scriptures on truth. "Who Am I?" reviews three Bible characters from the lesson. Perhaps you will want to make up more of these quizzes.

Memory Verse: Ephesians 4:25

Lesson 12

Learning to Forgive

Genesis 42—46; Luke 23; Acts 6:9-15; 7

Introduction to Lesson

Memory Verse Review

Put the lesson titles on one side of the chalkboard and the memory verse references on the other. Let pupils match the lessons and verses, after looking up the references. (Check the answers by noting the memory verses at the end of each lesson.)

Understanding the Rules	Ephesians 4:25
Following Jesus' Example	Matthew 6:14
Worshiping God	John 14:15
Sharing in the Lord's Work	John 4:24
Praying Every Day	2 Corinthians 9:7
Reading God's Word	John 13:17
Learning Obedience	1 Thessalonians 5:17
Choosing Friends	Romans 12:18
Getting Along With Others	John 15:13
Learning Self-Control	Luke 2:52
Telling the Truth	Ephesians 4:26
Learning to Forgive	2 Timothy 3:16

The Bible Lesson

Do you think it is an easy thing to forgive? When someone wrongs you, it is hard to be friendly with that person, and forgive him, isn't it? And yet Jesus told Peter that we should forgive "seventy times seven." That means we should never stop forgiving people, no matter how many times they do wrong things to us. Jesus also said that we should not only forgive our friends when they do unkind things to us, but we should also forgive our enemies. In our lesson today we shall learn about people who were willing to forgive.

Before Jesus came . . .

One of the greatest stories of forgiveness is in the first book of the Bible.

Joseph Forgives His Brothers

Joseph, one of twelve brothers, was the favorite son of Jacob. His ten older brothers were jealous of him and decided to get rid of him. They secretly sold him to some traders on their way to Egypt, and then lied to their father, saying that Joseph had been killed by wild beasts. Joseph went from being a slave in Egypt to second in command to Pharaoh, king of Egypt. When a famine came, only Egypt had extra grain to sell to people from other countries. Joseph's brothers traveled to Egypt to buy grain. Joseph, being a ruler, had the power to punish his brothers. Instead he chose to forgive them. He invited them to bring Jacob and all of their families to live in Egypt.

After Jesus came . . .

Jesus is the perfect example of someone who is forgiving.

Jesus Forgives His Enemies

While Jesus lived on earth, He went about doing good: healing the sick, making the blind see, and raising the dead. He also gave God's message to the people, telling them to repent and live as God wanted them to live. The religious leaders of the Jews resented Jesus' popularity with the people. They knew that if the people followed Jesus, they would no longer be the leaders. These evil men began to plot against Jesus. Finally they succeeded in having Jesus condemned to death by crucifixion. Just before Jesus died on the cross, He prayed, "Father, forgive them; for they know not what they do" (Luke 23:34). Jesus' example gives us the true meaning of forgiveness.

Stephen Forgives His Enemies

Among the first deacons, chosen by the church in Jerusalem, was a man named Stephen. He was a man of faith who did "great wonders and miracles among the people."

Some of the enemies of Jesus stirred up the people by telling them that Stephen was speaking against God. He was brought before the Jewish council. Stephen stood up to speak, telling the members of the council that Jesus was the Savior who had been promised, that He had been crucified, and that He had risen from the grave.

When Stephen finished speaking, the council members were so angry that they rushed upon him, dragged him out of the city, and stoned him. Just before he died, Stephen prayed, "Lord, lay not this sin to their charge." He followed Jesus' example and forgave the enemies who put him to death.

The Lesson Applied

From the time the first man sinned, God planned a way for sin to be forgiven. In God's own time the Savior came, Jesus, God's own Son. He died on the cross that we might be forgiven of our sins. "For God so loved the world, that he gave his only begotten Son, that whosoever believeth in him should not perish, but have everlasting life" (John 3:16).

When we become Christians, we repent of our sins. And when we repent, God is ready to forgive us. "If we confess our sins, he is faithful and just to forgive us our sins, and to cleanse us from all unrighteousness" (1 John 1:9). None of us deserves forgiveness, yet God does it because He loves us. That is the way we must forgive others.

Questions for Discussion: How often will God forgive us? Is there such a thing as forgiving without forgetting?

The Lesson Quiz

1. What did Joseph's brothers do to him?

(They sold him as a slave to traders.)

2. What happened when Joseph's brothers went down to Egypt to buy grain?

(Joseph forgave them for the things they had done to him.)

3. What good things did Jesus do while He was on earth?

(He healed the sick, raised the dead, etc., and taught God's Word.)

4. Why did the religious leaders plot against Jesus?

(They were jealous of His popularity. The people were following Jesus' teachings instead of theirs.)

5. What did Jesus' enemies do to Him?

(They had Him crucified.)

6. What did Jesus pray just before He died?

("Father, forgive them; for they know not what they do.")

7. Who was Stephen?

(One of the deacons in the church at Jerusalem.)

8. Why did the members of the Jewish council stone Stephen?

(He preached about Jesus.)

9. What did Stephen say just before he died?

("Lord, lay not this sin to their charge.")

10. What was God's plan for the forgiveness of our sins?

(Jesus, God's Son, gave His life on the cross for our sins.)

Additional Lesson Activities

1. The Parable of the Unforgiving Servant

Let pupils act out Jesus' parable in Matthew 18:23-35.

2. Review Quiz

Using the ten questions from each of the lessons (1-12) in this series, have a quiz between two teams from the class.

Workbook Page

Page 29 contains two puzzles that review portions of the Bible stories from this lesson. Again, the King James Version of the Bible is quoted. Are pupils copying their memory verses in their scrolls?

Memory Verse: Matthew 6:14

Lesson 13

Telling Others About Jesus

Isaiah 9:6; Micah 5:2; Daniel 9:25; Matthew 28:19, 20; Mark 16:15, 16; Acts 8:1-8, 26-40; 16:6-34

Introduction to Lesson

Titles Given to Jesus

Place the assignment below on the chalkboard. Let pupils look up the various titles given to Jesus and write them in the blank spaces.

L ________ (John 8:12)
A ________ and ________ (Revelation 22:13)
M ________ (Daniel 9:25)
B ________ (Matthew 9:15)

O ______ __________ ______ (John 1:18)
F ________ (Colossians 1:15)

G ______ ________ (John 10:11)
O ________ ______ ______ (Revelation 22:16)
D ________ (John 10:7)

(Answers: Light, Alpha and Omega, Messiah, bridegroom, only begotten Son, firstborn, good shepherd, offspring of David, door.)

The Bible Lesson

From the beginning God planned to send His Son to be the Savior of the world.

Before Jesus came . . .

Isaiah prophesied about seven hundred years before Jesus came: "For unto us a child is born . . . his name shall be called Wonderful, Counselor, The mighty God, The everlasting Father, The Prince of Peace" (Isaiah 9:6).

Micah foretold: "Bethlehem . . . out of thee shall he come forth unto me that is to be ruler in Israel" (Micah 5:2).

Daniel told of Messiah the Prince (Daniel 9:25).

These and other prophets did not know when the Savior would come, but they believed that God would keep His promises. God did send the Savior, His only begotten Son. (Read aloud John 3:16.)

After Jesus came . . .

Jesus came to earth, lived a sinless life, and then gave His life for the sins of the world. He made it possible for us to be forgiven. He arose from the grave and made it possible for us to have eternal life.

Philip, the Preacher

When the enemies of Jesus began to persecute the church in Jerusalem, the Christians "went every where preaching the word."

Among these Christians was a man named Philip. He had been chosen to be one of the first deacons (Acts 6:5). Philip traveled to Samaria and preached Christ to the people there. The people listened to Philip, and they were astonished at the miracles he did. Through the power of the Holy Spirit he could heal people. There was much joy in the city where Philip preached, because many people believed in Jesus and were baptized.

Then the angel of the Lord told Philip to go south on the road from Jerusalem to Gaza. As he walked along the road, Philip saw an important official from Ethiopia, who served as treasurer for Candace, queen of the Ethiopians. This man had been to Jerusalem to worship God. As he rode along in his chariot, he was reading aloud from the book of Isaiah the prophet.

The Holy Spirit told Philip to join the man. Philip ran up to the chariot and asked him, "Do you understand what you are reading?"

The Ethiopian answered, "How can I unless someone should guide me?" He asked Philip to come up and sit with him in the chariot. Philip explained that the prophet Isaiah was telling about Jesus. Philip began to preach to the Ethiopian man about Jesus.

As they traveled they came by a pool of water. The Ethiopian said, "Here is water. Is there any reason why I can't be baptized?"

Philip answered, "If you believe with all your heart, you may be baptized."

He said to Philip, "I believe that Jesus Christ is the Son of God."

They went down into the pool of water, and Philip baptized the Ethiopian. When they were come up out of the water, the Holy Spirit took Philip away. The Ethiopian went on his way rejoicing.

Paul's Vision

The apostle Paul, guided by the Holy Spirit, traveled to many cities and preached the gospel. During one night Paul had a vision from the Lord. A man from Macedonia appeared to him and said, "Come over into Macedonia, and help us."

Paul's group then went to Philippi, an important city in Macedonia. There they had some wonderful opportunities to witness about Jesus. A businesswoman named Lydia, and others from her household, heard Paul teach about Jesus. They believed and were baptized.

Later, Paul cast an evil spirit from a young woman who told fortunes. Her masters were angry because they no longer could make money from her powers, and they had Paul and Silas put in jail. At midnight the Lord sent an earthquake and all the prisoners' chains were loosened. The jailer would have killed himself, but Paul called out, "Don't harm yourself! We are all here." The jailer asked Paul and Silas, "What must I do to be saved?"

Paul and Silas told him to believe on the Lord Jesus Christ. They taught him and his family the Word of the Lord. That same hour of the night the jailer and his family were baptized. They, too, rejoiced.

The Lesson Applied

The apostles and disciples were not the only ones who had the responsibility of telling others about Jesus. The command Jesus gave, sometimes called the Great Commission, is for us, too.

Questions for Discussion: What does the word "missionary" mean? What specific things can we do to help missionaries? How can we find out more about the missionaries supported by our church?

The Lesson Quiz

1. What three prophets told about the coming of the Messiah?

(Isaiah, Micah, Daniel—among others.)

2. What command did Jesus give before He ascended into Heaven?

("Go ye into all the world, and preach the gospel.")

3. What did the Christians in Jerusalem do when they were persecuted?

("They . . . went every where preaching the word.")

4. What preacher was sent by the Lord to a road south of Jerusalem?

(Philip.)

5. Who was traveling along the road, and what was he reading?

(An Ethiopian, treasurer to Queen Candace, was riding in his chariot, reading the prophet Isaiah.)

6. After Philip preached to him about Jesus, what did the Ethiopian ask?

(He asked to be baptized.)

7. Where was Paul when he had a vision of a man asking him to come to his country?

(Paul was in Troas.)

8. What did the man say to Paul in the vision?

("Come over into Macedonia, and help us.")

9. What businesswoman of Philippi believed and was baptized?

(Lydia.)

10. What other person and his household believed in Jesus and was baptized?

(The Philippian jailer.)

Additional Lesson Activities

1. Mission Project

If your pupils have not had a mission project during this series, introduce one at this time. Select a mission family that is supported by your congregation, or choose a children's home, nursing home, or a mission school. Let pupils help with the plans.

2. Make Invitations

Let pupils make simple invitations to give to their friends and acquaintances who do not go to Sunday school. Provide construction paper, felt-tipped pens, colorful seals or pictures to be cut out. Help them with the wording of the invitations. Be sure to include the name of your class and the church's name and address.

Workbook Page

Page 30 of the Workbook contains two puzzles that review the New Testament stories from this lesson. Check your answers with those on pages 62-64.

Memory Verse: Mark 16:15

Part Three

Adventures With Peter

In these lessons we will be having some adventures with the apostle Peter. We see him first as a humble fisherman who becomes interested in the teachings and the miracles of Jesus. When Jesus calls him, he leaves his fishing business and his home in order to follow Jesus.

At first, Peter seems to be very sincere and enthusiastic as he works with Jesus—and he is. He stands up before the other disciples and says to Jesus, "Thou art the Christ, the Son of the living God." But when a test comes, Peter loses his courage and denies his Lord. However, he soon repents and because Jesus knows that Peter means it this time, He gives Peter the task of preaching the first gospel sermon to the Jews and also to the Gentiles. He preaches on the Day of Pentecost when three thousand people become Christians. He preaches to Cornelius, a Gentile, and this soldier and his family become Christians.

Peter's life as a Christian is not an easy one. The rulers of the people do not want anyone to preach about Jesus, and so they persecute all Christians, especially the apostles. Many times Peter is thrown into prison, and tradition says—the Bible does not tell us—that he is finally crucified head downward. But through all of these hardships, Peter is never sorry that he has decided to follow Jesus. He is glad that he is able to suffer for his Master, and he teaches other Christians that they, too, should not become discouraged. "If any man suffer as a Christian," writes Peter, "let him not be ashamed; but let him glorify God on this behalf." This means that we should never be ashamed to suffer for Christ, but we should thank God that we have the opportunity to do so.

We find Peter preaching to those who were not Christians, and teaching those who already had accepted Christ as their Savior. He shows them that it is not enough just to become Christians. They should be trying every day to be better Christians. His two letters encourage people to be faithful to the Lord.

Peter is an outstanding and colorful character in the New Testament. The Bible does not tell us what he looked like, but it is easy to picture him as a big man, rugged in body and in speech. He is quick to become angry, quick to speak, and impulsive in action. His great love for Christ helps him to become a great leader for Christ.

As you present this series of lessons, think of Peter with both his courage and his weaknesses. Help the students see that God can use them, even though they do not always measure up to God's standards.

There is much in the present-day conception of Peter than has no Scriptural basis. Stick to the Biblical accounts and do not confuse your students. (Read Acts 10:25, 26.)

Make a "Surprise" Theme Chart

You will need two pieces of lightweight poster board, 16 x 19", felt-tipped pens, pencil, scissors, and glue for this theme chart.

On the first piece of poster board, position a cutout figure of Peter in the center. (Use the pattern on page 58.) Carefully draw and cut open three sides of the 2" square "doors" as indicated in figure 1. Letter the title, "Adventures With Peter."

Place the first piece of poster board on top of the second, and open the doors. Trace lightly around the openings, so you will locate the exact places for the drawings of the symbols.

Add the symbols from each lesson, as indicated in figure 2. These symbols are found with the lessons on the workbook pages. You may trace them or sketch them freehand. Add color if you wish. Allow at least a one-inch border for glue.

After adding the symbols to the second piece, check the spacing with the first piece before gluing the two pieces together. Add white glue on the border (figure 2).

Each week as you tell the story (or stories), you will open one or more of the "doors" to show the symbol or symbols for that lesson. These symbols will help students remember the stories. They will be eager to see what is behind each "door."

The theme chart may be used in different ways to review the lessons.

figure 1

figure 2

Memory Verses: Words to Remember

Each memory verse in this thirteen-week series is taken from one of these four situations:

1. Conversation between Jesus and Peter.
2. Peter's preaching and teaching.
3. Jesus' speaking to Peter.
4. Peter's writings.

Students are to copy the words from the memory verses as indicated in their workbooks. These verses will help to reinforce the study of Peter's life, and the lessons from his life that apply to us.

Lesson 1

Peter Becomes a "Fisher of Men"

Matthew 4:18-22; Mark 1:14-20; Luke 5:1-11; John 1:35-42

Introduction to Lesson

Some Interesting Facts About Peter

Give these assignments to pupils (individuals or small groups) and let them find the answers.

1. His names
   John 1:40, 42
2. His homes
   John 1:44; Mark 1:21, 29
3. His family
   Matthew 8:14; Mark 1:30; Luke 4:38; 1 Corinthians 9:5
4. His business
   Matthew 4:18; Luke 5:3, 10

Let pupils or groups give reports on their findings.

The Bible Lesson

All through the Old Testament history, the Jewish people had been waiting for God to send the Savior to the earth. Many times during these years God had spoken of His promise to send the Messiah.

When the right time came, Jesus, God's Son, came to earth. He was born to Mary in the little village of Bethlehem. He grew up in the town of Nazareth. When He was thirty years of age, He was baptized in the Jordan River by John the Baptist. Then Jesus began His ministry. He told the people of God's love for them, what they should do to have their sins forgiven, and how to live as God wanted them to live.

The first we hear of Peter, one of Jesus' disciples, is in John 1:35-42. His brother, Andrew, had been led to Jesus by John the Baptist. When Andrew was sure that Jesus truly was the Savior for whom the people had been waiting so long, he went to find his brother, Peter. "I have found the Messiah," he said, and he brought Peter to Jesus.

Peter, who also was called Simon, was the son of Jonas. At the time he began following Jesus, he was married and lived in Capernaum. He and his brother Andrew were in the fishing business. Peter was a rough fisherman, making his living by catching and selling fish. Although he sometimes did and said things without thinking, he wanted to be sure he was doing the right thing when he became acquainted with Jesus. He did not immediately "leave all to follow Jesus." He must have spent a great deal of his time with Jesus, listening to Him as He preached to the people, and seeing many of the miracles that Jesus did. Since Jesus was then living in Capernaum, Peter and Andrew spent part of their time at their work.

One day while they were casting a net into the sea, Jesus came by. "Follow me," He said, "and I will make you fishers of men." Peter and Andrew left their nets and went with Jesus.

A little farther on two other brothers, James and John, were mending their nets. Jesus called them, too, and they went with Him. Jesus wanted these men to travel with Him so that He might teach them to bring people to God.

Sometime after this, Jesus was preaching to the people on the shore of the Sea of Galilee. When the people began to crowd around Him, He looked behind Him and saw Peter's fishing boat tied up by the shore. Peter must have been listening to Jesus as He preached, for when Jesus stepped into the boat, Peter pushed the boat out a short distance from the shore and Jesus continued His preaching.

When Jesus finished speaking to the people, He asked Peter to take the boat out into the lake and let down his nets. At first Peter began to argue with Jesus, saying they had fished all night and had caught nothing. But Peter probably remembered all the wonderful things he had seen Jesus do in the past and he said, "If You say You want me to do it, I will." The fishermen rowed out into the lake and let down their nets. Immediately the nets were full of fish! Peter called to his partners, James and John, who were in another boat. They came and helped gather in the great catch of fish. Peter was amazed at this great miracle of Jesus, and he bowed down before the Master.

Jesus turned to Peter and said, "From now on you shall catch men." Peter was now convinced that Jesus was truly the Son of God. Without a moment's hesitation he, with Andrew, James, and John, left their boats and nets and followed Jesus.

The Lesson Applied

Jesus is calling us today through His Word, the Bible, for He still needs faithful people to become "fishers of men." Perhaps it will not be necessary for you to give up your home or your work, in order to follow Jesus, as did His apostles. Jesus does expect us to be willing to give up all we have for Him. He expects us to put Him first in our lives.

Questions for Discussion: How can we be "fishers of men" today? Why did Jesus call these men to help Him? Couldn't He have done the work by himself?

The Lesson Quiz

1. Who led Andrew to believe in Jesus?
   (John the Baptist.)
2. Whom did Andrew bring to Jesus?
   (His brother, Simon Peter.)
3. What kind of work did Peter do?
   (He was a fisherman.)
4. What were Peter and Andrew doing when Jesus called them?
   (They were casting a net into the sea.)
5. What did Jesus tell them?
   ("Follow me, and I will make you fishers of men.")
6. What were James and John doing when Jesus called them?
   (They were mending their nets.)
7. After Jesus finished preaching to the people from Peter's boat, what did He tell Peter to do?
   (Take the boat out and let down the nets.)
8. What did Peter tell Jesus?
   (They had fished all night and had caught nothing, but they would do what Jesus said to do.)
9. What happened when they let down the nets?
   (Immediately the nets were full of fish.)
10. When they brought the fish to shore, what did Jesus say to Peter and the others who were with him?
    (From now on you shall catch men.)

Additional Lesson Activities

1. Read-aloud Poem

Read the following poem about Peter, and let pupils call out the missing words that complete the rhymes.

By the shores of Lake Gennesaret,
Two fishermen washed out their _ _ _,
And spread it in the morning sun,
Because their night of work was _ _ _ _.
Yet all their toil had been for nought,
A single fish they had not _ _ _ _ _ _ _.
Then Jesus came, ere they should sleep,
And said, "Launch out into the _ _ _ _."
Poor Simon sighed, reluctant still,
But to the Master said, "I _ _ _ _."
And soon they found they could not pull
The net to ship, it was so _ _ _ _.
So Simon called his partners' names,
The ever faithful John and _ _ _ _ _.
At once responding to his call,
They helped to land the mighty _ _ _ _.
The brimming net broke through and spilled,
But not before each boat was _ _ _ _ _ _.
So greatly did this bounty please,
That Simon fell at Jesus' _ _ _ _ _.
Then Jesus spoke to him again,
And said, "Henceforth thou shalt catch _ _ _!"
Forsaking all, when this they heard,
They followed Him to preach the _ _ _ _.

2. Posters

Let pupils make posters with the message, "Be a fisher of men," to remind them to invite others to come and learn about Jesus.

Workbook Page

On page 34 of the Workbook you will find two puzzles, "Peter's Occupation" and "Scrambled Names." These will help students recall facts from the Bible story. Answers to the puzzles are on pages 62-64 of the Workbook. Be sure to work the puzzles in your copy of the Workbook (in the back of this teacher's manual) before assigning them to the pupils. Be sure to have students finish the Bible verses each week in the section: *Words to Remember.*

Words to Remember

"And Jesus said unto them, Come ye after me, and I will make you to become fishers of men" (Mark 1:17).

Lesson 2

Peter's Faith in Jesus

Matthew 8; 10; 14; 16:13-25; Mark 8:27-38; Luke 9:18-27

Introduction to Lesson

The Twelve Apostles

Write the numbers from 1-12 on the chalkboard. Let students read Matthew 10:2-4, and list the names of the twelve apostles.

The Bible Lesson

From among His followers, Jesus chose twelve men as His special helpers. Who were they? (Let students call out the names of the apostles.)

As Jesus traveled about Galilee, preaching, teaching, and healing, great crowds of people from places as far away as Jerusalem followed Him. His close followers were with Him and saw great miracles. One day Jesus went to Peter's house, and healed Peter's mother-in-law, who was sick with a fever. He also healed lepers, stopped storms on the Sea of Galilee, caused blind men to see, cast demons from people, and brought people back to life.

Jesus sent His apostles out to preach to the Jews. They also were to heal the sick, cleanse the lepers, raise the dead, and cast out devils. Jesus warned the twelve that their mission could be dangerous. Many people would hate them and persecute them because they would not want to hear the message of Jesus. The twelve apostles went out into the cities to preach the gospel and heal people.

Again Jesus was with the apostles for more teaching and miracles, and then He told them to get into a boat and go to the other side of the Sea of Galilee. After Jesus had sent the crowds away He went up into a mountain to pray, where He could be alone.

While the apostles were crossing the sea, a wind came up suddenly. The boat was tossed about by the waves. In the darkness of the night, Jesus came near the boat, walking on the water!

When the twelve men saw Jesus walking on the water, they were afraid. "It is a spirit!" they cried out.

But Jesus spoke to them immediately. "Be of good cheer; it is I; be not afraid."

Peter called out to Jesus, "If it is You, Lord, tell me to come to You on the water."

Jesus answered, "Come!" Peter lowered himself out of the ship, and started to walk on the water toward Jesus. But when Peter looked up and saw the waves, he was afraid and started to sink.

Peter cried, "Lord, save me!"

Jesus stretched out His hand and caught Peter. "O you of little faith," He said to Peter, "why did you doubt?"

When Peter and Jesus entered the ship, the wind stopped. The apostles came and worshiped Jesus, saying, "Truly You are the Son of God."

Some time later, near Caesarea Philippi, Jesus was with His apostles. "You have been among the people and have heard them talking about Me. Tell me, who do they think I am?" Jesus did not have to ask this question in order to know what the people thought about Him. He knew what they were thinking. When Jesus asked His followers what the people thought of Him, He was testing them to see if they really knew who He was.

Peter spoke up, answering for the group. That was just like Peter, always the first to speak up or to act! "Some of the people think You are one of the prophets come back to life—Jeremiah or Elijah. Others think that You are John the Baptist, who has come back from the dead."

When Peter finished speaking, Jesus asked, "But who do you say that I am?"

Without a moment's hesitation, Peter answered Jesus' question. "You are the Christ, the Son of the living God."

Jesus blessed Peter because of his faith. "No man has told you this," He said. "God has revealed it to you. On this truth I shall build my church. Nothing shall be able to destroy it." Then Jesus reminded them that if they were to be true disciples they must be willing to suffer for Him. "If any man will come after me," said Jesus, "let him deny himself, and take up his cross, and follow me."

Peter's faith sometimes was weak, as it was when he started to sink in the waves. But again his faith would be strong, as it was when he stated that Jesus was the Christ, the Son of the living

God. After some more tests of faith, Peter became very strong and gave his whole life to the preaching of the gospel.

The Lesson Applied

When we decide to follow Christ, we, too, must make that "good confession" by saying, "I believe that Jesus is the Christ, the Son of the living God." As we make that confession we must remember that we are promising Christ that we will be faithful to Him for the rest of our lives. We will "deny" ourselves when necessary, in order to do those things that He would have us do. We must be ready and willing to confess His name not just once, but by every word and action all of our lives.

Questions for Discussion: How often should we confess Christ? What other ways can we confess our faith besides talking about it?

The Lesson Quiz

1. What miracles of Jesus did the apostles see?
   (Healing the sick, casting out demons, causing the blind to see, stopping storms on the sea, raising the dead.)
2. When Jesus sent out the twelve apostles, what were they to do?
   (Preach to the Jews, heal the sick, cleanse the lepers, raise the dead, cast out demons.)
3. What happened while Jesus was praying on the mountain, and the apostles were in a ship on the sea?
   (A storm came up and waves tossed the ship.)
4. What did the apostles think when they saw Jesus walking toward them on the water?
   (They thought He was a spirit.)
5. What happened to Peter when he tried to walk on the water?
   (He started to sink, and cried, "Lord, save me!")
6. When Jesus saved Peter from drowning, and they had entered the ship, what did the apostles say?
   ("Truly You are the Son of God.")
7. Some time later, at Caesarea Philippi, what question did Jesus ask Peter?
   ("Who do people think I am?")
8. What did Peter reply?
   ("Some say You are John the Baptist come back to life, or Jeremiah or Elijah.")
9. When Jesus said to Peter, "But who do you say that I am?" what was Peter's answer?
   ("You are the Christ, the Son of the living God.")
10. How did Jesus say that Peter knew this?
    (God had revealed it to him.)

Additional Lesson Activities

1. Bible Word Hunt

Put this list of Scriptures on the chalkboard. Let students look them up and read them silently. They are to guess what word is common to all the Scriptures listed. (Answer: FAITH)

Mark 11:22	Hebrews 11:1
Mark 4:40	James 2:17
Luke 17:5	Hebrews 11:6

2. Another Confession

Find another "good confession" in Acts 8:36, 37. Who made this confession? What did he say?

Workbook Page

On page 35 of the Workbook you will find a "Word Maze" that reviews the lesson Scripture.

Students will need their Bibles for the exercise entitled "Faith. . . ." You will want to discuss the meanings of these three important verses of Scripture.

Answers for the puzzles are on pages 62-64 of the Workbook.

Words to Remember

"He saith unto them, But whom say ye that I am? And Simon Peter answered and said, Thou art the Christ, the Son of the living God" (Matthew 16:15, 16).

Lesson 3

Peter Learns Some Lessons

Matthew 17:1-9; John 13:1-17; Matthew 26:36-56

Introduction to Lesson

In the first of the three stories in this lesson, Moses and Elijah appear with Jesus on the "Mount of Transfiguration." Let students review briefly the lives of these two great Old Testament leaders. Refer to lessons 4 and 10 of Part One, Adventures With Bible People. Use the lesson quizzes, workbook quizzes, or other material. On the chalkboard, place this question: "What do you remember about Moses and Elijah?" Students may write facts on the chalkboard, or discuss them.

The Bible Lesson

Today we are going to look at three events in Peter's life when he learned some very important lessons.

The Transfiguration

On some occasions, instead of taking all twelve apostles with Him, Jesus took only three: Peter, James, and John. Soon after Peter's confession of his faith in Jesus, Jesus took these three men up into a high mountain. While He was talking with them, suddenly there seemed to be a bright light surrounding Jesus. His face, and even His clothing, seemed to shine. While the three men looked in wonder, two men appeared with Jesus. One of these men was Moses and the other was the prophet Elijah. As the men began to talk with Jesus, Peter spoke up. "Let us build three tabernacles here: one for Jesus, one for Moses, and one for Elijah." Then a cloud covered the figures, and the voice of God spoke: "This is my beloved Son, in whom I am well pleased; hear ye him."

Peter, James, and John fell to the ground and covered their faces. Jesus came and touched them and told them not to be afraid. They raised their heads and "saw no man, save Jesus only."

This great event let them know that although Moses and Elijah were great leaders, God wanted people to listen to the teachings of Jesus and obey them. Peter realized that it was wrong to suggest building three tabernacles. Jesus was greater than Moses and Elijah. Only He was worthy of their worship and praise.

(Read aloud Matthew 17:1-9.)

The Last Supper

The last night before Jesus was to be crucified, He gathered His disciples together for the Passover. This was the last supper He was to have with them before His death. But before they sat down to eat, Jesus did a very unusual thing. He took a basin of water and a towel, and kneeling down began to wash the disciples' feet. It was very dusty and hot in Palestine. Whenever people were invited to a house for a meal, a servant would wash the feet of the guests. But when Jesus, the Son of God, began doing something that a servant was supposed to do, the disciples could not understand it. When Jesus came to Peter, Peter got excited and said he would not let Jesus wash his feet. But when Jesus said that Peter could not be one of His disciples unless he allowed Him to do this, Peter agreed.

Then Jesus explained why He had done this. He said that He wanted His followers to be willing to do anything for Him, even the unpleasant things. If Jesus was willing to do the work of a servant, His followers should be willing to do these humble things for Him and for others.

(Read aloud John 13:12-17.)

In the Garden

When the Passover supper was over, Jesus and the apostles joined in singing a hymn together. Then Jesus led His disciples out to the Mount of Olives and into the little garden called Gethsemane.

Jesus knew the time had come for His enemies to carry out their evil plan. He wanted to be alone to pray for strength. He left His disciples near the entrance of the garden and took Peter, James, and John farther into the garden. He asked them to watch while He went a little further to pray. Three times when Jesus came back to them, after praying to His heavenly Father, He found them asleep. Jesus woke them up and sadly asked them, "Could you not watch with me for one hour?" How ashamed they must have felt to think that they could not stay awake while their Master prayed.

Suddenly the enemies of Jesus came into the garden to arrest Jesus. Peter angrily took his sword and slashed at the servant of the high priest, cutting off his ear. Jesus healed the man's ear, and said to Peter, "Put up your sword. Those who take the sword shall perish with the sword."

(Read aloud Matthew 26:47-52.)

The Lesson Applied

Peter had to learn many lessons before he could become the fine Christian worker that he later became. Here are three of the lessons:

1. Jesus was greater than any man, and so only His teachings must be obeyed. We must listen only to Him.
2. The followers of Christ must be willing to do even the most humble tasks for Him and for others.
3. The kingdom of God was not to be defended by the sword. Its only weapon would be love.

These lessons are just as important for us to learn as they were for Peter.

Questions for Discussion: Why did Jesus allow Peter, James, and John to see Him in His glory? Why was the lesson Jesus taught (when He washed the disciples' feet) important?

The Lesson Quiz

1. What three disciples spent much time with Jesus?

    (Peter, James, and John.)

2. What happened to Jesus while Peter, James, and John were with Him on the mountain?

    (His face and clothing seemed to shine brightly. Jesus is said to have been "transfigured.")

3. Who appeared with Jesus?

    (Moses and Elijah.)

4. What did Peter suggest building?

    (Three tabernacles: one for Moses, one for Elijah, and one for Jesus.)

5. What did God say at this time?

    ("This is my beloved Son . . . hear ye him.")

6. What meal did Jesus and His disciples eat the night before Jesus' crucifixion?

    (The Passover, also referred to as the "last supper.")

7. Why did Jesus wash His disciples' feet?

    (To teach them that they must be willing to do humble tasks for Him and for others.)

8. What did Peter, James, and John do while Jesus was praying in the garden?

    (They slept.)

9. What did Peter do to the high priest's servant?

    (He cut off the man's ear.)

10. What did Jesus do?

    (He healed the man's ear, and rebuked Peter.)

Additional Lesson Activities

1. Draw Pictures

Let pupils choose one of the three events in today's lesson, and draw a picture of it. Provide felt-tipped pens, crayons, colored chalk, or other drawing materials. (See the project, "A Shoe-box Movie," on page 31 of the Workbook. This activity may be a part of that project.)

2. Memory Verse Review

Provide three 3 x 5 cards (different colors if possible) for each pupil. Let them write the first three memory verses on the cards, and begin to review the verses. Pupils may wish to continue this activity throughout the series on Peter.

3. Eyewitness Account

Let students find Peter's account of the transfiguration in his second letter (2 Peter 1:16-18).

Workbook Page

On page 36 of the Workbook, you will find three puzzles to review the Bible stories. Answers to the puzzles are on pages 62-64 of the Workbook.

Words to Remember

"Watch and pray, that ye enter not into temptation: the spirit indeed is willing, but the flesh is weak" (Matthew 26:41).

Lesson 4

Peter Denies Christ

Luke 22:19-34, 54-62

Introduction to Lesson

Put this list of characteristics on the chalkboard. Let students cross out the ones that do not apply to Peter. Discuss the characteristics that remain, and let students tell in what events of Peter's life these characteristics were demonstrated. (Use only the stories that have appeared thus far in the study of Peter's life.)

1. Impulsive	6. Enthusiastic
2. Quiet	7. Leader
3. Outspoken	8. Hard worker
4. Hesitant	9. Selfish
5. Bold	10. Energetic

The Bible Lesson

For about three and a half years Jesus had traveled from one end of Palestine to the other, telling the people about God and His love for them. He had healed the sick people, opened the eyes of the blind, given hearing to the deaf, and raised the dead. He had gathered the little children around Him, saying, "Suffer little children, and forbid them not to come unto me; for of such is the kingdom of heaven." Jesus had left His beautiful home in Heaven in order to come to earth to show people how they could have their sins forgiven, and someday live with Him in that heavenly home that God has prepared.

Since Jesus had done all of these things, it would seem that everyone would love Him, but this was not so. The religious leaders of the people (the scribes, Pharisees, and Sadducees) were jealous of Jesus. They were looking for an opportunity to find an excuse to kill Him. Jesus knew what they were trying to do. When He called His disciples together for that last supper, He knew that this was to be His last time with them before His death. The hour was approaching when He would be crucified. He also knew what the disciples would do when He was arrested. Jesus told Simon Peter that Satan would be testing him. "I have prayed for you, that your faith won't fail!" Jesus told him.

Peter answered and said, "Lord, I am ready to go with You, both into prison, and to death."

Jesus turned to Peter and said, "I tell you, Peter, the cock shall not crow this day before you will deny three times that you know Me."

Peter must have felt very unhappy about this. Surely Jesus was wrong. Hadn't Peter loved Jesus enough to be willing to leave his fishing business and to follow Him? Hadn't he already confessed his faith in Jesus? Hadn't he been one of the three disciples who had been chosen to see Christ's transfiguration on the mountain? How could Jesus say that Peter would deny knowing Him?

When the soldiers, led by Judas, one of Jesus' own disciples, came into the Garden to arrest Jesus, Peter was the first to face the enemies of the Lord. We have learned that Peter drew his sword to defend Jesus. But Peter lost his courage after this and fled, along with the other disciples.

He followed "afar off" and, after Jesus was taken into the palace of the high priest for trial, Peter stayed outside, warming himself by the fire. It was then that some of the crowd began to accuse Peter of being one of Jesus' disciples. Because of fear, or because he was ashamed, Peter denied that he was a disciple of Jesus.

Again he was questioned and again he replied that he was not a disciple. A third time he was questioned, and he cursed and swore, saying he did not even know Jesus.

At that moment a cock crowed. Jesus, who was being led out of the palace, looked down at Peter. Peter remembered that Jesus had said he would deny Him three times before the cock should crow. When Peter realized what he had done, he went out into the night and wept bitterly. He had openly denied knowing the very One whom he had confessed so recently as being the Son of God, and the One for whom he had promised to die if necessary. How terrible the next few days must have been to Peter as he saw His Master being dragged out of the city, nailed to a cross, and left to die on the hill called Calvary. It certainly would be a dark picture if it had ended there. But in our next lesson we will learn of the joy and hope of Christ's resurrection from the dead, and of Peter's repentance.

The Lesson Applied

Confessing our faith in Christ and accepting Him as our Savior is not a very hard thing for us to do. The real test of our faith and loyalty to Him comes when we begin to live for Him.

Some of our friends may laugh at us for being Christians; they may turn against us because we will not do the things that we know are not right. It is then that we may be tempted to deny our Savior, to be ashamed to let others know we are His followers. Because it is easier to follow the crowd than to be laughed at, we may turn against the One who died for us.

If this is one of your problems, just think about Peter and how bad he felt when he turned against Jesus.

Questions for Discussion: What would you have done if you had been Peter? Name some ways we deny Jesus other than by lying as Peter did.

The Lesson Quiz

1. Why had Jesus prayed for Peter?
   (Because Satan was going to test him. Jesus prayed that Peter's faith wouldn't fail.)
2. What did Peter say about this?
   (He said he was ready to go to prison or to die for Jesus.)
3. What did Jesus say that Peter was going to do?
   (He said that Peter would deny knowing Him three times.)
4. Who led the soldiers when they came to arrest Jesus?
   (Judas, one of Jesus' disciples.)
5. What did Peter do when he saw the soldiers coming to arrest Jesus?
   (He drew his sword and cut off an ear of the high priest's servant.)
6. What did Peter do when he saw that Jesus was not going to fight back?
   (He ran away.)
7. How did Peter follow Jesus "afar off"?
   (He went into the courtyard of the high priest's palace where Jesus was being tried. He warmed his hands over a fire.)
8. When some of the people accused Peter of being one of Jesus' disciples, what did Peter say?
   (Peter said three times that he did not know Jesus.)
9. When Peter had denied three times that he knew Jesus, what did he see and hear?
   (He saw Jesus being led out, and he heard the cock crow.)
10. What did Peter do?
    (He was ashamed and he went out and cried.)

Additional Learning Activities

1. Overcoming Temptation

Peter gave in to Satan's temptation and denied knowing Jesus. How did his Master, Jesus, respond to Satan's temptations? Read Matthew 4:1-11.

2. Read Other Gospel Accounts

Let students look up this event in the other Gospel accounts: Matthew 26:69-75
Mark 14:53, 54, 66-72
John 18:15-18, 25-27

Compare these with the passage in Luke 22:54-62.

3. Discuss the Word "Deny"

Let students look up the meaning of "deny" in a dictionary. Explain why it was wrong for Peter to deny Jesus (lesson 4), but it was right for Peter and all of us to deny ourselves (lesson 2).

Workbook Page

You'll find a "Crossword Review" on page 37 of the Workbook. All words are found in Luke 22. Be sure to work the puzzle before class time and check your answers with those on pages 62-64 of the Workbook.

Words to Remember

"But I have prayed for thee, that thy faith fail not: and when thou art converted, strengthen thy brethren" (Luke 22:32).

Lesson 5

Peter's Love for Jesus

John 20:1-10, 19-21; 21:1-19

Introduction to Lesson

Put this assignment on the chalkboard:
Read Matthew 18:21, 22

1. What did Peter ask Jesus?
2. What was Jesus' answer?
3. What was the meaning of Jesus' answer?

(Discuss how Peter must have felt after the events of last week's lesson. He may have recalled Jesus' teaching on forgiveness, but he didn't think he'd have the opportunity to ask Jesus to forgive him.)

The Bible Lesson

What a heavy heart Peter must have had! He had denied his Lord. Although he was sorry and had wept over his sin, he had not been able to tell Jesus how he felt and to ask Him for forgiveness. Jesus had been crucified, and had been placed in the tomb. These were long, lonely days for Peter and all the rest of those who loved Jesus.

Then early in the morning of the first day of the week, some of the women who had known and loved Jesus came to put spices on His body. But when they came to the tomb, they found that the stone had been rolled away from the entrance and the tomb was empty!

An angel spoke to them saying, "I know you are looking for Jesus, but He is not here. He wants to meet His disciples in Galilee. Go tell them."

One of the women, Mary Magdalene, ran into the city. There she found Peter and told him what she had seen. New hope came into his heart. Had not Christ said that He would rise from the dead? Could it be that the promise had come true? Without a moment's hesitation Peter, together with the apostle John, ran to the tomb; but John outran Peter and arrived there first. Mary was right! The tomb was empty. But where was Jesus?

Peter and John hurried back to the city. After they had gathered together many of Jesus' followers, they began talking about this wonderful thing they had heard. While they were talking, Jesus appeared in the room with them!

Soon after this Jesus' disciples went to Galilee to meet Jesus, just as He had asked them to do. They waited by the shore of the Sea of Galilee for some time, but Jesus did not come. Peter said, "I think I'll go fishing." The other disciples decided to go with him. They went down to the shore and got into a boat. They fished all night without catching a single fish.

The next morning Jesus appeared on the shore and called out to the fishermen, telling them to cast their net on the other side of the boat. They did not know who He was, but they obeyed. When they did, their net immediately was full of fish. John said to Peter, "It is the Lord!" When Peter realized that it was Jesus he became so excited that he jumped into the sea and waded to shore in order to reach Jesus as soon as possible.

When the rest of the disciples reached shore, they found that Jesus had built a fire and had prepared breakfast for them. While they were eating Jesus turned to Peter and asked him, "Peter, do you love Me?" Peter answered, "Lord, You know that I love You." Jesus asked this question three times, and Peter gave the same answer each time.

But Jesus wanted Peter to do more than say he loved Him. He wanted Peter to do something about it. Jesus said, "Feed my lambs" and "Feed my sheep." By "feeding" Jesus meant that Peter was to teach young and old people God's Word. Peter was to take care of God's people and guide them in the way they should go.

At last Peter knew that Jesus had forgiven him, and once again he was happy. He had learned his lesson, and he never would be so foolish again! And Peter kept his word.

The Lesson Applied

Jesus still has many "lambs" and "sheep" who need to be "fed" and tended. This work can be done only by those who truthfully say to the Lord, "You know that I love You."

Can Jesus look into your heart and know that you love Him enough to work for Him? You can start that work even though you are quite young. You can invite your friends and neighbors and your family to come to worship and Bible study. You can tell them some of the things you learn, and in this way help them to know more about

Jesus. You can listen closely to your Bible-school teacher and study your Bible so you will be able to teach others of God's love. These are just a few of the ways you can prove that you love Jesus.

Questions for Discussion: Will we be forgiven, as completely as Peter was, when we do wrong? Can you forgive others? What are some ways that we can work for Jesus?

The Lesson Quiz

1. What happened three days after Jesus was crucified?

(Jesus arose from the grave.)

2. What did Peter do when he heard that the tomb in which Christ had been buried was empty?

(He, along with John, ran to the tomb to see if the tomb really was empty.)

3. What happened when Peter and some of the other followers of Jesus were together talking about these things?

(Jesus appeared before them.)

4. Soon after this what did Peter and the other disciples do?

(They went to Galilee to meet Jesus, as He had asked them to do.)

5. After fishing all night, how many fish had they caught?

(None.)

6. Who appeared on the shore the next morning?

(Jesus.)

7. What did Jesus tell them to do, and what happened?

(Jesus told them to cast their nets on the other side of the boat. When they did, their nets were filled with fish.)

8. While the disciples were eating breakfast with Jesus on the shore, what did Jesus ask Peter?

("Peter, do you love me?")

9. What did Peter answer each of the three times?

("Lord, You know that I love You.")

10. What did Jesus mean when He said, "Feed my lambs" and "Feed my sheep"?

(Peter should teach young and old people the Word of God.)

Additional Lesson Activities

1. Shoe-box Movie

Are the students working on the project for this series of lessons that is described in their workbooks on page 31? In these first five lessons there are many scenes that can be sketched showing Peter's adventures:

Jesus calls Peter to follow Him.

The great catch of fish, after which Jesus tells Peter he will be a "fisher of men."

Peter's "good confession" at Caesarea Philippi.

The transfiguration.

The last supper.

In the Garden of Gethsemane.

Peter's denial of Christ.

Peter and John at the empty tomb.

Jesus appears to Peter and the others in Jerusalem.

Another great catch of fish, when the disciples do not recognize Jesus right away.

Jesus eats breakfast on the shore with Peter and six other disciples.

Jesus questions Peter and tells him to feed His lambs and sheep.

2. Peter's Letter

Read Peter's advice to the elders in 1 Peter 5:2-4. How does this compare with John 21:15-17?

Workbook Page

On page 38 of the Workbook you'll find a "Memory Verse Match-up," reviewing the first five memory verses, and "Peter Goes Fishing," an acrostic.

Words to Remember

"He saith unto him the third time, Simon, son of Jonas, lovest thou me? Peter was grieved because he said unto him the third time, Lovest thou me? And he said unto him, Lord, thou knowest all things; thou knowest that I love thee. Jesus saith unto him, Feed my sheep" (John 21:17).

Lesson 6

Peter Preaches to the Jews

Matthew 28:19, 20; Acts 1:4-14; 2:1-42

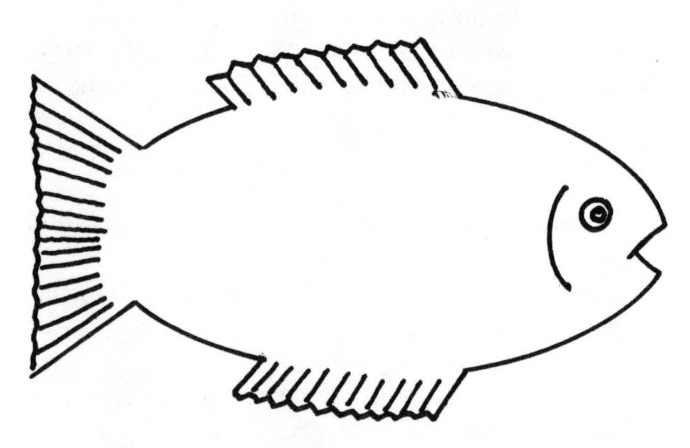

Introduction to Lesson

The first five lessons on Peter's life are connected with events in Jesus' ministry. Review these lessons about Jesus and Peter by using the quizzes included with the lessons. Divide the class into two teams, "Andrew" and "Peter." Cut fish shapes from construction paper using the pattern on this page. Provide two nets, one for each team. For each correct answer, a team receives a fish in its net. At the end of the quiz, let each team count its fish. The team with the biggest "catch" wins.

(Note: The quiz questions for each lesson always should be used in the order given, because each question builds on the answer to the previous question.)

The Bible Lesson

After Jesus arose from the dead, He stayed on the earth for forty days. During this time, He gave His disciples their final instructions about the work they were to do for Him. His command to spread the gospel, sometimes called the "Great Commission," is found in Matthew 28:19, 20. (Read these verses aloud.) Then Jesus went back to be with His Father in Heaven. The account of His ascension is found in Acts 1:9-11. (Read these verses aloud.)

Jesus had told His followers to wait in Jerusalem. There they would be baptized with the Holy Spirit not many days later.

The disciples, filled with wonder because of the things that they had seen, went down from the mountain and into the city of Jerusalem. They awaited the great power that Jesus had said He would send to them. Each day they met together for prayer in an upper room. Other disciples gathered there with them. Ten days after Jesus had gone back to Heaven, the promised power of the Holy Spirit came to the apostles. The sound of a rushing mighty wind filled the house where they were sitting. Tongues of fire appeared upon each of the apostles. Suddenly they were able to speak in other languages!

Thousands of people were in Jerusalem for the Jewish feast of Pentecost. Many Jews had come from other countries, and they were amazed when they heard these men from Galilee speaking the wonderful works of God in their native languages.

Peter went out and stood before a crowd of people. He began preaching to them about Christ. He spoke of the prophet Joel who foretold signs and wonders that would happen. He told how Jesus of Nazareth had been approved of God by miracles, wonders, and signs. Peter spoke boldly: "But you took Him and crucified Him! God has raised Him up and He is now seated at the right hand of God." Peter continued, "Therefore let all the house of Israel know that God has made this same Jesus, whom you have crucified, both Lord and Christ!"

The people were shocked and saddened because of what they had done. They began asking Peter and the other apostles, "What shall we do?"

Peter replied, "Repent, and be baptized every one of you in the name of Jesus Christ for the remission of sins, and you shall receive the gift of the Holy Spirit." Three thousand people repented of their sins and were baptized. They were added to the church that Jesus had said He would establish.

These new Christians continued faithfully in the apostles' doctrine (teaching), fellowship (sharing), breaking of bread (Communion or Lord's Supper), and prayer (talking to God). They also proved their love for Christ by helping others and by telling others of God's love.

Peter, who earlier had been fearful and discouraged, now was a courageous Christian, and a preacher of the gospel!

The Lesson Applied

When Peter preached the first gospel sermon in Jerusalem on the Day of Pentecost, he was following Jesus' command. "Ye shall be my witnesses," Jesus had said, "in Jerusalem, and in all Judea, and in Samaria, and unto the uttermost part of the earth" (Acts 1:8). Later Peter traveled around to other cities to spread the gospel, but he began in Jerusalem.

Perhaps someday you will have the opportunity of becoming a missionary and going to a faraway country to tell about Jesus. But until that time, you can do your part to tell others in your own neighborhood. There are many people around you who do not know Christ.

If you wait until you are older to work for Jesus, perhaps your next-door neighbor or a friend at school may never learn to love and follow Christ.

We all should be interested in mission work at home and abroad, but let's not forget that we have a job to do right where we are, now!

Questions for Discussion: What are some of the ways that we can go "into all the world, and preach the gospel"? How can we be courageous Christians?

The Lesson Quiz

1. How long did Jesus remain on the earth after His resurrection?

   (For forty days.)

2. What command did Jesus give His apostles before He went back to Heaven?

   ("Go ye into all the world, and preach the gospel.")

3. Where were the apostles told to wait for the promise of the Father?

   (In Jerusalem.)

4. What happened ten days after Jesus returned to Heaven?

   (The Holy Spirit came upon the apostles, accompanied by these signs: sound of rushing mighty wind and tongues of fire.)

5. On what Jewish feast day did this event take place?

   (The Day of Pentecost.)

6. When the Holy Spirit came upon the apostles, what unusual thing could they do?

   (They could speak in many languages.)

7. After Peter preached about Jesus, what did the people ask?

   ("What shall we do?")

8. What did Peter answer?

   ("Repent, and be baptized.")

9. How many people gladly received Peter's message and were baptized?

   (Three thousand.)

10. How did those early Christians show their faithfulness?

    (They continued steadfastly in the apostles' doctrine, fellowship, breaking of bread, and prayer.)

Additional Lesson Activities

1. Missionary Project

Let pupils begin a missionary project, such as starting a fund to send a gift of money to one of the missionaries supported by your congregation.

2. Posters

Let pupils make posters with missionary messages. Emphasize the work being done by missionaries your congregation supports. Ask permission to place the posters on bulletin boards in classrooms or hallways throughout the building.

Workbook Page

On page 39 of the Workbook there are two puzzles, "Acrostic Clues" and "Match the Meanings."

Words to Remember

"Then Peter said unto them, Repent, and be baptized every one of you in the name of Jesus Christ for the remission of sins, and ye shall receive the gift of the Holy Ghost" (Acts 2:38).

Lesson 7

A Lame Man Is Healed

Acts 3:1-20; 4:1-22

Introduction to Lesson

On the chalkboard place the following list of people and places:

1. Andrew	6. Elijah
2. James	7. Caesarea Philippi
3. John	8. Jerusalem
4. Galilee	9. Calvary
5. Moses	10. Mount of Olives

Let students tell how each person or place is connected with an event in Peter's life.

The Bible Lesson

In our last lesson we learned how Peter had preached in Jerusalem on the Day of Pentecost, and three thousand people had become Christians. The church that Jesus had promised had begun!

But that was just the beginning of the work that the apostles had to do. There were many more thousands of people who had not obeyed the gospel.

In order to prove to people that Christ was the Son of God, and the apostles were His spokesmen, the Holy Spirit gave the apostles power to do miracles. Our lesson today is about one of those miracles.

One day when Peter and John went to the temple to pray, they saw a lame man begging by the gate called Beautiful. The man had been crippled from birth, and he had never walked. As the apostles were about to go into the temple, the crippled man called out to them and asked them for some money. Peter stopped and looked down at the man. "We do not have any money to give you," he said, "but we have something else to give you. In the name of Jesus Christ of Nazareth rise up and walk!"

Peter took the man by the hand and lifted him up. The man could feel the strength coming into his feet. The next moment he was walking and leaping and praising God!

Since this miracle was done at one of the entrances leading into the temple, a great crowd of people must have seen it. In a moment an excited crowd had gathered around Peter and John. Peter took this opportunity to preach to the people about Jesus, saying that it was in the name of Jesus that this man had been healed.

News of the miracle soon spread to the Jewish rulers. Peter and John were arrested. This gave the apostles another opportunity to preach! This time they spoke to the Jewish rulers, accusing them of being the ones who had caused Christ, the Son of God, to be put to death. Peter, who had once been so afraid of getting into trouble that he had denied knowing Christ, now was standing up before the wicked rulers of the people, pointing out their sins and asking them to repent.

The rulers wanted to keep Peter and John in prison, but they were afraid of the reaction of the people. Everyone knew that a great miracle had been done by the apostles. If the two men had been kept in prison, the people might have started a riot. Therefore the rulers let them go, commanding them not to preach any more in the name of Jesus. Peter then turned to them and said, "We cannot obey you and God at the same time, so we shall do what God wants us to do."

The rulers again threatened the apostles, but allowed them to go free. Peter and John went out and continued to preach in the name of Jesus!

The Lesson Applied

When the apostles first began to preach, the people wondered how these men could say such wonderful things and do such wonderful deeds. But then they began to understand that it was because these men "had been with Jesus." That is what makes Christians different from other people.

If we live close to Jesus each day by reading the Bible, praying to Him, thinking of Him during the day, and trying to do what He would have us to do at all times, people will begin to ask, "I wonder why those people are so kind and patient and always so ready to help others? Why is it that they do not get into trouble as other people do?" The answer will be the same each time: "They are Christians."

The closer we walk with Christ the more like Him we will become. What a wonderful thing it is that we can walk each day with the Son of God!

Questions for Discussion: Why don't church leaders today perform miracles such as Peter did? Should the words "good Christian" ever be used to describe someone? Explain.

The Lesson Quiz

1. What did Jesus do to prove to the people that the apostles were His followers?

(He gave them the power to do miracles through the Holy Spirit.)

2. How long had the man at the temple gate been crippled?

(All his life.)

3. For what did the crippled man ask the apostles?

(He asked them for money.)

4. What did Peter say to him?

(Peter said they had no money to give him, but they would give him something else: "In the name of Jesus Christ of Nazareth rise up and walk.")

5. After Peter lifted him up, what did the man do?

(He walked, and leaped, and praised God.)

6. What did the rulers of the people do to Peter and John?

(They arrested them and took them to prison.)

7. What did Peter do?

(He preached to the Jewish rulers.)

8. Why did the rulers not keep Peter and John in prison?

(They were afraid of what the people would do.)

9. When they released the apostles, what did the rulers command them not to do?

(They commanded them not to teach or preach in the name of Jesus.)

10. Did the apostles obey the rulers?

(No. They said, "We must obey God rather than men.")

Additional Lesson Activities

1. A Change in Peter

Let pupils write paragraphs about the change in Peter's life after Jesus' resurrection. Contrast Peter's former fearfulness with his courage.

2. "Stay Close to Jesus" Calendars

Let pupils make calendars with monthly schedules of praying and reading the Bible, to help them stay close to Jesus. Use the illustration below to make the calendars. Enlarge the pattern to 7" square. Make photo copies, or use a stencil and duplicate the sheet so that each student has two copies. Let students fill in the month names and dates. Instruct them to check off each day when they read the Bible and pray. (You may wish to provide Bible seals and "praying hands" seals as awards.)

MONTH:						
SUN.	MON.	TUES.	WED.	THURS.	FRI.	SAT.

Workbook Page

Page 40 contains two puzzles: an acrostic, "Find the Missing Words," and "Three-way Match-up."

Words to Remember

"Then Peter said, Silver and gold have I none; but such as I have give I thee: In the name of Jesus Christ of Nazareth rise up and walk" (Acts 3:6).

Lesson 8

A Lesson About Honesty

Acts 4:23-37; 5:1-14

Introduction to Lesson

Answer to a Prayer

Let students silently read the prayer of the disciples in Acts 4:29, and the answer to the prayer in Acts 4:31. Ask students to find two words that appear in both verses (boldness and word). Students will report their answers in the Bible lesson that follows.

The Bible Lesson

Peter and John, after healing the lame man and preaching to the crowds that gathered, had been taken before the Jewish council. They had been warned not to teach about Jesus, but they were determined to obey God and not men. As soon as they were released, they went to the place where their fellow Christians were meeting, and reported all that had happened to them.

This group of Christians then lifted up their voices in prayer to God. What was one thing they asked God? (Acts 4:29.) How did God answer? (Acts 4:31.) What does "boldness" mean? What "word" were they speaking?

There were thousands of Christians in Jerusalem at this time. Some were wealthy, and others were very poor. Those with money shared with the others, so that no one lacked food or clothing. Some of the Christians owned houses and lands, and they sold them and brought the money to the apostles. The apostles then distributed the money to those who were in need. One of those who shared was Barnabas. He sold the land he owned, and brought the money to the apostles. It may have been a large sum of money—no one knows. Perhaps Barnabas was commended before the group for his generosity—no one knows.

A husband and wife, who belonged to this group of Christians, decided to sell their land, too, and bring the money to the apostles. Maybe they wanted to be commended for their generosity before all the people, but they didn't want to give all the money. They agreed to keep back part of the price, and bring the rest to the apostles as though they were giving the whole amount.

The husband, Ananias, brought the money to the apostles. Peter, who had special knowledge given to him by the Lord, said to Ananias, "Why has Satan filled your heart to lie to the Holy Spirit, and keep back part of the price? The land was yours. After it was sold, the money was yours. You haven't lied to men, but to God."

Peter wanted Ananias to know that he didn't have to give all the money; he could have given just part of it. The sin was in pretending that all of the money was given.

When Ananias heard Peter's words, he fell down dead! Some young men nearby came and carried him out, and buried him immediately.

About three hours later, Sapphira, the wife of Ananias, came to the apostles. She had not heard about her husband's sudden death. Peter said to her, giving her an opportunity to tell the truth, "Tell me if you sold the land for this amount of money?"

Sapphira answered, "Yes, we sold it for that much money."

Peter said, "Why have the two of you agreed to tempt the Spirit of the Lord? Behold, the young men who buried your husband are at the door. They will carry you out, too."

At that moment Sapphira fell dead. The young men carried her body out and buried her beside her husband. Great fear came over the Christians when they heard these things.

This was sudden and harsh punishment, but God wanted to teach the people that it is a terrible thing to lie to God. He wants people to be honest.

The Lesson Applied

Peter knew what it meant to sacrifice for Christ. He gave up a good fishing business in order to become a "fisher of men." Barnabas sold his property, and gave all the money to the apostles to distribute to the needy. But no command was given for all the people to give all their money. Ananias and Sapphira did not have to sell their land. They did not have to give the whole amount to the apostles. But they were dishonest; they pretended they had given more than they had.

Jesus does not want us to say we are giving more money than we really are giving, or to say that we are doing all we can for Jesus when we could be doing much more.

The sin of dishonesty was listed in the Commandments that God gave the Jewish people. (Read Leviticus 19:11.)

If we are to grow in the Christian life, we must be honest in all things.

Questions for Discussion: Is it a sin to be rich? How much money and time should a Christian give to the Lord's work? In what situation is it hardest to be honest? In what ways are people dishonest today?

The Lesson Quiz

1. How did the early Christians share with each other?

(Those who had possessions sold them and brought the money to the apostles, who gave it to those in need.)

2. What man sold his land and brought the money to the apostles?

(Barnabas.)

3. What husband and wife sold a possession and brought some money?

(Ananias and Sapphira).

4. What had they agreed to do, before bringing the money?

(They agreed to keep back part of the price.)

5. To whom had Ananias and Sapphira lied?

(To the Holy Spirit and to God.)

6. What happened to Ananias when Peter accused him of lying to God?

(He fell dead, and was taken out and buried.)

7. How much later did Sapphira come to Peter?

(About three hours.)

8. What lie did she tell Peter?

(That the land had been sold for the amount of money they had brought.)

9. What happened to Sapphira?

(She fell dead, and was carried out and buried beside her husband.)

10. How did the people react when they heard about Ananias and Sapphira?

(Great fear came upon all the church.)

Additional Lesson Activities

1. Bible Word Hunt

Let students look up these Scriptures on the subject of "honesty."

Romans 12:17
2 Corinthians 8:21
2 Corinthians 13:7
1 Peter 2:12
Romans 13:13
1 Thessalonians 4:12
Hebrews 13:18
1 Timothy 2:2
Philippians 4:8

2. Our "Fair Share"

Let students figure out how much of their time and money they are giving to the Lord's work. No judgments are to be made by others. Let each one decide if he or she is being honest with God. (Suggest that students include only the money they earn or receive as allowance, not money that is given to them by parents for the offering.)

Workbook Page

"Make It Right," on page 41, is the story of Ananias and Sapphira. It is to be corrected—false statements are to be crossed out. Be sure that each pupil understands what is true and what is false in the story. Pupils will need their Bibles to answer the question, "What Does God's Word Say About Telling Lies?"

Words to Remember

"For he that will love life, and see good days, let him refrain his tongue from evil, and his lips that they speak no guile" (1 Peter 3:10).

Lesson 9

Peter Encounters Simon the Sorcerer

Acts 8:1-25

Introduction to Lesson

The most prominent Bible character in the first twelve chapters of the Book of Acts is Peter. However, other apostles and disciples are mentioned, and pupils need to understand how they fit into the narrative of the Acts of the Apostles. Let pupils look up information on these men listed in the first part of Acts 8:

1. Saul: Acts 7:58; 8:1, 3 (persecutor turned preacher)
2. Stephen: Acts 6:5-8; 7:59, 60; 8:2 (first Christian martyr)
3. Philip: Acts 6:5, 6; 8:4-8 (not the apostle, but an evangelist)

The Bible Lesson

So many people were becoming Christians in Jerusalem that the Jewish leaders were afraid of losing their power. They began persecuting the church. Who was the first to give his life for his faith? Who was one of the main persecutors? (Let students report on the Scriptures from the introduction.)

The Christians began to scatter to other parts of the country because of the persecution. Wherever they went, they spread the gospel. Who went to Samaria to preach? (Let students report on the Scriptures about Philip.)

The people of Samaria paid attention to the things that Philip said and did. God had given him the power to do miracles. He healed the sick and the crippled people, and cast out demons.

In Samaria lived a man named Simon, who was a sorcerer. He practiced witchcraft and trickery, and was able to deceive many people. He pretended to be a great person, and some people believed that he received great power from God. But when these people heard Philip preach, they believed what he said about the kingdom of God, and about Jesus. Many men and women were baptized. Even Simon believed when he heard Philip's messages and saw the miracles Philip did. Simon also was baptized.

When the apostles at Jerusalem heard that the people in Samaria were becoming followers of Jesus, they sent Peter and John to see them. Peter and John, being apostles, were able to give others the power to do miracles by laying their hands on them.

Simon decided that he wanted the power to give this gift to others. He offered to pay Peter and John if they would give him this power of the Holy Spirit.

Peter said to Simon, "Let your money perish with you, because you think that the gift of God may be purchased! Your heart is not right in the sight of God! Repent of this wickedness and pray to God, so that the evil thoughts in your heart may be forgiven."

Simon was sorry for what he had done. He said to Peter, "Pray to the Lord for me, that none of these things you're speaking about will come upon me."

Simon hadn't wanted the power to lead people to Christ, but to do miracles that were much greater than his magic tricks. Peter had told Simon that if he did not change his ways, he was in danger of losing eternal life with Jesus in Heaven. When Simon's sin was pointed out to him, he wanted to be forgiven. One of the many wonderful things about God is that He will forgive us when we are truly sorry for what we have done wrong.

After his experience with Simon the sorcerer, Peter, with John, went back to Jerusalem. On the way they preached the gospel in many villages of Samaria.

The Lesson Applied

When we become Christians, we are to leave behind our old way of life. Simon the sorcerer had to learn this lesson, and ask forgiveness for the wrong he did. We must be willing to give up anything that keeps us from being true disciples of our Master.

When we grow old enough to go to work, we never should do any kind of work that would bring shame to the name of Christ—even if we could earn more money doing that kind of work. Remember Jesus' words, "Seek ye first the kingdom of God, and his righteousness; and all these things shall be added unto you" (Matthew 6:33).

Questions for Discussion: What does it mean to repent? What kinds of work can Christians do? What kinds of work should Christians not do?

The Lesson Quiz

1. Who preached and did miracles in Samaria?
   (Philip the evangelist.)
2. How did the people react when they heard Philip preach and saw the miracles?
   (They believed and were baptized.)
3. What was the name of a famous sorcerer in Samaria?
   (Simon.)
4. What did Simon do after he believed and was baptized?
   (He continued with Philip, watching the miracles he did.)
5. What apostles were sent to Samaria to give the power of the Holy Spirit to some of the new Christians?
   (Peter and John.)
6. Why did Simon offer money to Peter and John?
   (He wanted to buy the power to give the gift of the Holy Spirit to others.)
7. What did Peter tell Simon to do?
   (To repent and pray.)
8. What did Simon then ask Peter to do?
   (To pray for him.)
9. Where did Peter and John preach before they returned to Jerusalem?
   (In many villages of the Samaritans.)
10. What did they preach?
    (The gospel.)

Additional Lesson Activities

1. Peter's Travels

Put a simple map outline on the chalkboard. (Copy the map sketch on this page, enlarging it to fit your chalkboard. Or, use a large piece of poster board and draw the map with felt-tipped

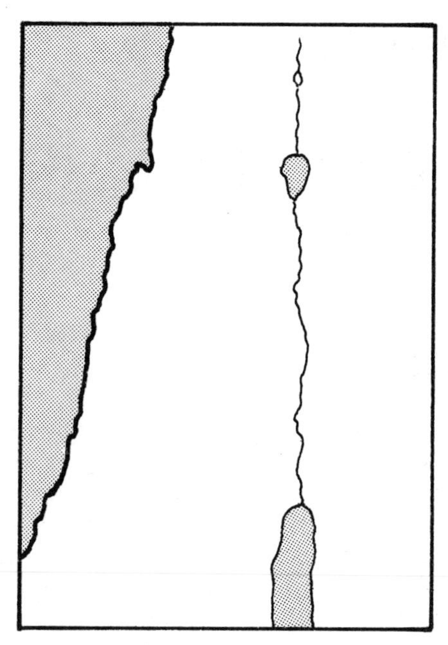

pen.) Let pupils add the following places to the map, telling what event of Peter's life is connected with each place:

Capernaum
Sea of Galilee
Caesarea Philippi
Jerusalem
Samaria

2. Research on "Repentance" and "Forgiveness"

Let pupils look up the words "repentance" and "forgiveness" in a concordance. They may make lists of Scriptures and look them up. Some may wish to write brief reports on the Bible meanings of these two terms.

3. Philip's Activities

Let pupils read about Philip's adventure when he left Samaria (Acts 8:26-40).

Workbook Page

A "Crossword Quiz" on page 42 reviews the lesson Scripture. (Always work the puzzles before class time and check your answers with those in the answer section of the Workbook, pages 62-64.)

Words to Remember

"The Lord knoweth how to deliver the godly out of temptation, and to reserve the unjust unto the day of judgment to be punished" (2 Peter 2:9).

Lesson 10

More Miracles

Acts 9:31-43

Introduction to Lesson

Map Review and Preview

Provide a large map of Bible lands and let students find the places mentioned previously: Capernaum, Sea of Galilee, Caesarea Philippi, Jerusalem, and Samaria. Let students tell what happened at these places. Add two new towns: Lydda, Joppa. These places are the scenes of two miracles in today's lesson.

The Bible Lesson

Something wonderful happened that caused the great persecution of the church to stop for a time. The main leader of the fight against the Christians had become a Christian! Saul, later to be called Paul, was now a follower of Christ. The churches in Judea, Galilee, and Samaria began to grow. The people were walking in the fear of the Lord, and not the fear of persecution.

Before Jesus went back to Heaven, He had promised that "signs" and "wonders" would help His apostles prove that they were working in His name. As people saw these miracles, they believed in Jesus.

Sick people were brought into the streets and laid on beds and couches, in hope that even the shadow of Peter might pass over them and they would be healed. Great crowds from the cities around Jerusalem brought sick people and those who were demon-possessed, and all were healed. The name of Peter was known throughout the whole area.

Peter traveled to various cities, teaching, preaching, and healing in the name of Jesus. One day he visited the Christians in the town of Lydda. (Have a student point to Lydda on the map.) A man named Aeneas lived there, and he had a disease called "palsy." He had been in bed for eight years. Peter said to him, "Aeneas, Jesus Christ makes you completely well! Rise up!" Aeneas arose immediately, healed of his disease. When the people who lived at Lydda saw this miracle, they turned to the Lord.

Nearby, in a town called Joppa, there lived a disciple of Jesus—a Christian woman named Dorcas. She also was known by the name, Tabitha. She was a helpful person who made clothing for many needy people.

Dorcas became ill, and died. The people prepared her for burial, and laid her on a bed in an upper room.

Some of the Christians knew that Peter was in Lydda, so they sent two men to ask him to come quickly. Peter came without delay, and he was brought into the room where Dorcas lay. The widows and others whom Dorcas had helped stood there crying. They showed Peter the clothes that Dorcas had made for them.

Peter told all of them to leave the room. Then he kneeled down and prayed. Turning to the body, he said, "Tabitha, arise!" She opened her eyes. When she saw Peter, she sat up. He gave her his hand, and lifted her up.

The widows and the other Christians waiting outside the room were called by Peter. Imagine their surprise when they saw Dorcas, alive and well once more!

News of this miracle spread throughout Joppa, and many people believed in the Lord.

Peter stayed for many days in Joppa with a man named Simon. He was a tanner, and lived by the sea. Peter soon would have a very unusual experience at that house in Joppa, as we'll learn in next week's lesson. The "signs" and "wonders" that God had promised the apostles would continue to bring people to believe in Jesus!

The Lesson Applied

God gave a special gift to Peter, and he was able to heal people and even bring them back to life. Peter used this gift to help many people. The miracles caused them to believe in Jesus, as Peter preached to them. God was glorified through Peter's gift.

Dorcas also had a gift that God had given her. She had a talent for making clothing, and she helped many needy people.

Whatever talent God gives to a person should be used to bring glory to God. What talents do you have now that you can use for the glory of God?

Questions for Discussion: What talents do you see being used by adults in your congregation? What talents are being used by young people?

The Lesson Quiz

1. What did Jesus promise His apostles to prove they were working in His name?
(Signs and wonders—miracles.)
2. Where did Peter go to visit some Christians?
(Lydda.)
3. What sick man did Peter heal in Jesus' name at Lydda?
(Aeneas.)
4. What disciple lived in Joppa?
(Dorcas, also called Tabitha.)
5. What good works did Dorcas do?
(Made clothing for needy people.)
6. What happened to Dorcas while Peter was in Lydda?
(She became sick and died.)
7. When Peter was brought to the place where Dorcas' body lay, what did he do?
(He sent everyone out, then kneeled and prayed. He told Dorcas to arise.)
8. What did Dorcas do when Peter spoke?
(She opened her eyes and sat up.)
9. What did Peter do after he gave her his hand and lifted her up?
(He called the widows and other Christians, and presented Dorcas alive.)
10. When the news spread through Joppa, how did the people react?
(Many believed in the Lord.)

Additional Lesson Activities

1. Plan a Project
Let pupils discuss various projects that they could do to help others in need. If possible, let them find ways to use their time and talents, rather than giving money for some cause. Consider projects such as collecting good used clothing for a mission, putting on a program at a nursing home, doing housework or running errands for elderly neighbors, or making doll clothes or toys for a children's home.

2. Interviews
Let pupils make a list of questions to use in interviewing Christian workers about their jobs. Include staff workers such as ministers and youth ministers, and volunteers such as Sunday-school teachers, youth sponsors, etc. Pupils may report on their interviews at the next session.

3. Review Quiz
Use "The Lesson Quiz" questions for the first ten lessons on Peter (total of 100 questions). Divide into two teams, have a "spelldown," or use some other method to add some excitement to the review.

4. Review Game
Call out the names of these Bible characters associated with Peter, and see how quickly pupils can tell in a sentence or two Peter's connection with that person.

Aeneas	Simon
Philip	Barnabas
Andrew	Sapphira
Jesus	John
Dorcas	James

Workbook Page

On page 43 "Which Verse?" reviews the lesson Scripture. Under the title, "Talents and Abilities That I Can Use for the Lord," encourage pupils to list gifts that God has given them. They may need some prompting.

Words to Remember

"And above all things have fervent charity among yourselves: for charity shall cover the multitude of sins" (1 Peter 4:8).

Lesson 11

Peter Preaches to the Gentiles

Acts 10; 11:1-18

Introduction to Lesson

In Acts 1:8, Jesus said that the disciples would be His witnesses in Jerusalem, Judea, Samaria, and the uttermost part of the earth. Let students look up these Scriptures and tell where the gospel had been preached:

Acts 8:1, 4	Acts 8:25
Acts 2:14	Acts 6:7
Acts 8:5	Acts 9:31

The good news was being spread in many cities, but thus far only to the Jews in those cities. The Gentiles—all people who were not Jews—had not received the message. Today's lesson is about the first Gentile to become a Christian.

The Bible Lesson

As far back as the time of Adam and Eve, God promised that one day He would send a Savior to the world. God planned that His Son would be born into a special family when it was time for Him to come to earth. This family or nation has been called by these names through the years: Hebrews, Israelites, Jews. Abraham was the "father" of this great nation.

All people who were not Jews were called Gentiles. According to Jewish law, Gentiles were considered as being "unclean" and Jews would not associate with them.

God's Son was born into a Jewish family, but Jesus came to save everyone who would believe on Him. Because the Jews were God's chosen people, they had the first opportunity to become Christians. Peter preached the first sermon to the Jews on the Day of Pentecost.

Today we are going to see that Peter was the first to preach to the Gentiles, too. Peter was reluctant, because he believed that Jews should not associate with Gentiles. God had to teach him a special lesson.

Living in the town of Caesarea was a man by the name of Cornelius. He was a Gentile, but he believed in God and prayed to Him. He was a soldier in the Roman army, but he was known for his kindness and good deeds.

One day God appeared to this man in a vision. He told him to send his servants to a city called Joppa. There they would find a man named Peter. "You will find him at the home of Simon, the tanner, who lives by the sea," Cornelius was told. Peter would tell Cornelius what God wanted him to do.

Cornelius immediately sent two of his servants and a trusted soldier to Joppa to find Peter.

While the messengers from Cornelius were on their way, Peter also saw a vision that was sent by God. As Peter prayed upon the rooftop of the house, he saw a large sheet being lowered from Heaven. In this sheet were all kinds of animals that the Jews, according to their laws, considered "unclean." These "unclean" animals were forbidden to Jews to eat. A voice spoke to Peter and told him to kill and eat one of the animals. Peter refused, saying that it was not lawful for him to eat unclean animals. The voice replied, "What God has made clean you must not call common or unclean." This same thing happened three times. As Peter thought on this, the men sent by Cornelius arrived in Joppa, and were inquiring at the house of Simon whether or not Peter was there.

God spoke to Peter. "There are three men waiting at the gate. Go down and talk with them, for I have sent them." Peter went to meet the men. They explained who they were and why they had come. The three stayed that night in Joppa. The next morning they all prepared to go to the home of Cornelius.

As Peter entered the Gentile's house, Cornelius bowed down before him. But Peter told him to rise, saying, "Stand up! I am a man, just as you are!" In the house, Peter found that Cornelius had gathered together his relatives and friends to hear the message from God.

Peter said to them, "You know that it is against Jewish law for a Jew to associate with a Gentile. But God has showed me that I should not call any man 'common' or 'unclean.' I came to you as soon as you sent for me. May I ask why you wanted me to come?"

Cornelius then explained how the Lord had told him to send to Joppa for a man named Peter, who would tell him all things that God has commanded.

Peter said, "I see that God is no respecter of persons. In every nation the person who fears God and does what is right is accepted with Him." Then Peter began to preach about Jesus. The Holy Spirit came upon all those who heard the word. Peter commanded them to be baptized in the name of the Lord! Cornelius and his household were the first Gentiles to become followers of Christ.

Some of the Jews who had become Christians did not approve of Peter going into the house of a Gentile. Peter talked with them and explained the vision that God had sent him. They finally realized that God was allowing the Gentiles to become Christians, too. God loves all people, and He wants them to follow Jesus, His Son.

The Lesson Applied

Have you ever seen people who refused to have anything to do with people who are poor, or handicapped, or unattractive? Have you seen people who are mistreated because they come from another country or have skin of a different color? We should be kind and friendly to everyone, because God loves them as much as He loves us.

Watch for those who are being treated unkindly by others, and try to be extra kind and friendly to them. Show God's love to all people you meet.

Questions for Discussion: Are there any groups of people in the world who are better than other people? Can a person be a Christian and hate other races or nations of people?

The Lesson Quiz

1. Who were God's chosen people?
   (Israelites, also called Hebrews, Jews.)
2. What man did God choose to be the "father" of this special nation of people?
   (Abraham.)
3. Why did God want to have this special nation of people?
   (The Savior was to come from this nation.)
4. Who were the Gentiles?
   (All people who were not Jews.)
5. How did Jews feel toward Gentiles?
   (They did not associate with them.)
6. How did God show Peter that the Gentiles could become Christians?
   (By a vision of animals in a sheet.)
7. Who was the first Gentile to become a Christian?
   (Cornelius.)
8. When Peter arrived at the home of Cornelius who else was there?
   (Family and close friends of Cornelius.)
9. How did the Jews who had become Christians feel about Peter going into the home of a Gentile?
   (They thought he had done wrong.)
10. How did Peter convince them that God loves all people and wants all of them to follow Jesus?
    (He told them of his vision and its meaning.)

Additional Lesson Activities

1. Posters

Let pupils make posters using drawings or pictures of boys and girls from many different countries. Choose a Scripture motto such as "God so loved the world," "Go ye into all the world," or "He is Lord of all."

2. Promises

Let pupils write promises to God, telling how they will show kindness to certain persons this week. No one should see what someone else has written—these are promises between the pupils and the Lord.

Workbook Page

On page 44 you'll find two puzzles, "Choose the Right Word" (Acts 10) and "Peter's Report" (Acts 11).

Words to Remember

"Then Peter opened his mouth, and said, Of a truth I perceive that God is no respecter of persons" (Acts 10:34).

Lesson 12

Peter Is Put in Prison

Acts 12:1-23

Introduction to Lesson

Put these scrambled names on the chalkboard and let students unscramble them (Acts 12:1-19).

1. R E E T P
2. R E O H D
3. H D O A R
4. G L E N A
5. M R Y A
6. H J N O K A M R
7. S E A M J
8. S J W E

The Bible Lesson

It was not easy to be a Christian when the church began. The rulers of the people were afraid they would lose their power over the people, so they persecuted the Christians in many ways. King Herod had many of them thrown into prison, and even ordered the death of James, the brother of John. When Herod saw that James' death pleased the Jewish rulers, he decided to have Peter thrown into prison. Peter was one of the well-known leaders of the church, and Herod wanted to be sure that Peter would not escape. A large company of soldiers guarded the prison. Chains were put on Peter's wrists, and he was placed between two soldiers. That night Peter must have made himself as comfortable as he could between the two guards, and he went to sleep.

Many Christians were meeting in the home of Mary, John Mark's mother. They were praying to God, asking Him to be with Peter. The answers to those prayers came in a very surprising way!

God sent an angel to the prison where Peter was sleeping. The angel touched Peter and said, "Get up quickly!" Peter awakened and the angel helped him up. When he did this, the chains fell off his hands. The angel told Peter to put on his robe and sandals and follow him. After passing the guards, they came to the gate. When Peter and the angel reached the iron gate that led into the city, the gate opened by itself. The angel then left Peter. He continued on his way to the house where the Christians were praying for him.

Peter knocked at the door of the gate, and a young girl named Rhoda came to see who it was. She was quite surprised and happy to see Peter. She left him standing there while she ran back into the house to tell the other Christians. They would not believe it really was Peter. They thought perhaps that he had been killed in prison, and that his spirit was at the door.

However, Peter continued knocking at the gate, and they finally came to let him in. They were astonished to see him! He told them all that had happened to him in prison. Once again the disciples' faith was strengthened.

The next day, when King Herod heard that Peter had escaped, he became so angry that he ordered the keepers of the prison to be killed. Later King Herod went before the people and made a great speech. He wanted the people to think that he was some kind of a god. Because of this and many other sins that Herod had done, God sent an angel to take Herod's life.

God is with those who trust and obey Him, and He is against those who work against Him.

The Lesson Applied

There will be many times in your life, as you try to be a Christian, that unpleasant things will happen to you. You may become discouraged and say to yourself, "I have tried to live as Christ would have me live. I wonder why He has let these things happen to me. Maybe God doesn't take care of us after all!" If you should ever feel that way, just remember that God never forgets us and never stops loving us.

Perhaps Peter wondered why God allowed him to be put into prison, not once, but several times.

When things seem to go wrong, remember how much the early Christians had to suffer. The Bible says they rejoiced "that they were counted worthy to suffer shame for his name."

Remember, too, how much the early Christians prayed. Acts 12:5 says that "prayer was made without ceasing" by the church for Peter while he was in prison. Acts 12:12 says that "many were gathered together praying." God answers prayer.

Questions for Discussion: Will God be with us everywhere we go? What does it mean to "pray without ceasing"?

The Lesson Quiz

1. What wicked king persecuted the Christians?

(King Herod.)

2. What did he do to James, the brother of John?

(He had James killed.)

3. What did he do to Peter?

(He put Peter in prison.)

4. Whom did God send to Peter while he was in prison?

(An angel.)

5. When the angel told Peter to arise quickly, what happened?

(The chains fell off Peter's hands.)

6. When the angel left Peter, where did Peter go?

(To the house of Mary, John Mark's mother, where the Christians were praying.)

7. Who came to the door when Peter knocked?

(A young girl named Rhoda.)

8. How did the Christians react when they saw Peter?

(They were astonished.)

9. What did King Herod do when he found that Peter had escaped?

(He ordered the guards to be killed.)

10. What happened to King Herod later when he gave a great speech to the people?

(The Lord sent an angel to take his life.)

Additional Lesson Activities

1. Prayer Thoughts

Let pupils write out prayers that the Christians might have prayed for Peter.

2. Pantomime the Story

Let pupils act out the story as it is being read from Acts 12:1-23. Here are the characters:

Herod	guards	Rhoda
James	soldiers	Christians
Peter	angel	another angel

Here are the scenes:

Herod's palace   Prison   Mary's house

Here is the action:

1. Herod orders his guards to kill James.
2. Herod orders his guards to put Peter in prison. They bring him in, heavily guarded.
3. Christians are meeting to pray for Peter.
4. Peter, chained to two soldiers, sleeps in prison.
5. Angel enters, raises Peter up, tells him to put on his sandals and his outer cloak. Peter obeys orders, and follows angel out of prison.
6. Angel departs, and Peter goes to the house of Mary.
7. Peter knocks, and Rhoda comes to door.
8. Rhoda leaves Peter at door, and hurries to tell the rest that he has come. Peter continues knocking.
9. Several come to the door and see Peter. They are astonished.
10. Peter enters, beckons for silence, and explains to them what has happened to him. Then he departs.
11. Soldiers look for Peter in the prison.
12. Herod orders the prison keepers put to death.
13. Herod sits on his throne, making a great speech.
14. The Lord's angel "smites" him and he dies immediately.

Workbook Page

The first puzzle on page 45 reviews the lesson Scripture: "First and Last (Acts 12)." The second puzzle reviews twelve of the stories about Peter that have been studied in this series.

Words to Remember

"Yet if any man suffer as a Christian, let him not be ashamed; but let him glorify God on this behalf" (1 Peter 4:16).

Lesson 13

Peter Writes Some Letters

1 and 2 Peter

Introduction to Lesson

Let students finish the sentences to see how much they know about Peter:

1. Peter's occupation was. . . .
2. Jesus called Peter to be a. . . .
3. Jesus told Peter to feed. . . .
4. Peter preached the first. . . .
5. Through God's power, Peter. . . .
6. Peter preached to the first. . . .
7. An angel helped Peter. . . .
8. Peter wrote. . . .

The Bible Lesson

Everyone likes to receive letters. When you are sick, a letter from a friend seems to make you feel better; when you are lonely or sad, you feel happy again when the mailman brings a letter; and when a letter arrives inviting you to spend a week with Grandma or asking if you would like to go camping with Uncle John—well, nothing is nicer than receiving such a letter.

Nearly all of the books of the New Testament are letters! They were written by disciples of Jesus to other Christians or to churches. Paul wrote many of these letters. When Paul became a Christian, he also became a missionary and traveled to many countries and preached wherever he went. After he returned from those missionary journeys, he was anxious for the new Christians in those churches to live as Christ wanted them to live. He wrote them letters, telling them the way God wanted them to live. He also wrote letters to individuals, such as Timothy and Titus.

Peter wrote two letters in the New Testament. They are called 1 Peter and 2 Peter. The first verse of the first chapter of each one tells to whom the letters were sent. God told Peter what to write. The messages of these letters help us today.

In Peter's first letter, he tells the Christians that they should be happy, even though they may suffer many hardships. He reminds them of Christ's love for them, and of the home He has gone to prepare for them in Heaven. He also says that Christians should love one another and be good citizens. "You are to walk in the steps of Jesus," he wrote, "for we follow His example." He says that if Christians will do these things they will set a good example for others to follow.

Peter speaks of Satan and tells how dangerous he is. "The devil as a roaring lion walks about, seeking those he may devour."

Peter's second letter may have been written just before he was put to death. He speaks of his coming death, saying he wanted to remind them of things they should do, since he would not always be able to guide them. In his last letter, he warns Christians that wicked men would try to turn them away from Christ and that others would laugh at them because they were looking for Christ's second coming. But he pleads with them to be faithful to Christ and to be ready for that great day when Christ will return for His followers. He closed the letter by saying, "Grow in grace, and in the knowledge of our Lord and Savior Jesus Christ."

Christians today are still reading these letters written by Peter, and they are still trying to live lives that are pleasing to the Master. As we live for Christ, and as we work for Him, we, too, are waiting for that wonderful day. Christ will come in the clouds to take us to the beautiful home in Heaven that He is preparing for us.

Peter's two short letters have helped many thousands of people to become better Christians.

The Lesson Applied

Let's look at one part of Peter's second letter. These verses are very helpful to Christians: 2 Peter 1:5-7.

First, Peter said to have FAITH. (This means believing that Jesus is God's Son, and accepting His words as true.) Then other things are to be added to faith:

VIRTUE (This means living a good, clean life.)
KNOWLEDGE (This means studying the Bible and knowing what God would have you do.)
TEMPERANCE (This means not overdoing anything such as playing too much, eating too much; also avoiding things that are harmful to your body.)

PATIENCE (This means controlling your temper, not getting angry if you can't have everything you want the moment you want it.)

GODLINESS (This means thinking about God and Jesus and trying to live the right way.)

BROTHERLY KINDNESS (Treating everyone in a kindly way, whether he is young or old, friend or stranger; whether he is a member of your family or not.)

LOVE (Obeying God and living for Him; never knowingly hurting or being unkind to someone else.)

Questions for Discussion: To whom were Peter's letters sent? Why are Peter's letters helpful to people today? How can we use letters to help other people?

The Lesson Quiz

1. What books of the New Testament were written by Peter?
   (First and 2 Peter.)
2. Where did Peter get the messages he put in his letters?
   (God told Peter what to write.)
3. What does it mean to have faith in Christ?
   (Believing that He is God's Son, and that His teachings are true.)
4. What is virtue?
   (Being clean and pure in our lives.)
5. How do we get knowledge?
   (By reading God's Word.)
6. What does "temperance" mean?
   (Not overdoing things, such as overeating; not doing things that are harmful to our bodies.)
7. How can we be patient?
   (Learn to control our tempers.)
8. What is "godliness"?
   (Trying to live like Jesus.)
9. How can we show "brotherly kindness"?
   (By treating everyone kindly, no matter who he or she is.)
10. What are we to add to our faith?
    (Virtue, knowledge, temperance, patience, godliness, brotherly kindness, love.)

Additional Lesson Activities

1. Write Letters

Let pupils write short notes on postal cards and send them to people who are ill. They can make the cards pretty by adding flowers or scenes cut from old greeting cards, pasting them in the corners of the postal cards.

Cards also may be sent to absentees from the Sunday-school class or youth meetings.

Let pupils write cheerful letters to shut-ins or patients in nursing homes and hospitals.

2. Make a Chart

Let pupils make charts with the eight items (Faith to Love) listed on the left side. At the close of each day they may read each item on the chart and decide if they have really lived up to that goal. They may place check marks beside the ones they have accomplished. Challenge them to see how many check marks they have at the end of the month.

Workbook Page

"Fill in the Blanks" on page 46 reviews 2 Peter 1:5-7. "Scrambled Letters" contains verses from Peter's first letter.

Words to Remember

"But grow in grace, and in the knowledge of our Lord and Saviour Jesus Christ. To him be glory both now and for ever. Amen" (2 Peter 3:18).

Part Four

Adventures in Bible Lands

The lessons in this last section of *Adventures Through the Bible* are planned to give pupils an introduction to Bible geography. Six cities in Israel, three bodies of water, the land of Egypt, and seven mountains are included. Cities on the map are indicated by circles; mountains are indicated by triangles. (The pupil's map on page 61 of the workbook is exactly the same as the map on the opposite page of this book—but the names have been omitted for the pupils. At the end of the study, have pupils add the names to the map.)

Most of the geographical places studied have stories from both the Old and New Testaments. Be sure to emphasize where these stories are found in the Bible, as well as where they are found on the map.

Provide resource material for pupils to use in the additional lesson activities suggested. Maps, Bible encyclopedias and atlases, and other reference books are available in Christian bookstores, or may be ordered from religious publishers. Some of these books are prepared especially for children. Perhaps your more advanced pupils will add the provinces, other mountains, cities, and additional geographical locations to your magnetic map described below.

Magnetic Map

To make a special visual aid to use during this study of Bible lands, you will need the following materials:

a map of the area to be studied (enlarge the map on page 61 of the pupil's workbook, where nothing is identified)

a metal sheet the same size as the map (cookie sheet, or stove-top protector, etc.)

two or three magnetic rubber strips

several 3 x 5 cards or a sheet of lightweight cardboard

felt-tip pen, glue, scissors, and a large spring-type clip to attach the map to the metal backing

Letter the names of the towns, bodies of water, countries, and mountains on small rectangles of lightweight cardboard. On the back of each one, glue a small piece (¼″) of magnetic strip. These names may be attached and removed again and again to review the lessons of Bible geography.

Small pictures, such as Bible picture cards or pictures cut from Sunday-school papers, also may be mounted on pieces of cardboard with magnetic strips glued on the backs. Place these scenes near the towns or bodies of water with which they are connected. Books of seals that contain small scenes from Bible stories may be used, too.

Bulletin Board Ideas

Help your pupils to connect the countries mentioned in the Bible with countries in the Middle East.

Ancient Names	Modern Names
Babylon and Babylonia	Iraq
Assyria	Syria and Iraq
Arabia	Saudi Arabia, Jordan
Persia	Iran
Canaan, Palestine	Israel

For the past several years, countries in the Middle East have been in the news. Clip newspaper articles and headlines that mention countries such as Israel, Jordan, Lebanon, Iran, Saudi Arabia, Iraq, Syria, Egypt, Cyprus, Sudan, Turkey, and Yemen. Encourage pupils also to collect these clippings. Provide a bulletin board where these items may be displayed.

If you have a large map of Bible lands, place it in the center of the bulletin board. Attach the clippings or headlines around the edge of the map. Tape one end of a piece of ribbon or string to a clipping, and the other end to the country on the map.

Many newspaper articles will refer to Islam, the chief religion of the Middle East. Some research into this subject would be helpful, in order that you may be able to explain the basic beliefs of Islam to your pupils. Compare their false doctrines with Scriptural truths.

Project for Pupils

A Relief Map of Palestine

Pages 47 and 48 of the pupil's workbook contain directions and a pattern for making a relief map of Palestine. You may want to share some of these explanations with your pupils as they prepare to work on their maps.

1. A "relief" map shows the contours of the land: mountains, valleys, etc. (These are scaled down, and may not be completely accurate, but they give an idea of the topography of the land.) The coloring of the map is significant, too. Shades of green are used for fertile areas, tans or browns for mountainous areas, and light browns or yellows for desert areas.

2. Palestine is the name given to the land of Israel in the time of Christ. The boundaries have changed somewhat through the years, but the territory of Canaan (Old Testament), Palestine (New Testament), and Israel (the name of the land today) is basically the same.

3. This relief map includes the major mountains of Israel, although not all of them will be studied in this series of lessons. (Lebanon, Gilboa, and Tabor are not mentioned in any of the stories.) Mountains in other lands, Nebo and Sinai, are included in the lessons but not on the relief map.

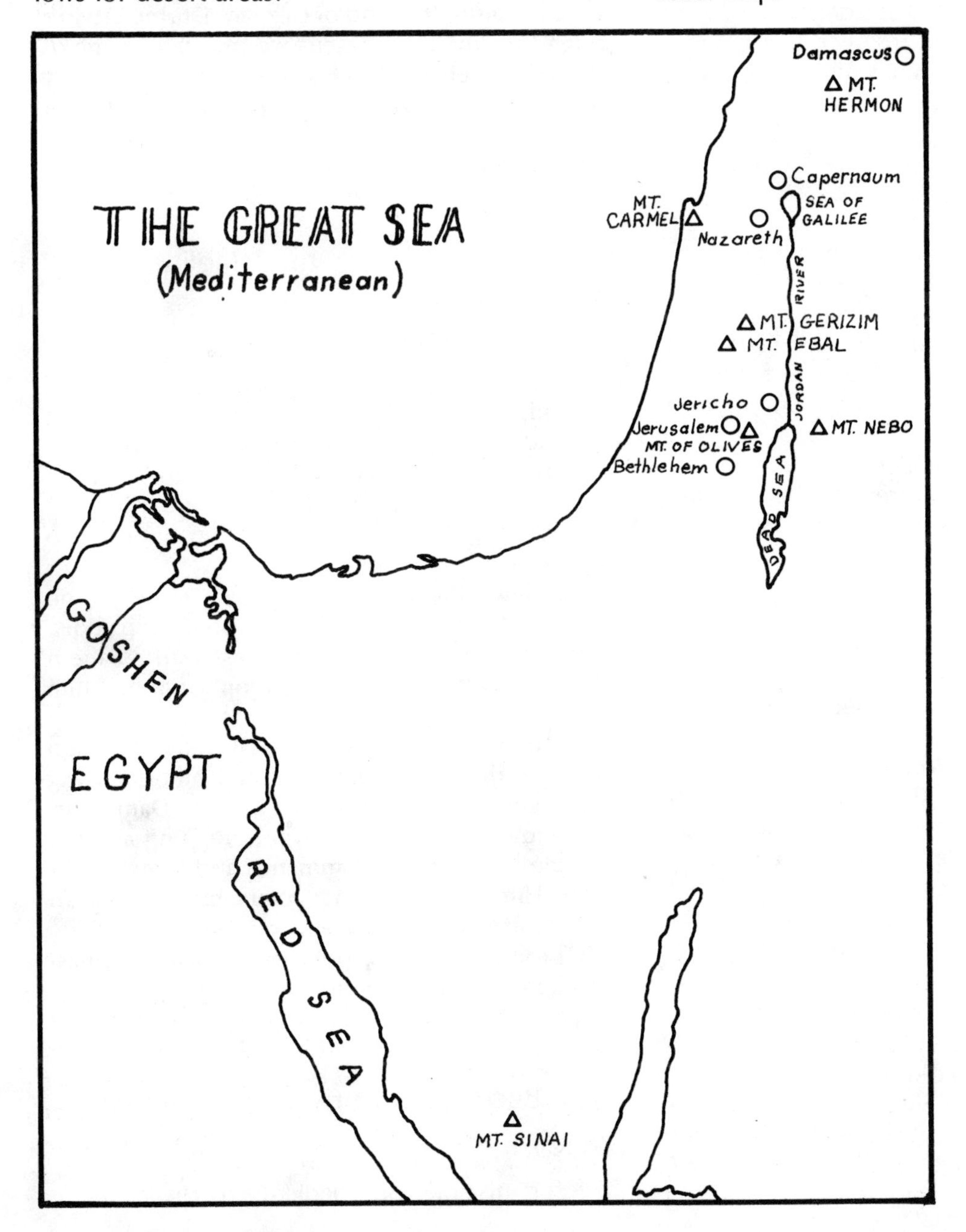

Geography Game

Practice going down the map, naming only the cities and bodies of water.

Damascus
Capernaum
Sea of Galilee
Nazareth
Jordan River
Jericho
Jerusalem
Bethlehem
Dead Sea

Next, note Egypt on the left, and add Goshen and the Red Sea.

Finally, coming up from the bottom of the map, name the mountains.

Sinai
Nebo
Olivet (Olives)
Ebal
Gerizim
Carmel
Hermon

(Teach your pupils to name the places this way, too. Make a game of learning Bible geography!)

Lesson 1

Damascus

Introduction to Lesson

(Introduce the bulletin-board display suggested on page 86. Encourage pupils to bring in headlines and clippings.)

Point out the city of Damascus in Syria. Explain to the class that Damascus is considered to be one of the oldest cities in the world. It is mentioned in connection with many Bible events, and still is inhabited today.

The Bible Lesson

(Write the following names on the chalkboard: Abraham, Lot, King David, King Joash, Saul, and Ananias. Let pupils identify as many of them as they can. Ask which are from the Old Testament and which are from the New Testament. Explain that all of these Bible people are mentioned in connection with the city of Damascus.)

(The following Bible stories may be told as they appear below, or the Scriptures may be assigned to four pupils for reports.)

Abraham Rescues Lot

(Genesis 14:8—15:2)

Abraham, the man God had chosen to be the father of a great nation, had settled in the land of Canaan. His nephew, Lot, and his family had moved their tents and belongings near the city of Sodom. Several kings of the surrounding cities were at war, and the people of Sodom and all their possessions were taken away by an enemy king. When Abraham heard that Lot had been taken captive, he armed three hundred and eighteen trained servants of his household. They pursued the invaders to Hobah, on the left side of the city of Damascus. There he was able to rescue Lot, his family and possessions, and bring them back to their own land. Abraham refused to accept any reward from the king of Sodom for what he had done. The word of the Lord came to him in a vision: "Fear not . . . I am your shield and your great reward."

David Captures the City

(2 Samuel 8:3-8)

Many years after Abraham's time, David became king over Israel. He spent much of his time in battles with the heathen nations who were trying to capture the land of Canaan. During David's reign the city of Damascus was ruled by some of these heathen people. David marched to the city with his armies, captured it, and put a garrison of soldiers there. The Syrians became servants of King David.

The Syrians Capture the Israelites

(2 Chronicles 24)

Many years after the time of David, Joash became king of Israel. As long as Jehoiada, a priest of God, lived, Joash did what was right in the sight of God. He even collected money and repaired the great temple that had fallen into ruin. He placed a chest near the door of the temple and encouraged the people to give their offerings to the Lord.

But after the good priest died, some of the people forgot God and began to worship idols. When the son of the good priest warned them that they were doing wrong, King Joash had him stoned to death.

Then the Syrian army invaded Israel. They killed many of the people and captured others, taking them back to their king who lived in Damascus. The Bible points out that when the king and the people forgot God's commands and turned away from Him, God punished them by allowing an enemy army to capture and kill them.

(These three Bible stories took place in Damascus before Jesus came to earth.)

Saul Becomes a Christian at Damascus

(Acts 9:1-27)

Jesus' disciples, in obedience to His last command, were going everywhere preaching about Him. The Jews began to persecute the Christians, killing many of them and putting others in prison. One man who was determined to get rid of the Christians was Saul. One day he was on his way to the city of Damascus to arrest some Christians. A great light, brighter than the sun, shone down on him from Heaven. Jesus spoke to him, "Saul, Saul, why are you persecuting Me?"

Saul answered with a question: "Who are You, Lord?"

"I am Jesus," He answered. He told Saul to go into Damascus and wait there. Someone would tell him what he must do.

Saul was blinded by the light and had to be led by his companions into the city, where he stayed three days. God spoke to a Christian named Ananias and told him to go to a certain house on the street called Straight. There he would find Saul. When Ananias reached the house where Saul was, he first healed him of his blindness. Then he gave Saul God's message, and Saul was baptized. Saul became a messenger for God and began to preach about Jesus.

The Lesson Applied

As we study the Bible, especially the Old Testament, we find that God's people were involved in many battles for their land. The heathen nations surrounding them wanted their territory. But as long as the Israelites obeyed God's commands, He was with them and helped them win their battles.

Saul had been an enemy of Jesus. When Saul became a Christian, he immediately began trying to get others to follow Jesus. This made the enemies of Jesus angry, and they tried to kill Saul. Saul had to put His trust in the Lord to help him be victorious.

Christians today have battles, too. Satan is the enemy, and he is always trying to get people to disobey God. We must put our trust in God and obey Him. He will be with us and help us win the victory over Satan.

Questions for Discussion: What "battles" do Christians have today? How can we resist Satan's attacks?

The Lesson Quiz

1. Where is the ancient city of Damascus?
(Syria.)

2. Whom did Abraham rescue from a place near the city of Damascus?
(His nephew, Lot.)

3. What king of Israel captured Damascus?
(David.)

4. What king forgot God and let his people worship idols, after the good priest, Jehoiada, died?
(Joash.)

5. When the Syrians captured the Israelites, during Joash's reign, where did they take them?
(Back to their king in Damascus.)

6. To what great city was Saul going to persecute the Christians?
(Damascus.)

7. What happened to him on the way?
(A great light from Heaven blinded him.)

8. When the light appeared, who spoke to Saul, and what did He say?
(Jesus told Saul who He was, and He told Saul to go into Damascus where he would receive more instructions.)

9. After Saul received his sight, what did he do?
(He was baptized.)

10. How did Saul escape from the Jews?
(He was let down over the city wall in a basket.)

Additional Lesson Activities

1. A Relief Map

Let pupils begin the map project described on pages 47 and 48 in the pupil's workbook.

2. Set of Description Cards

Provide a 3 x 5 card for each pupil. Each one is to write the name "Damascus" on one side of the card and a description of Damascus on the other side. Sample description: "One of the oldest known cities in history, in the land of Syria. King David once captured the city. Saul was on his way to this city when Jesus spoke to him."

(These cards are to be made for all of the Bible places in this series of lessons. They will be used in a review game.)

Workbook Page

On page 49 of the pupil's workbook there are two puzzles. "Find Out" is an acrostic, and "Match the Verses" is a review using one verse from each of the four Bible stories. Check your answers on page 64.

Memory Verse: 1 Corinthians 15:57

Lesson 2

The Sea of Galilee

Introduction to Lesson

Place the following Scriptures on the chalkboard, and let pupils find four names for the same body of water:

1. Numbers 34:11 (Sea of Chinnereth)
2. Matthew 4:18 (Sea of Galilee)
3. Luke 5:1 (Sea of Gennesaret)
4. John 6:1 (Sea of Tiberias)

The land of Palestine, now called Israel, is a small country filled with mountains, and hills, and valleys. There are desert lands and rich farm lands. It has a river and two seas (large lakes): the Jordan River, the Dead Sea, and the Sea of Galilee.

The Sea of Galilee is about six to eight miles across at the widest part, and about twelve miles long. It is called Chinnereth in the Old Testament, and Galilee, Gennesaret, and Tiberias in the New Testament.

The Bible Lesson

(Many wonderful things happened during the life of Jesus on and around this lake. But first we will mention one incident from the Old Testament concerning the "Sea of Chinnereth.")

Dividing the Promised Land

(Deuteronomy 3:16-24)

Each of the twelve tribes of Israel was to receive a certain section of the land. They first had to conquer the heathen enemies who lived there. The men of the tribes that received land on the east side of Jordan could leave their wives and children there while they helped conquer the land on the west side.

Two tribes on the east bordered the Sea of Chinnereth: a half-tribe of Manasseh and Gad. The tribe of Naphtali bordered the sea on the west.

God promised to be with His people in the battles. Moses told Joshua, "You have seen what the Lord has done to the two kings who fought us. He will do the same to the other kingdoms through which you pass. Do not fear them, for the Lord your God will fight for you." Then Moses prayed to God, "O Lord God, what god in Heaven or earth can do such great works as You do, or have such power and might!"

The Calling of the Four Fishermen

(Matthew 4:18-22)

One day Peter and Andrew were fishing in the Sea of Galilee when Jesus passed by on the shore. He called out to them, "Follow me, and I will make you fishers of men." Peter and Andrew left their nets and followed Him. Farther along the shore Jesus saw James and John sitting in their fishing boat with their father, mending nets. "Follow me," Jesus said to them. James and John left their father and their work and went with Jesus.

Jesus Preaches From the Boat

(Luke 5:1-11)

One day Jesus was preaching to a great crowd on the shore of Galilee. He stepped into a boat that was nearby and had Simon Peter, who owned the boat, push it out a little way from the shore. Jesus sat down in the boat and continued to teach the people. When He had finished, He told Simon Peter to row the boat out into the lake and let down the nets. Simon said they had fished all night and had caught nothing, but he would let down the nets again if Jesus wanted him to. When the nets were pulled in, they were so full of fish that they were breaking. The fish filled two boats.

Peter was astonished, and he bowed low before Jesus and said, "Depart from me; for I am a sinful man, O Lord."

Jesus said to him, "Don't be afraid! From now on, you will catch men!"

Jesus Stills the Storm

(Luke 8:22-25)

Jesus had been teaching the people, and He was very tired. He and His disciples got into a boat and started rowing toward the other side of the Sea of Galilee. Jesus went to sleep in the back part of the boat. A sudden storm came up. The wind blew and the waves dashed against the boat until it seemed the boat would turn over. The disciples were afraid and awakened Jesus. He stood up in the boat and said, "Peace, be still." The wind stopped and the sea was quiet once more. The disciples were astonished. They looked at each other and said, "What manner of man is this! for he commandeth even the winds and water, and they obey him."

Jesus Walks on the Water
(John 6:1-21)

After Jesus had preached to a great multitude one day on the shores of Galilee, He fed them with five loaves of bread and two fish. It was late afternoon, so He told His disciples to get into a boat and row to the other side of the lake while He went up on a mountain to pray. A storm came up when the boat was in the middle of the lake. Suddenly the disciples saw Jesus walking on the water toward their boat. "It is I," He said, "be not afraid." He entered the boat, and immediately it was at the shore!

The Lesson Applied

God's great power is seen in stories from the Old Testament, when He guided His people in reaching the promised land. The Sea of Galilee was included in that area.

God's Son, Jesus, showed His great power in miracles, and many of them took place on or near the Sea of Galilee.

As we study and think about these events in God's Word, we realize that God wants us to believe in Jesus as His Son. Only One who came from God could do the things that Jesus did.

Questions for Discussion: Why is it important to believe that Jesus is the Son of God? How can we be "fishers of men" today?

The Lesson Quiz

1. Which of the three tribes had the Sea of Galilee as part of their border?
(Manasseh, Gad, and Naphtali.)
2. Why did Moses tell Joshua not to be afraid?
(Because God would fight for him in the battles to conquer the promised land.)
3. What were Peter and Andrew doing when Jesus called them to follow Him?
(Fishing in the Sea of Galilee.)
4. What did four fishermen decide to do when Jesus called them?
(They left their work and followed Him.)
5. In whose boat did Jesus sit while He taught the people gathered on the shore of Galilee?
(Peter's.)
6. After Jesus finished teaching, what did He ask Peter to do?
(Row out into the lake and cast down his nets.)
7. When Peter saw the great catch of fish, what did He say to Jesus?
("Depart from me; for I am a sinful man, O Lord.")
8. What did Jesus answer?
("Don't be afraid! From now on, you will catch men.")
9. What did Jesus do when the disciples awakened Him during a storm on the Sea of Galilee?
(He said to the winds and the sea, "Peace, be still," and the storm ceased.)
10. In what other way did Jesus show His great power on the Sea of Galilee?
(He walked on the water.)

Additional Lesson Activities

1. Seascapes

Let pupils choose one of the events connected with the Sea of Galilee and draw or paint a picture of it. Obtain some photographs of the Sea of Galilee to provide backgrounds for the pupils to copy. Display pupils' scenes on a large bulletin board.

2. Set of Description Cards

Provide a 3 x 5 card for each pupil to add to his set of description cards. On one side of the card the pupil will write the name "Sea of Galilee." On the other side a description is written. Suggested description: "A body of water, 6-8 miles wide and 12 miles long, from which the Jordan River flows down to the Dead Sea. Here Jesus called fishermen to be His followers, calmed the storms, and walked on the water."

Workbook Page

On page 50 of the pupil's workbook, two puzzles review the lesson: "What Happened Here?" and "A Puzzle." Check your answers on page 64.

Memory Verse: Matthew 8:27

Lesson 3

Capernaum

Introduction to Lesson

If possible, provide two maps: one showing Canaan as divided among the twelve tribes, and one showing Palestine in the time of Christ. On the first map show a city named "Chinnereth" at the top part of the Sea of Galilee. On the second map, the city of Capernaum is in almost the same location. Let pupils look at these maps and make comparisons. Explain that Capernaum is not mentioned in the Old Testament, but the city of Chinnereth is found in Joshua 19:35.

The Bible Lesson

(Many events from Jesus' life took place in and around the city of Capernaum.)

Jesus Heals in Capernaum

(Mark 1:21-34)

Once when Jesus was in Capernaum, He went into the synagogue on the Sabbath Day and taught the people. When He had finished teaching, He healed a man who had an unclean spirit. Jesus went to Peter's home, and found that Peter's mother-in-law was very sick with a fever. Jesus healed her, and immediately she was able to rise and help serve the meal. In the evening, just as the sun was setting, a great crowd came to Peter's house, bringing people who were sick or crippled. Jesus healed them, too.

Jesus Heals the Man With Palsy

(Mark 2:1-12)

In the city of Capernaum, Jesus healed a man who was sick of the palsy. Four friends brought the man to Jesus. There was such a crowd of people in and around the house where Jesus was teaching and healing that the friends of the sick man were unable to get him to Jesus. They took the sick man up on the roof of the house, made a hole in the roof, and lowered the man on his bed until he was in front of Jesus. Jesus said to the man, "Son, your sins are forgiven." The religious leaders in the crowd were very critical. "Only God can forgive sins," they thought to themselves. Jesus could read their thoughts, and to show that He had the power to forgive sins, He told the sick man to arise, take up his bed, and walk. Immediately the man was well.

Jairus' Daughter

(Mark 5:21-24, 35-43)

One day while Jesus was teaching, Jairus, a ruler of the synagogue in Capernaum, came and fell at His feet. "My little daughter is sick," Jairus said. "Come and put your hands on her that she may be healed." Jesus started to go with him, but others wanted help and Jesus was delayed.

A servant came to Jairus and said, "It is too late; the child is dead." But Jesus told Jairus not to be afraid, but to believe. When they reached the home of Jairus, many people were weeping. Jesus sent them away. He went into the room where the little girl lay, taking with Him the parents of the girl and three of His disciples. He took the little girl by the hand, spoke to her, and she got up. She was alive and well again! Jesus had raised her from the dead.

The Centurion's Servant Healed

(Matthew 8:5-13)

One day when Jesus was coming into Capernaum, a centurion (Roman captain of one hundred soldiers) came to Him saying, "Lord, my servant is very ill at my house."

Jesus answered, "I will come and heal him."

But the centurion replied, "Lord, I am not worthy for You to come into my house. Just speak the word, and my servant will be healed. I know what it means to have authority—I give orders to my servants and they obey me."

Jesus marveled at the man's faith! "Go your way. As you have believed, it will be done." And the centurion's servant was healed that same hour!

The Calling of Matthew

(Matthew 9:9-13)

Matthew, one of Jesus' disciples, had been a publican (tax collector) before he followed Jesus. When Jesus came by, he had been sitting at the place in the city of Capernaum where he collected taxes. No doubt Jesus had been nearby many times, teaching and preaching, and Matthew must have heard Him. Jesus knew that Matthew would be a good worker for Him, and He called to him, "Follow me." Matthew went with Jesus as one of His disciples.

To those who criticized Jesus for associating with despised tax collectors, Jesus explained, "I came to call sinners, not the righteous, to repentance."

The Lesson Applied

Why did Jesus do so many miracles? One reason was because He loved people and wanted to help them. But the most important reason for the miracles was to prove that Jesus is the Son of God. Although the people listened to the wonderful lessons that Jesus taught, they were not sure that Jesus was God's Son until they saw His miracles.

We do not need to see miracles today to believe that Jesus is God's Son. We can read about all these great miracles in the Bible, and we know that God's Word is true. We can have eternal life when we believe in Jesus as the Son of God and obey His commands.

Questions for Discussion: How did the people in these Bible stories show their faith in Jesus? How can we show faith in Jesus? Why must we obey as well as believe?

The Lesson Quiz

1. Where is the city of Capernaum?
(On the shore of the Sea of Galilee.)

2. On one busy Sabbath Day in Capernaum, what miracles did Jesus do?
(He healed a man in the synagogue, Peter's mother-in-law, and a great crowd of sick and crippled people who came to Peter's house in the evening.)

3. How did the man with palsy get to Jesus?
(Four friends brought him and let him down through the roof of the house.)

4. What did Jesus say first to the sick man?
("Your sins are forgiven.")

5. Who criticized Jesus, thinking that only God can forgive sins?
(The religious leaders.)

6. What did Jesus then say to the sick man, to prove that He had power to forgive sins?
(He told the man to take up his bed and walk.)

7. What did Jesus do for the daughter of Jairus?
(He brought her back to life.)

8. Who came to ask Jesus to heal his servant?
(A centurion—Roman captain.)

9. How did Jesus heal the centurion's servant?
(He spoke the word, and the man was healed without Jesus going to the house.)

10. What disciple did Jesus call in Capernaum?
(Matthew.)

Additional Lesson Activities

1. "First-person" Stories

Let each pupil choose one of the following people who lived in Capernaum and write a "first-person" story about what Jesus did for him or her: Peter's mother-in-law, the man with palsy, the daughter of Jairus, the centurion's servant, Matthew.

2. Set of Description Cards

Each pupil should add another 3 x 5 card to his set. On one side the name "Capernaum" is lettered, and on the other a description of Capernaum is given. Suggested description: "A city on the west shore of the Sea of Galilee. Here Jesus performed many miracles, including healing the sick and raising the dead. Matthew, a tax collector there, was called to be a follower of Jesus."

Workbook Page

"What's the Word?" on page 51 of the pupil's workbook reviews the stories about Jesus in Capernaum. Answers are on page 64 of the workbook. "Map Study" is a simple review of the three places studied in the first three lessons. Check the map on page 87 of this book for the correct names.

Encourage pupils to think of ways that they can show faith in Jesus. Write them on the lines provided.

Memory Verses: John 20:30, 31

Lesson 4

Nazareth

Introduction to Lesson

(Display a map of Palestine in the time of Christ.) When Jesus was on earth, the land of Palestine was divided into provinces. In the north was Galilee. Below Galilee was Samaria, then Judea. On the other side of the Jordan River was Perea. On the other side of the Sea of Galilee was a section called Decapolis, meaning "ten cities." The city of Nazareth was in the province of Galilee. (Point to Nazareth.)

Jesus spent much of His life in Galilee. He lived in Nazareth and Capernaum, but He traveled to other cities of the province.

The Bible Lesson

(All of our stories about Nazareth are from the New Testament. They are all connected with the life of Christ.)

An Angel Is Sent to Mary

(Luke 1:26-38)

In the city of Nazareth lived a young woman named Mary. She was to be married to Joseph, a carpenter, who also lived in Nazareth. One day an angel, named Gabriel, was sent from God to give Mary a very special message. When Gabriel appeared to her, he told Mary that the Lord was with her, and that she was blessed among women. Mary was frightened and wondered what this meant. Gabriel said, "Do not be afraid, Mary, for you have found favor with God. You will have a son, and His name will be called Jesus. He will be great and will rule over the house of Jacob. His kingdom will never end."

When Mary replied that she could not understand how this could happen, Gabriel explained: "The Holy Spirit will come upon you, and the child that will be born will be the Son of God." Gabriel then told Mary that her elderly cousin, Elisabeth, who lived in Judea, was going to have a child also! With God, nothing shall be impossible!

Mary said, "Behold the handmaid of the Lord; be it unto me according to thy word." Then Gabriel departed. Everything happened just as Gabriel, God's messenger, had said!

Joseph, Mary, and Jesus Return to Nazareth

(Luke 2:39-52)

Joseph and Mary had traveled from Nazareth to Bethlehem for the taxing commanded by the Roman emperor. While they were in Bethlehem, Jesus was born. According to the laws that God had given, hundreds of years before, parents had certain duties to carry out when a child was born. They were to offer sacrifices at the temple in Jerusalem. When Joseph and Mary had done these things, they were ready to return to their town of Nazareth. But God warned Joseph in a dream to take Mary and Jesus down to Egypt, to escape from King Herod who had ordered all the boy babies to be killed. After Herod's death, Joseph and Mary took Jesus back to Nazareth. Very little is known of Jesus' childhood, except for a trip He made to the temple when He was twelve. God's Word tells us that after the journey to the temple, He returned to Nazareth with Mary and Joseph and was obedient to them. He grew in wisdom, stature, and in favor with God and man.

Jesus Visits the Synagogue in Nazareth

(Luke 4:14-32)

After Jesus' baptism and temptation, He returned to Galilee and began His ministry. He came to Nazareth, where He had been brought up, and went into the synagogue on the Sabbath Day.

When Jesus stood up to read the Scriptures, He was handed the book of the prophet Isaiah. Jesus opened the book and read these words: (Read aloud Luke 4:18, 19). Then He closed the book, gave it to the minister, and sat down. Everyone was watching Him as He began to speak. "This day is this Scripture fulfilled in your ears." As Jesus taught them, they were amazed. "Isn't this Joseph's son?" they asked. They could not believe that someone who had grown up in their city could be the One sent from God. They could not accept His claim to be the Savior. They became angry and rushed Him out of the synagogue, to the edge of a cliff. They were going to throw Him down over the side of the hill and kill Him, but Jesus passed through them and went on His way to Capernaum. They were powerless to harm the Son of God! As far as we know, Jesus never went back to His home in Nazareth.

The Lesson Applied

(Assign the Scripture references to pupils and call on them to read the verses as you proceed through this lesson application.)

A person who lives in a certain town or state often is referred to by the name of the town or state. For example, a person from New York is called a "New Yorker," and a person from California is called a "Californian." Jesus lived in Nazareth, and He was called a Nazarene. (Read Matthew 2:23.)

All through His ministry, as He preached and taught and healed people, Jesus was known as "Jesus of Nazareth." (Read Mark 1:24; Luke 4:34; and John 1:45.) When Jesus was crucified, Pilate had a sign made to put on the cross. It said that "Jesus of Nazareth" was the "King of the Jews." (Read John 19:19.) After Jesus went back to Heaven, the apostles referred to Him as "Jesus of Nazareth." (Read Acts 10:38.)

It is sad to think that although the Son of God was known as "Jesus of Nazareth" the people of Nazareth rejected Him! John wrote, "He came unto his own, and his own received him not." But John went on to say, "But as many as received him, to them gave he power to become the sons of God, even to them that believe on his name" (John 1:11, 12).

Sometimes when we try to win our friends and relatives to Jesus, they won't listen. We have to remember that Jesus, too, was not always received by His own people. When some rejected Him, He went to others. He didn't stop preaching and teaching. He continued to go about doing good, and God was with Him. God will be with us as we try to follow Jesus, our perfect example.

Questions for Discussion: Why is it sometimes hard to win our relatives and close friends to Jesus? How should we act when others refuse to come and learn about Jesus?

The Lesson Quiz

1. What angel did God send to give Mary a special message?
(Gabriel.)
2. Where did Mary live?
(Nazareth.)
3. What was the angel's message?
(Mary was to become the mother of Jesus.)
4. In what city did Jesus grow up?
(Nazareth.)
5. What trip did Jesus take when He was twelve?
(He went from Nazareth to Jerusalem.)
6. What was Jesus' attitude toward Mary and Joseph when they went back to Nazareth, after the trip to the temple?
(He was obedient to them.)
7. What happened in the synagogue at Nazareth when Jesus spoke to the people?
(They became angry at His teachings.)
8. Where did the angry mob take Jesus?
(They took Him out of the synagogue to the edge of a cliff.)
9. How did Jesus get away from them?
(He passed through the crowd unharmed.)
10. When did Jesus visit Nazareth again?
(As far as we know He never went back.)

Additional Lesson Activities

1. Other Towns in Galilee
Let pupils look at maps and Bible research materials and find other towns in Galilee where Jesus taught or performed miracles: Cana, Nain, Tiberias, Capernaum.
2. Set of Description Cards
Let pupils add "Nazareth" to their sets of cards.

Workbook Page

The "Crossword Review" on page 52 of the pupil's workbook provides a Scripture reference for each answer. Check your answers with those on page 64 of the workbook. Have pupils add a circle to the map on page 51 and label it Nazareth.

Memory Verse: Acts 10:38

Lesson 5

The Jordan River

Introduction to Lesson

Place the following scrambled names on the chalkboard along with these directions:

"Can you unscramble the names of these Bible people who had important events happen to them in or near the Jordan River?"

H A J I E L	(Elijah)
M A N A N A	(Naaman)
S H U A O J	(Joshua)
E S I L A H	(Elisha)
S E U J S	(Jesus)
H O N J	(John)

The Bible Lesson

(Many wonderful and interesting things happened in and around the Jordan River. This river is the largest in Palestine (Israel), being about 100 miles long. It is very crooked and winding.)

Crossing the Jordan
(Joshua 3)

Moses had led God's people from the land of Egypt through the wilderness to the borders of Canaan, the promised land. God allowed Moses to look across the Jordan to the promised land before he died. Then God buried Moses on the mountain. Joshua was chosen to lead the people into the land that God had given them; but the Jordan River lay between them and this land. God told Joshua to have the priests carrying the ark of the covenant step into the water. When they did, the waters parted, making a dry path. The people walked across and entered the land.

Elijah Goes to Heaven
(2 Kings 2:1-18)

Elijah had been a faithful messenger for the Lord. The time came for his life on earth to end. God was going to take him to Heaven in a whirlwind!

Before Elijah and the younger prophet, Elisha, came to the place where Elijah was to be taken up, they had to cross the Jordan River. Elijah took off his cloak and struck the water with it. The waters parted and made a dry path for them, just as they had done when the Israelites crossed over with Joshua. After Elijah had gone up to Heaven, Elisha, who was to take Elijah's place, had to cross the Jordan again. He took the cloak that Elijah had left with him, and by striking the water with it, he was able to make a path through the river.

The Healing of Naaman
(2 Kings 5)

Many years after the Israelites went into the promised land they began to forget God. Because of this God allowed their enemies to come in and take many of the people away to other countries as slaves. Among these captives was a young girl who was placed in the home of an army captain in Syria. This captain, whose name was Naaman, was a great man—but he had the dread disease of leprosy. When the young girl heard about it she told her mistress, Naaman's wife, that a prophet in Israel could heal him of his leprosy. Naaman went to Israel, and Elisha sent his servant to tell him to go to the Jordan River and dip himself in it seven times. At first Naaman was very angry. "The rivers in my own country are cleaner and better than the Jordan," he said. But his servants begged him to do as the prophet had said. "If he had asked you to do some great thing, you would do it," they said. Naaman finally decided to obey. He went to the Jordan River and dipped once, twice, five times, six times, and still he was not cured. But when he went down the seventh time, he came up completely healed of his leprosy!

Jesus and John the Baptist
(Matthew 3)

The baptism of Jesus also was in the Jordan River! John the Baptist was preaching near there, asking the people to prepare for the coming of the Savior by repenting of their sins and being baptized. While John was there, Jesus came to be baptized. John knew who Jesus was; he knew that He was the Son of God. "You should baptize me," John said. But Jesus said that He wanted to be baptized to "fulfil all righteousness." This meant that Jesus wanted to do everything that God had commanded. John baptized Him, and as Jesus came up out of the water, the Spirit of God came upon Jesus in the form of a dove. A voice came from Heaven: "This is my beloved Son, in whom I am well pleased."

The Lesson Applied

The stories that we have heard, about events connected with the Jordan River, teach us some important lessons in obedience. The two great prophets, Elijah and Elisha, were chosen by God because they were obedient to His will, and God blessed them. Naaman could not see why he had to dip in the Jordan River when the rivers in his own country were much nicer. But when he did what the prophet of God told him to do, he was cured of his leprosy. When the priests obeyed Joshua's orders, the waters parted.

Jesus is the greatest example of obedience. He did everything that was right. His obedience to God was complete—perfect.

There will be many times in our lives when we will ask the question, "Why is it wrong for me to do this certain thing?" or "Why do I have to do that?" If the Bible says we are to live a certain way, we should trust God enough to know that His way is best, even though we cannot always understand His ways. When we grow older and look back over our lives, we may then see why God led us in those ways. Just as God was pleased with His Son, Jesus, God is pleased when we obey Him.

Questions for Discussion: Are children obeying God when they obey their parents? How do we know what God wants us to do?

The Lesson Quiz

1. Who led the Israelites over the Jordan River?
(Joshua.)
2. How did Elijah get across the Jordan River?
(He struck the water with his cloak and the waters parted.)
3. Who took Elijah's place after he went up into Heaven?
(Elisha.)
4. What was the name of the army officer in Syria who had leprosy?
(Naaman.)
5. What prophet told him how he could be cured?
(Elisha.)
6. What did Elisha tell Naaman to do?
(To dip in the Jordan River seven times.)
7. What happened when Naaman obeyed?
(He was cured of leprosy.)
8. Who was preaching and baptizing at the Jordan River?
(John the Baptist.)
9. Who came to John to be baptized?
(Jesus.)
10. What happened after Jesus was baptized?
(The Spirit of God came in the form of a dove, and God said, "This is my beloved Son, in whom I am well pleased.")

Additional Lesson Activities

1. Compare Rivers
Let pupils compare the Jordan River, the largest river in Israel, with the largest river in their area. Provide Bible encyclopedias and other reference books.
2. Set of Description Cards
The fifth card should be added to each pupil's set. On one side "Jordan River" is to be lettered. On the other side a description is to be added. Suggested description: "A winding river, about 100 miles long, that flows from the Sea of Galilee to the Dead Sea. Naaman dipped in this river seven times to be cured of leprosy. Jesus was baptized in this river by John the Baptist."

Workbook Page

"Crossword Clues," on page 53 of the pupil's workbook, lists four chapters where answers to the questions may be found. You may wish to divide your class into two groups and assign two chapters to each group with the accompanying questions:

Bible chapters	Across:	Down:
Joshua 3	10	7,11,15
2 Kings 2	2	
2 Kings 5	5,8,15,16	1,4,6,14
Matthew 3	3,12,13,17	3,9,10

Check the answers on page 64 of the workbook.

Memory Verses: Matthew 3:16, 17

Lesson 6

Jericho

Introduction to Lesson

On the chalkboard, place this chart:

Place	*Old Testament People*	*New Testament People*
Damascus		
Sea of Galilee		
Capernaum		
Jordan River		
Nazareth		

Put these names on 3 x 5 cards, and let pupils tape them in the right places: DAVID, SAUL, ANDREW, PETER, JAIRUS, MATTHEW, ELIJAH, NAAMAN, JOHN THE BAPTIST, ABRAHAM, JAMES, JOHN, MARY, JOSEPH.

(Answers for above chart)

Damascus: David, Abraham (Old Testament), Saul (New Testament); Sea of Galilee: Peter, Andrew, James, John (New Testament); Capernaum: Matthew, Jairus (New Testament); Jordan River: Naaman, Elijah (Old Testament), John the Baptist (New Testament); Nazareth: Mary, Joseph (New Testament).

The Bible Lesson

(Jericho was an ancient fortified city in Canaan. It was five miles west of Jordan and eighteen miles from Jerusalem. Some very important events in both the Old and New Testaments took place in Jericho.)

Joshua Takes the City
(Joshua 6)

Moses had led the Israelites out of Egypt, through the Red Sea, and for forty years in the wilderness. He had brought them to the very edge of the promised land of Canaan. Here Moses died. Joshua took his place as leader.

Many years had passed since Jacob's family had left Canaan to go down into Egypt at the time of the great famine. During that time, heathen people had taken possession of the land and had built great walled cities. Now that God was bringing His people back to live in this land, the heathen people had to be driven out. Jericho was the first city that Joshua was to take.

According to God's plan, Joshua marched the Israelites around the city once every day for six days. On the seventh day they marched around the city seven times. As they were going around the last time, Joshua commanded all the people to shout while the priests blew trumpets. The walls of Jericho fell, and Joshua and his soldiers were able to rush in and capture the city. Joshua said that anyone who tried to rebuild the city would be cursed.

Jesus Heals Two Blind Men
(Matthew 20:29-34)

The city of Jericho mentioned in the New Testament probably was a mile south of the place where the old city had stood. King Herod had made it his summer home and had built many beautiful buildings there.

One day when Jesus and His disciples were leaving Jericho, a great crowd followed them. Two blind men, sitting by the wayside, heard that Jesus was passing by. They cried out, "Have mercy on us, O Lord!"

Jesus called to them, "What do you want Me to do for you?"

They said to Him, "Lord, that our eyes may be opened."

Jesus had compassion on them and touched their eyes. Immediately they could see! The two men who had been blind began to follow Jesus with the crowd.

Zaccheus Meets Jesus
(Luke 19:1-10)

One day as Jesus was passing through Jericho, Zaccheus, a very wealthy tax collector, wanted to see Him. Zaccheus was not very tall. Because of the large crowd, he could not see Jesus. He climbed a sycamore tree to get a better view. When Jesus came by, He looked up and saw Zaccheus.

"Come down," Jesus said to him. "Today I must go to your house."

Zaccheus hurried down and received Jesus joyfully. The people in the crowd began to murmur, "Jesus is going to be the guest of a sinner!" Many people considered tax collectors the worst kind of people and would not associate with them.

At his house, Zaccheus told Jesus that he would give half of his possessions to the poor. "If I have taken anything from any person falsely, I will give him back four times as much as I took."

Jesus said, "This day salvation has come to this house. The Son of man is come to seek and to save the lost."

(Review the three stories by dividing the class into three groups of varying numbers and having the pupils act out the stories. A large group could present the scene of Joshua and the battle of Jericho. Three pupils could present the story of Jesus and the two blind men. A small group also could act out the story of Jesus and Zaccheus.)

The Lesson Applied

The power of God can be seen in the story of Joshua conquering the city of Jericho. The power of Jesus, God's Son, can be seen in the story of the two blind men who received their sight.

When Zaccheus met Jesus, he recognized Him as the Son of God. He believed, and he repented of his wrongdoing. He showed by his actions that his life had been changed.

Jesus came to bring salvation to all who are lost. He wants everyone to believe in Him as the Son of God. He wants all people to repent of doing wrong.

When people accept Jesus as Lord and Savior, they confess their faith before others and are baptized in obedience to His command.

Christians show others by their lives that they are changed persons!

Questions for Discussion: How did Joshua show that he believed in God? How did the blind men show their faith in Jesus? How can we show that we believe in Jesus? How can we show that we have repented?

The Lesson Quiz

1. What was the first city the Israelites captured?

(Jericho.)

2. How was the city captured?

(The Israelites marched around it once every day for six days and seven times on the seventh day. They shouted and blew trumpets, and the walls of Jericho fell down.)

3. What men called to Jesus just outside the city of Jericho?

(Two blind men.)

4. What did they ask Jesus to do?

(Open their eyes.)

5. What happened when Jesus touched their eyes?

(Immediately they could see.)

6. Why did Zaccheus climb a tree to see Jesus?

(He was short and couldn't see because of the crowd.)

7. What kind of man was Zaccheus?

(A rich tax collector, despised by the Jews.)

8. What happened when Jesus went to be his guest?

(The people began to murmur that Jesus was eating with sinners.)

9. What promise did Zaccheus make?

(He would give half his possessions to the poor, and he would restore four times as much as he had taken falsely.)

10. Why did Jesus say the "Son of man" had come?

(To seek and to save the lost.)

Additional Lesson Activities

1. More Stories About Jericho

Let pupils look up these references and learn about other events connected with Jericho: Joshua 2; 2 Samuel 10:1-5; 1 Kings 16:34; Luke 10:30-37.

2. Set of Description Cards

Each pupil should add a sixth card to his set. "Jericho" should be written on one side, and a description written on the other side. Example: "An ancient city, five miles west of the Jordan River. This was the first city in the promised land conquered by Joshua and the Israelites. Zaccheus, a tax collector, lived there in Jesus' day."

Workbook Page

On page 54 of the pupil's workbook, "Find the Word" and "Four-way Matching" review the Bible stories that took place in Jericho. Also, there are eight Scripture references for verses that contain the word "salvation." Have pupils look up these verses and discuss them.

Answers are on page 64 of the workbook.

Memory Verse: Luke 19:10

Lesson 7

Jerusalem

Introduction to Lesson

Divide pupils into small groups. Using their sets of description cards, let them take turns reading descriptions of Bible places while others guess the names. Then let them read the names and have others give the descriptions. Bible events that took place at these locations should be included in the descriptions.

The Bible Lesson

(The city of Jerusalem is the most important city in Israel. It was the capital city, and the great temple of God was built there on Mount Moriah. Many events in the life of Jesus took place in Jerusalem.)

David Takes Jerusalem

(2 Samuel 5:1-10)

When David became king of Israel, there was still some of the land that had not been taken from the people of Canaan. Among these places was a heavily fortified city that belonged to the Jebusites. The people there were proud of their strong walls and fine army.

King David challenged his men to climb up the wall gutters and lead the way for his army. David and his soldiers took the city, and he made it the capital of the nation. He built a beautiful palace and planned for the temple of God to be built there. The city was called Jerusalem.

David's son, King Solomon, later built the great temple of God in the capital city.

Nehemiah Rebuilds the Walls of Jerusalem

(Book of Nehemiah)

When the Israelites turned away from God, He punished them by allowing their enemies to come into the country, capture it, and take the people away as slaves. The city of Jerusalem was captured and destroyed, and its people scattered as slaves throughout surrounding countries.

Nehemiah was a Jew living in Shushan, the palace of King Artaxerxes. He was the king's cupbearer. One day his brother and other men from Judah came to see him. They brought word that the people who were left in Jerusalem were having hard times. The broken walls and burned gates of Jerusalem never had been repaired or replaced. Nehemiah was very sad when he heard this news. He cried and prayed and asked God to help him. Then he went to the king and asked permission to go back to Jerusalem and help his people rebuild the city walls. The king allowed him to go. When Nehemiah arrived, he said to the Jews, "Come, let us build up the wall of Jerusalem. God is with me, and the king has given permission."

"Let us rise up and build!" the people answered. They worked hard and soon the walls were repaired.

Jesus in Jerusalem

(Luke 2:42-52; Luke 19:45, 46)

Many years passed from the time of Nehemiah until the coming of Jesus. During that time the city of Jerusalem was ruled over by many different countries. Enemy armies completely destroyed the city two times. Finally, just a few years before the birth of Jesus, the city was taken over by the Romans.

The first time Jesus was in Jerusalem was when He was about forty days old. He was brought by Mary and Joseph to be dedicated to God, according to God's laws. The next time He visited the city was when He was twelve. He went with His parents to the Passover feast.

The final week of Jesus' life before His crucifixion was spent in or near the city of Jerusalem. He entered the city as a king, riding on a colt and having the praise of the people. He drove the money changers out of the temple. At the close of the week Jesus and His disciples ate the Passover meal together in an upper room in Jerusalem. At the end of the meal Jesus asked them to remember Him by eating the bread and drinking the cup. Jesus was arrested in the Garden of Gethsemane and put on trial in Jerusalem. He carried His cross through the streets of the city, and He was crucified and buried just outside its gates. Forty days after His resurrection, Jesus ascended to Heaven from a mountain not far from Jerusalem.

The Church Begins

(Acts 1, 2)

Before Jesus went back to Heaven, He told His followers to return to Jerusalem and wait for the promise of God. They would receive power when the Holy Spirit came upon them, and they would be His witnesses in Jerusalem, Judea, Samaria, and the uttermost part of the earth.

On the Day of Pentecost, ten days after Jesus' ascension, the Holy Spirit came upon Peter and the other apostles. They preached the gospel, and three thousand people were baptized. This was the beginning of the church of Jesus Christ.

The New Jerusalem

(Revelation 21)

God gave the apostle John a vision of what Heaven would be like. He called Heaven the "New Jerusalem" and gave a beautiful description of it. There are no words wonderful enough to help us understand how great it will be. We know that Jesus and God will be there; and there will be no pain or sorrow or crying or death. All those whose names are written in the Lamb's book of life will live there forever.

The Lesson Applied

God promised the land of Israel to His chosen people. He promised a Savior. He promised to send the Holy Spirit. God keeps every promise that He makes. He promises that those who become followers of Jesus will someday live in Heaven with Him.

We are to keep our promises, too. When we accept Jesus as our Lord and Savior, we are promising to give our lives to Him for eternity.

Questions for Discussion: What are some of God's promises to us? Why is it important that we keep the promises we have made to God? To others?

The Lesson Quiz

1. What king of Israel captured the fortified city of the Jebusites?
(David.)
2. What was the name of this new capital city?
(Jerusalem.)
3. What happened to the city of Jerusalem when the Israelites continued in their disobedience to God?
(The city was captured by enemy armies, and many people were taken away to other lands.)
4. Who came back to help rebuild the walls?
(Nehemiah.)
5. How old was Jesus when He went with Mary and Joseph to the Passover in Jerusalem?
(Twelve years old.)
6. In the final week of Jesus' ministry, what were some of the events that took place in or near Jerusalem?
(Triumphal entry, cleansing the temple, the last supper, trials, crucifixion, burial, resurrection.)
7. On what day did the Holy Spirit come to the apostles, as God and Jesus had promised?
(Day of Pentecost.)
8. How many were baptized when they heard the gospel message?
(Three thousand.)
9. What place is called the "New Jerusalem"?
(Heaven.)
10. What are some things the Bible tells us about Heaven?
(God and Jesus will be there; there will be no pain, death, sorrow, crying.)

Additional Lesson Activities

1. Other Names for Jerusalem

Let pupils look up these Scriptures and find seven other names for Jerusalem: Genesis 14:18; Joshua 18:28; 1 Kings 8:1; 2 Chronicles 25:28; Nehemiah 11:1; Psalm 46:4; Psalm 48:2.

2. Set of Description Cards

The seventh card for each pupil should have "Jerusalem" on one side and a description of Jerusalem on the other side.

Workbook Page

The puzzle, "Fill the Blanks," reviews some Scriptures about the church that began on the Day of Pentecost. The "New Jerusalem" Word Search is taken from Revelation 21. These puzzles are on page 55 of the pupil's workbook.

Memory Verse: Revelation 22:14

Lesson 8

Bethlehem

Introduction to Lesson

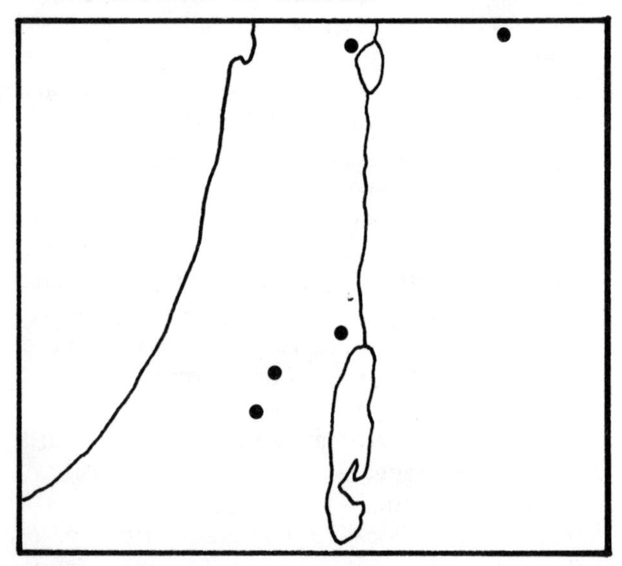

Place this simple drawing on the chalkboard (You don't have to be an artist!) and let pupils identify these places:

Damascus	Jordan River
Sea of Galilee	Jericho
Nazareth	Jerusalem

Ask if anyone knows what city is just below Jerusalem. If no one knows, display a map of Israel. Then have a pupil add Bethlehem to the map.

The Bible Lesson

(The "little town of Bethlehem" is about six miles south of Jerusalem. Many events from the Old and New Testaments took place in this historic spot. It is one of the oldest towns in Israel, and it is mentioned in Genesis, the first book.)

The Death of Rachel
(Genesis 35:9-20)

God had appeared to Jacob, the grandson of Abraham, and repeated the promise that He had made to Abraham: from Jacob's family would come a great nation. God changed Jacob's name to Israel.

While he was working for Laban, he fell in love with one of Laban's daughters, Rachel. He promised Laban that he would work for him seven years if he could marry Rachel. Laban agreed to this, but after the seven years were over he made Rachel change places with her older sister, Leah. When the wedding was over, Jacob found he had been tricked into marrying the wrong girl. But he loved Rachel so much that he was willing to work another seven years to marry her. After many years, Jacob and his family went back to his home in Canaan. Near Bethlehem Rachel died, and Jacob sadly buried her there. Rachel was the mother of Joseph and Benjamin, and Jacob loved these two children very much.

The Story of Ruth
(The Book of Ruth)

During the time of the judges, before there were kings over the nation of Israel, a woman named Naomi, her husband Elimelech, and their sons, Mahlon and Chilion, lived in Bethlehem. When a famine came to that area, they left Bethlehem and traveled to Moab. There Naomi's husband and both of her sons died. Naomi decided to go back to her home in Bethlehem. Both of her daughters-in-law, Ruth and Orpah, started back with her. But Orpah turned back.

In Bethlehem Ruth met a wealthy farmer named Boaz, who was distantly related to Naomi's family. With Naomi's blessing, Ruth married Boaz, and a son was born to them. His name was Obed, and he became the father of Jesse. Jesse had a son named David, who was a shepherd in the hills around Bethlehem. David became the greatest king of Israel!

The Birth of Jesus
(Luke 2:1-20; Matthew 2:1-11)

Hundreds of years after David was born in Bethlehem, another king was born there.

Joseph and Mary, who lived in Nazareth, had to journey to Bethlehem because of a decree concerning taxes made by the Roman emperor. Everyone had to go to the city of his ancestors, and Joseph was descended from the family of David. While they were in Bethlehem, Mary's baby, Jesus—the Son of God—was born! The news of the Savior's birth was announced by angels to shepherds out in the fields. The shepherds hurried to Bethlehem and found Mary and Joseph and the baby in a manger. When they returned, they spread the news everywhere they went. They praised God for all the things that they had heard and seen.

Mary and Joseph stayed in Bethlehem for some time. They were living in a house there when some unusual visitors arrived. Wise-men, following a star, came from the East to bring gifts to the "King of the Jews." When they saw the young child, they fell down and worshiped Him. Opening their treasures, they presented gold, frankincense, and myrrh.

Hundreds of years before Jesus was born, God had given a message to the prophet Micah: "But thou, Bethlehem . . . though thou be little among the thousands of Judah, yet out of thee shall he come forth unto me that is to be ruler in Israel." Bethlehem was a small but very important town.

The Lesson Applied

The name "Bethlehem" has a beautiful sound to our ears because of the wonderful things we remember when we hear it. Everything in the Bible about Bethlehem makes us think of love—the love of Jacob for Rachel and for his sons Joseph and Benjamin; the love of Ruth for Naomi and for Boaz; the love of David for God; and, most of all, the love that God showed us when He sent Jesus to be the Savior.

When people hear your name, what do they think of? Some names are disliked because they make us think of evil people and evil deeds. We should act in such a way that when people see us, they will think of Christ; and, thinking of Him, they will think of love and joy and peace.

Questions for Discussion: How did Jacob show his love for Rachel? How did Ruth show her love for Naomi? How did God show His love for the world? How can we show our love for God and others?

The Lesson Quiz

1. Where did Jacob bury Rachel?
(Near the city of Bethlehem.)

2. Why did Naomi, her husband, and her two sons have to leave their home in Bethlehem?
(Because there was a famine in the land.)

3. Where did they go?
(To the land of Moab.)

4. What happened to them there?
(Naomi's husband and her two sons died.)

5. What did Naomi do?
(She went back to her home in Bethlehem.)

6. Who went with her?
(Her daughter-in-law, Ruth.)

7. What happened to Ruth?
(She met and married a relative of Naomi's named Boaz.)

8. What king was the great-grandson of Ruth?
(David.)

9. What is the greatest thing that happened in the city of Bethlehem?
(Jesus was born there.)

10. Who were the first people to hear the news that Jesus, the Savior, was born?
(The shepherds who were watching their flocks on the hills near Bethlehem.)

Additional Lesson Activities

1. "Show Your Love" Projects

Encourage pupils to plan some sharing projects; to find ways in which they can show their love for God and others.

2. Other Bible People and Bethlehem

Let pupils find the names of a prophet, a judge, and a king who had connections with Bethlehem:
Judges 12:8
1 Samuel 16:4
2 Chronicles 11:6

3. Set of Description Cards

Each pupil should add "Bethlehem" to his set of description cards. Remember that the descriptions should not contain the name of the place.

Workbook Page

The first puzzle, "Guess My Name!" is a fun puzzle. The next one, "Match the Families," reviews some of the Bible people studied. In "Family History," some of Joseph's ancestors are given. Answers for these puzzles are on page 64 of the workbook.

Use any extra time to review the memory verses for lessons 1-8. Memory verses are listed at the end of each lesson in the workbook.

Memory Verse: John 3:16

Lesson 9

The Dead Sea

Introduction to Lesson

(Display map of Bible lands and point out the Dead Sea.)

The Dead Sea was called the Salt Sea or the Sea of the Plains in Bible times. It is about 40 miles long and 10 miles wide. The northern end is very deep, but the southern end is quite shallow in places. Six million tons of water flow from the Jordan River into the Dead Sea each day. No water flows out because there is no outlet! The water evaporates, and the Dead Sea contains a wealth of minerals. There is no life of any kind in the Dead Sea. Fish that are put into its waters die very quickly.

Many important Bible events are connected with the area around the Dead Sea.

The Bible Lesson

The Destruction of Sodom and Gomorrah

(Genesis 18:20-33; 19:1-29)

When Abraham and his nephew, Lot, reached the land of Canaan, they found it necessary to choose separate areas in which to live. Both had many flocks, herds, and servants. Abraham allowed Lot to choose his portion of the land first, and Lot decided to pitch his tents in the direction of Sodom, a very wicked city. Nearby was Gomorrah, another city that was filled with evil. It is believed by some that these two cities bordered the southern end of the Dead Sea. But others say the cities were at the northern end.

Finally the Lord decided to destroy the two cities, and He told Abraham of His plans. Abraham, wanting to spare his nephew's family and any other good people who might live there, asked if the Lord would destroy the good people along with the bad. He begged the Lord to spare Sodom if fifty good people could be found. The Lord agreed, but Abraham couldn't find fifty—or even ten—good people!

Two angels were sent to bring Lot and his family out of the city before the great destruction. But only Lot, his wife, and his two daughters escaped. Lot's wife disobeyed God, and looked back. She became a pillar of salt. The Lord rained fire and brimstone on the cities, and they were completely destroyed. Early the next morning Abraham went to the place where he had talked with the Lord. He saw smoke rising up where the cities had been. From that day until the present time no trace of those cities has been found! (Read 2 Peter 2:4-9.)

Boundaries of the Promised Land

(Numbers 33:50-56; 34:1-15)

Before the children of Israel entered the promised land, God told Moses how the land was to be divided. The southern end of the territory was to be from the coast of the Salt Sea (Dead Sea) eastward. Later, when the area around the Dead Sea was settled by the Israelites, the tribe of Judah was on one side and the tribe of Reuben was on the other. Below Reuben's territory was the land of Moab. God had promised this land to Abraham's descendants, and finally the promise was being fulfilled. "This shall be your land," God said, "but you will have to drive out the heathen peoples and destroy their images and their altars. If you do not drive them out, those who remain will bring trouble to you!"

God knew that any evil people who remained in the land would not only bring trouble to His people but would be a bad influence on Israel. In spite of this warning, the Israelites allowed some people to remain and trouble came just as God had said.

A Cave in Engedi

(1 Samuel 24)

King Saul was jealous of David and tried to kill him many times. One day he learned that David was in the wilderness of Engedi, an area near the Dead Sea. Saul took 3,000 soldiers and began to search for David in the high cliffs surrounding the sea. He went into a cave, not knowing that David and his men were hiding there. While Saul lay down in the cave, David secretly came behind him and cut off a piece of his clothing. But David would not allow his men to harm Saul, because the Lord had anointed Saul king. When Saul left the cave, David followed him and called, "My lord the king!" Then he told Saul that he had had the opportunity to kill him, but he would not kill one who had been chosen by the Lord. He showed Saul the piece of material cut from Saul's clothes. Then King Saul said to David, "You are more righteous than I am. You have been good to me, and I have done evil to you. I know now that you will surely be king of Israel."

The Lesson Applied

When Saul became king he was obedient to God's commands. But, as he became more powerful, he began to do things his way instead of God's way. His life was filled with evil. David chose to do good when he had the opportunity to do evil to Saul, and Saul knew that his days were coming to an end. Saul knew that God always keeps His promises, and that good wins over evil.

God punished the wicked cities of Sodom and Gomorrah, and He punished His own chosen people, the nation of Israel, when they were disobedient.

Sometimes in this world it may seem that evil is winning. But God's Word tells us even though the devil has many followers, and is trying every way to defeat the Lord, God will win the victory in the end.

Everyone has to make a choice whether to do good or evil, whether to follow the Lord or Satan. Are you on the winning side—the Lord's side?

Questions for Discussion: What are some choices that you have to make every day? Is this a true statement: "The devil made me do it"? How does Jesus help us make the right decisions?

The Lesson Quiz

1. What two wicked cities bordering the Dead Sea did God destroy?

(Sodom and Gomorrah.)

2. In which city did Abraham's nephew, Lot, live?

(Sodom.)

3. When Abraham learned that Sodom was to be destroyed, what did he ask God to do?

(Spare the city if at least ten righteous people could be found.)

4. Who did escape from Sodom?

(Lot, his wife, and two daughters. But his wife looked back and became a pillar of salt.)

5. How did God destroy the two cities?

(He rained fire and brimstone on them.)

6. When the promised land was divided among the twelve tribes, what two tribes were on opposite sides of the Dead Sea?

(Judah and Reuben.)

7. What warning did God give His people just before they went into the promised land?

(If they failed to drive out all the heathen people and destroy their images, they would always be troubled by these wicked people.)

8. Who hid in a cave in the wilderness of Engedi, near the Dead Sea?

(David and his men were hiding from King Saul.)

9. How did Saul know that David had the opportunity to kill him?

(He saw the piece of material that David had cut from his clothing while inside the cave.)

10. What did Saul say to David?

("You are more righteous than I am. I know now that you will surely be king of Israel.")

Additional Lesson Activities

1. The Dead Sea Scrolls

Let pupils do some research on the scrolls that were found in a cave at Qumran, near the Dead Sea, around 1947.

2. Masada

Another very interesting research project is to learn about the fortress called Masada, near the Dead Sea.

3. Set of Description Cards

Pupils should add the "Dead Sea" to their sets of description cards.

Workbook Page

The "Crossword Quiz" on page 57 of the pupil's workbook does not give a Scripture reference for each question. The lesson Scriptures are listed, and you may want to assign different passages to groups. Or, you may work the puzzle ahead of time and note in your book the verse references. Check your answers with those on page 64.

Memory Verse: Romans 12:21

Lesson 10

The Land of Egypt

Introduction to Lesson

Let pupils look in a concordance and see how many times "Egypt" or "Egyptian" appear in the Bible. Also, let pupils look at a map of Bible lands and see the distance from Israel to Egypt. Two special places in Egypt should be pointed out: Goshen and the Red Sea.

Provide encyclopedias and other reference books, and let pupils find interesting information about ancient Egypt and Egypt today. Note this interesting fact: The Great Pyramids of Giza were built hundreds of years before Abraham visited Egypt!

The Bible Lesson

(The ancient kingdom of Egypt was a world power for many centuries. Both the Old and New Testaments contain important events that took place in the land of Egypt.)

Abraham Visits Egypt

(Genesis 12:1-10; 13:1-4)

God had called Abraham (Abram) to leave his home and travel to a new land that God would show him. At the age of seventy-five Abraham took his wife, and his nephew, Lot, and all the servants and possessions and journeyed to the land of Canaan. The Lord appeared to Abraham and said, "I will give this land to your descendants." Abraham built an altar to the Lord in that place. Then he moved his family and belongings to a mountain east of Bethel, and there he also built an altar to the Lord. Abraham continued his journey, going toward the south. There was a serious famine so Abraham took his family out of the land of Canaan and down into Egypt, to find food for his family and cattle. The rich land around the Nile River in Egypt produced much food. When famines occurred in Canaan, people often could obtain food in Egypt. Later Abraham left Egypt and took his family back to Canaan. They went to Bethel, where Abraham had built an altar. He called on the name of the Lord.

The Children of Israel in Egypt

(Genesis 45:1-11; Exodus 1:8-22; 2:23—3:10)

Joseph, the great-grandson of Abraham, had been sold as a slave by his jealous brothers. The traders took Joseph to Egypt, where he became a slave, then a prisoner, and finally second in command to Pharaoh, king of Egypt. When a famine again came to Canaan, the brothers of Joseph came to Egypt for food. Finally Joseph revealed his true identity to his brothers, forgave them for the evil thing they had done, and invited them to live in Egypt. The Pharaoh allowed the relatives of Joseph to live in the area called Goshen. There the Israelites found much grazing land for their cattle and sheep.

Joseph's brothers and their families continued to stay in Egypt. For many years they were happy in that land. But after Joseph died the new king was afraid that this great nation of Israel would become so strong that they would take over the country. He made slaves of them and treated them cruelly. At last God answered their prayers and sent Moses to lead them to freedom.

Crossing the Red Sea

(Exodus 14)

Moses and his brother, Aaron, went before the Pharaoh and asked that the Israelites be allowed to leave Egypt. Pharaoh refused again and again, even though God sent terrible plagues upon the Egyptians. Finally, after the last plague—the death of the firstborn in every Egyptian home—the Pharaoh decided to let them go. Moses led them from the land of Goshen toward the Red Sea. God guided them by a pillar of cloud during the day and a pillar of fire by night.

After the Israelites were gone, the king was sorry. He started after them with his army—six hundred chariots. When the Israelites saw the Egyptians coming, they were afraid. The Red Sea was in front of them, mountains around them, and the Egyptian army behind them. But Moses told them that God would care for them.

God told Moses to stretch his rod over the sea. When Moses did this, God caused a great wind to blow. It blew back the sea so that there was a dry path. The Israelites crossed the sea, as the water stood like a high wall on either side of the path. The Egyptians started to follow the Israelites, but their chariot wheels fell off in the midst of the sea. Then God told Moses to stretch his hand over the sea again. When he did, the walls of water fell, covering the dry path. All the Egyptians were drowned.

The Baby Jesus Is Taken to Egypt

(Matthew 2:13-23)

When Jesus was born in Bethlehem, the Wise-men traveled to the palace of Herod in Jerusalem, asking for the "King of the Jews." Herod feared that another king was going to take his place, so he ordered that all the boy babies in Bethlehem be killed. But God warned Joseph in a dream, telling him to take Mary and Jesus and go to Egypt. The family lived in Egypt until the wicked king Herod was dead. Then they went back to Nazareth and lived there until Jesus was a man.

The Lesson Applied

Jealousy, or envy as the Bible also calls it, is a terrible thing. Jealousy caused Joseph's brothers to sell him as a slave. Jealousy made King Herod want to get rid of the baby Jesus.

Sometimes we may look at others and be jealous because they have better clothes, or they live in better homes, or they go to more exciting places on vacation.

Jealousy sometimes causes people to kill and steal. It is an evil thing. There should be no room for jealousy in the heart of a Christian!

Questions for Discussion: Why is it hard for a person who is jealous to make and keep friends? What can jealousy lead to?

The Lesson Quiz

1. Why did Abraham leave Canaan and go to Egypt?

(There was a famine, and Egypt often had food when other countries didn't.)

2. Who was sold by his brothers and taken down to Egypt as a slave?

(Joseph.)

3. What happened to Joseph's family when the famine came again to Canaan?

(They went down to Egypt to buy food. Later they came back with their families to live in Egypt.)

4. Why did their descendants wish to leave the land of Egypt many years later?

(The king made slaves of them and treated them cruelly.)

5. Whom did God choose to lead His people out of Egypt?

(Moses.)

6. What happened when Moses held his rod over the Red Sea?

(The waters parted and the Israelites crossed on dry land.)

7. What happened when the Egyptians tried to follow them?

(The waters came together again, and they were drowned.)

8. When Jesus was born, what cruel command did King Herod give?

(He ordered all boy babies killed.)

9. How was Jesus saved from death?

(God told Joseph in a dream to take Jesus and Mary to Egypt to live.)

10. When did they leave Egypt and go back to Nazareth to live?

(After King Herod had died.)

Additional Lesson Activities

1. "Jealousy" Posters

Let each pupil make a poster with a large heart in the center and the caption, "No Room for Jealousy." Words may be added to the heart such as: LOVE, KINDNESS, FORGIVENESS, etc.

2. Set of Description Cards

Pupils should add "Egypt" cards to their sets of description cards.

Workbook Page

On page 58 of the pupil's workbook, you will find a "True or False?" test that reviews the lesson facts. When you use this type of test, be sure to go over the answers in class. Correct any misconceptions that the pupils may have. "Map Problem" will help pupils locate places in Egypt. Have pupils look up, read, and discuss the Bible verses about jealousy and envy.

Memory Verse: James 3:16

Lesson 11

Bible Mountains—Part 1

Introduction to Lesson

Display a map of Bible lands and point out these three mountains: Mount Sinai, Mount Nebo, and the Mount of Olives. See if pupils can match the right mountains with these facts (mix them up on the chalkboard):

Mount Sinai	A mountain in the wilderness of Horeb, 2 peaks: 6,540 and 7,363 feet above sea level
Mount Nebo	A mountain in the land of Moab, near northeast shore of the Dead Sea
Mount of Olives (Olivet)	A flattened, rounded range with four summits, east of Jerusalem, 2,600 feet above sea level

The Bible Lesson

(Some of the most interesting stories in the Bible happened on mountains. We'll be studying seven mountains: three in this lesson and four in the next lesson. Of course there are many other mountains in the Bible lands that we won't have time to consider!)

Mount Sinai

(Exodus 3; 19; 20)

Mount Sinai, also called Horeb, is the scene of two important events in the Old Testament. It is believed that Moses was there, looking after the sheep of his father-in-law Jethro, when God spoke to him and told him he was to go into Egypt and lead the Israelites out of slavery. While Moses stopped to look at a bush that was on fire but not burning up, he heard God's voice speak to him from the bush. Moses obeyed God by going down to Egypt and leading the Israelites out of the country. On their journey toward Canaan, they passed this same mountain where God had spoken to Moses. While the people camped nearby, God called Moses up on the mountain and gave him the laws by which the people were to live. Some of these laws were the Ten Commandments, which were written on two tablets of stone. (Read aloud Exodus 20:1-17.)

Mount Nebo

(Deuteronomy 34)

Mount Nebo is in the land of Moab, and it overlooks the land of Canaan. Moses had led the Israelites on the long journey to the borders of the promised land. But God had told Moses that he could not enter the land. He had disobeyed God's command about providing water for the people.

Now the people were ready to cross over the Jordan River and enter Canaan. Moses knew that his work was over. He climbed Mount Nebo, and there God showed him the promised land. Moses could see the territories where the twelve tribes would settle, from the Sea of Galilee to the Dead Sea! "This is the land that I promised to Abraham, to Isaac, to Jacob, and to their children after them," God said. Moses died there on the mountain, and God buried him. To this day, no one knows where Moses was buried.

Mount of Olives

(Several events in the life of Jesus took place on the Mount of Olives.)

The Triumphal Entry (Luke 19:28-44)

For three and a half years Jesus spent His time preaching, teaching, healing, and helping others. Some believed that He was the Son of God, but many did not. Jesus headed for Jerusalem for the last time. When He and His disciples reached the Mount of Olives, He sent two of them into the village of Bethphage and told them where they would find a donkey that they were to bring back to Him. It was on this donkey that Jesus rode down the Mount of Olives into the city. The people met Him on the way, waving palm branches and praising God. They shouted, "Hosanna to the Son of David!" and "Blessed is he who comes in the name of the Lord!"

The Garden of Gethsemane (Matthew 26:36-56)

This garden was near the foot of the mount, on the western slope. Jesus, the Son of God, spent much time in prayer. After Jesus and His disciples had finished eating the Passover meal, they went to the Garden of Gethsemane. The disciples went to sleep while Jesus was praying. Suddenly Judas arrived with the soldiers, and Jesus was betrayed into their hands. Jesus was taken from the garden during the night to stand trial. His followers were afraid and ran away.

Jesus Goes Back to Heaven (Acts 1:9-12)

After Jesus was arrested, He was crucified and buried. But on the third day He arose from the dead. He stayed on earth for forty days after His resurrection, teaching His disciples the things He wanted them to do after He went back to Heaven. When the time came for Jesus to go, He took His eleven disciples up the Mount of Olives. While He was speaking to them, He was taken up into Heaven. Two angels told the men that Jesus would come again some day in the same manner that He had gone into Heaven.

The Lesson Applied

The first two mountains we talked about, Sinai and Nebo, were associated with the life of Moses. On Mount Sinai God gave Moses the Ten Commandments, along with other commands for His people. On Mount Nebo, God allowed Moses to view the promised land before he died. God was with Moses and the children of Israel all through their journey from Egypt to the borders of Canaan.

The third mountain, Olivet or the Mount of Olives, was just outside Jerusalem. There God was with His Son, Jesus, in the final week before His crucifixion.

(Read aloud Psalms 121 and 125:2.) We can know that God will be with us no matter what happens. Sometimes we have sadness or trouble in our lives, but God will give us strength to bear it. He will protect us from the power of Satan. He will be with us all the way. When we go to Heaven, we will be with Him forever.

Questions for Discussion: How can mountains remind us of God and His love? How do things that happened hundreds of years ago help us know that God will be with us?

The Lesson Quiz

1. What strange sight did Moses notice on the mountain while he was watching his sheep?
(A bush was in flames but was not burning up.)
2. What did God say to him from the bush?
(He asked Moses to lead the Israelites out of Egypt.)
3. On what mountain did God give Moses the Ten Commandments?
(Mount Sinai.)
4. On what mountain did Moses view the promised land?
(Mount Nebo.)
5. To what city did Jesus ride on a donkey?
(Jerusalem.)
6. In what garden on the Mount of Olives did Jesus go to pray?
(Garden of Gethsemane.)
7. Why were soldiers led by Judas into the garden?
(To arrest Jesus.)
8. How long was Jesus on earth after His resurrection?
(Forty days.)
9. Why did Jesus take His eleven disciples to the Mount of Olives?
(Jesus was going to ascend to Heaven.)
10. What did the two angels say after Jesus was taken into Heaven?
(Jesus would some day come again, just as He had gone into Heaven.)

Additional Lesson Activities

1. Mountain Mural—Part 1

Provide three 19 x 25 pieces of posterboard. Let pupils, working in three groups, pick one of the mountains and illustrate a scene. (Sinai: Moses receiving the Ten Commandments; Nebo: Moses viewing the promised land; Olivet: Jesus ascending into Heaven.) Continue this project with the next lesson and add three more Bible-mountain scenes. Arrange the mural scenes in chronological order.

2. Set of Description Cards

Each pupil will need three cards for the three mountains: Sinai, Nebo, Olivet.

Workbook Page

On page 59 of the pupil's workbook, review the facts and stories about the three mountains. Check your answers on page 64.

Memory Verse: Hebrews 13:6

Lesson 12

Bible Mountains—Part 2

Introduction to Lesson

Let pupils try to match these three mountains with the facts about them. (They are in correct order here. Mix them up on the chalkboard.)

Mount Gerizim and Mount Ebal	Two mountains in Samaria; 2,850 and 3,077 above sea level
Mount Carmel	Mountainous area that juts out into the Mediterranean Sea, 1,700 feet above sea level
Mount Hermon	Dome-shaped, rugged mountain near northeast boundary of Palestine, 9,200 feet above sea level

The Bible Lesson

Mount Gerizim and Mount Ebal

(Deuteronomy 11:22-32; Joshua 8:30-35)

After Moses died, Joshua led the children of Israel into the promised land. He built an altar to God in Mount Ebal, and he wrote on the stones there, in the presence of all the people, a copy of the law of Moses. All the people stood together to hear the reading of the law: half of them stood over against Mount Gerizim and half of them against Mount Ebal. Joshua read the blessings and the cursings to all the men, women, and children of the Israelites, and to the strangers who lived among them.

Mount Carmel

(1 Kings 18:16-40)

For a time God's people would obey His commands. Then they would turn away from God and begin to worship idols. During the years when the prophet Elijah was God's messenger, the king of Israel and his wicked wife led the people in worshiping idols. Elijah challenged the false prophets of the idol, Baal, to a contest on Mount Carmel.

Elijah proved to the people that the idols they were worshiping were not real and that God was the only God. He told King Ahab to gather together all the people and all the prophets of Baal. The heathen priests were to build an altar to Baal and put a sacrifice on it. They were to pray to their gods and beg them to send down fire on their altar to burn the sacrifice. Elijah would build an altar to God and ask God to send down fire also. The one who answered with fire would be the God the people were to worship. The priests of Baal prayed all day. They begged and pleaded but nothing happened.

Elijah built an altar and put on the wood and the sacrifice. Then he dug a trench around the altar. Three times he had four barrels of water poured over the sacrifice. Then he had the trench filled with water. Elijah prayed to God. Immediately, God sent fire from Heaven to burn not only the sacrifice but the altar as well! When the people saw it, they shouted, "The Lord, he is the God!"

Mount Hermon

(Matthew 16:13-17; Luke 9:28-36)

Mount Hermon is in the northern part of the land, and it is the highest mountain in Palestine. Jesus and His disciples had been in Caesarea Philippi, where Jesus had asked them, "Whom do men say that I am?" They had answered that some said Jesus was John the Baptist, Elijah, Jeremiah, or another of the prophets. Then Jesus asked, "Whom do you say that I am?" Simon Peter had answered, "You are the Christ, the Son of the living God."

Still later Jesus took three of His disciples, Peter, James, and John, up into the mountain to pray. As Jesus prayed His face and His clothing were shining brightly. Two prophets, Moses and Elijah (who had died hundreds of years before), appeared and talked with Jesus about His coming death. Peter, James, and John had been asleep. When they awoke, they saw Jesus in His glory, with the two prophets. Suddenly the prophets were gone, and Peter said, "Master, let us make three tabernacles; one for You, one for Moses, and one for Elijah." While he spoke a cloud covered them. God's voice came from the cloud, saying, "This is my beloved Son: hear Him."

The Lesson Applied

From the beginning, God had chosen certain people to be leaders and prophets for His people. Moses and Elijah were two who had been faithful messengers—prophets—to God's chosen people, the Jews. But when God sent His Son to earth to be the Savior, He wanted everyone to listen to Him. God still wants everyone to hear Jesus.

The New Testament is filled with the teachings of Jesus. We must read and study God's Word and try to put Jesus' teachings into practice in our lives.

Questions for Discussion: Since many false religions are being taught in the world, how can we know what is true? How can we help others learn about Jesus' teachings?

The Lesson Quiz

1. Where were Mount Gerizim and Mount Ebal?
(In Samaria.)
2. Who first told the people that if they would love the Lord and walk in His ways He would drive the heathen nations from the promised land?
(Moses.)
3. Who read the "blessings" and the "cursings" to the people when they stood between the two mountains?
(Joshua.)
4. What prophet of God challenged the false prophets of the heathen god Baal to a contest?
(Elijah.)
5. Where did the contest take place?
(Mount Carmel.)
6. What was the result of the contest?
(The people knew that the Lord was the true God, because He sent down fire from Heaven to burn up the sacrifice.)
7. On what high mountain in the northern part of the land did Jesus take three of His disciples?
(Mount Hermon.)
8. Who were the three disciples?
(Peter, James, and John.)
9. What two prophets appeared with Jesus?
(Moses and Elijah.)
10. What did God's voice say as the cloud covered them on the mountain?
("This is my beloved Son: hear Him.")

Additional Lesson Activities

1. Set of Description Cards
Each pupil should add the final three cards to his set: Mount Gerizim and Mount Ebal, Mount Carmel, Mount Hermon.
2. Teachings of the New Testament
All of the memory verses for the whole year's study are taken from the New Testament. Review them by looking them up and repeating them, according to books.

Matthew
3:16,17
6:14
8:27
16:15,16
26:41
28:19,20
Mark
1:17
16:15
Luke
2:52
19:10
22:32
John
3:16
4:24
13:17
14:15
15:13
20:30,31
21:17
Acts
2:38
3:6
10:34
10:38
Romans
8:28
10:17
12:18
12:21
1 Corinthians
15:57
2 Corinthians
9:7
Ephesians
4:25
4:26
6:10
Philippians
4:13
4:19
1 Thessalonians
5:17
2 Timothy
2:3
3:16
Hebrews
11:6
13:6
13:8
James
1:22
3:16
5:16
1 Peter
3:10
3:12
4:8
4:16
5:6
2 Peter
1:21
2:9
3:18
1 John
1:9
Revelation
22:14

3. Mountain Mural
Add three more sections to the mural begun last week: Mounts Gerizim and Ebal, Mount Carmel, and Mount Hermon. See page 108.

Workbook Page

Page 60 of the pupil's workbook contains a review quiz over the mountain facts and stories from this lesson, and a brief review over all the mountains studied in lessons 11 and 12.

Memory Verse: Romans 10:17

Lesson 13

"Adventures in Bible Lands" Review

Introduction to Lesson

Provide a simple map of the Bible places included in this series of lessons. Have circles for the cities and triangles for the mountains. Do not have any places identified. (You may wish to enlarge the map from page 61 of the workbook.)

Let pupils start at Damascus and go down the map, locating and naming all cities, seas, rivers, and other land areas. Then have pupils start at Mount Sinai and come up the map, locating and naming all the mountains studied.

The Bible Lesson

We have been learning about some important places in the Bible lands. We have found that many of these places were important in both the Old Testament and the New Testament. For example, Bethlehem was the birthplace of King David, and also of Jesus, the Son of God.

(Review the lessons by choosing as many of these ideas as you wish. Make this review session a time of fun as well as a time of study.)

1. Review Game With Description Cards

Divide pupils into groups of two. Each pupil has a set of description cards. Let pupils take turns. One reads the description of the place and lets the other guess what it is. The other may choose a place and ask for the description.

2. Erase the Place

On the chalkboard write the names of at least twelve places. Pupils are to tell an event from each place. The pupil who tells the event may erase the place from the chalkboard.

3. Match Places and People

Put two lists on the chalkboard: places on the left and people on the right. Let pupils match these by drawing chalk lines between them.

4. Point to the Place

Display a map of Bible lands. Call out events and let pupils point to the places on the map.

5. Scripture Hunt

Using the Scripture passages from the lessons, make a list of Bible verses that contain the names of the places studied. Call out one Scripture at a time. The pupil must find the verse and the name of the place before raising his hand. The first one gets to call out the place.

The Lesson Applied

We have been learning about events in Bible lands, and we have had lessons about God's people from the beginning of the nation of Israel to the time of Jesus and His followers. God gave commands to obey down through the years. When people obeyed they were blessed, and when they disobeyed they were punished.

When Jesus came to earth, He not only told God's commands, but He showed us how God wants us to live. He lived a perfect life, and then gave His life as a sacrifice for all our sins. He wants us to accept Him as Savior and Lord! Then He wants us to tell the good news to all the nations of the world! (Stress the memory verse here: Matthew 28:19, 20.)

The Lesson Quiz

Use the ten questions from each of the twelve previous lessons (total of 120 questions) for a comprehensive review quiz.

Additional Lesson Activities

1. Draw a Map

Let pupils draw freehand maps of the areas studied, without looking at a printed map.

2. Compare Ancient and Modern Maps

Let pupils compare maps of ancient Bible lands with modern maps of the Middle East.

Workbook Page

Pupils may continue to review the lessons by completing the exercises on page 61 of the workbook.

Memory Verses: Matthew 28:19, 20

Adventures Through the Bible

Pupil's Workbook

by Ivy M. Moody   revised by Dana Eynon

STANDARD PUBLISHING
Cincinnati, Ohio   3235

Part One: Adventures With Bible People

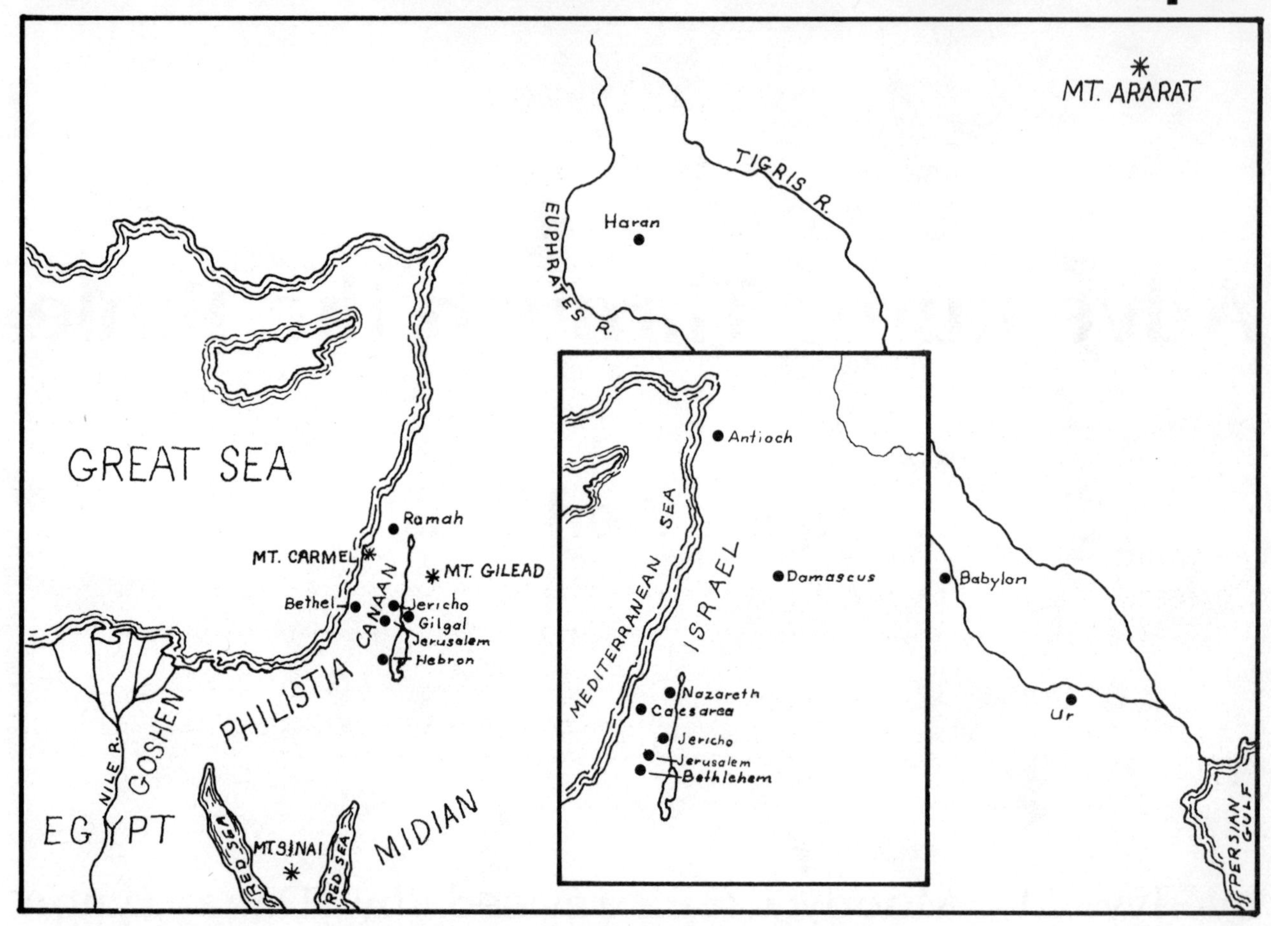

The Bible is a book of real adventures that happened many years ago.

(After each name are some of the places connected with the life of that person. Find these places on the map.)

1. Noah (MOUNT ARARAT)
2. Abraham (UR, HARAN, CANAAN, EGYPT)
3. Joseph (EGYPT, GOSHEN)
4. Moses (EGYPT, RED SEA, MOUNT SINAI)
5. Joshua (JORDAN RIVER, JERICHO)
6. Gideon (MOUNT GILEAD, MIDIAN)
7. Samuel (BETHEL, GILGAL, RAMAH)
8. Saul (ISRAEL, PHILISTIA)
9. David (HEBRON, JERUSALEM)
10. Elijah (MOUNT CARMEL)
11. Daniel (BABYLON)
12. Jesus (BETHLEHEM, NAZARETH, JERUSALEM, JORDAN RIVER)
13. Paul (DAMASCUS, ANTIOCH, CAESAREA, GREAT SEA)

Lesson 1
Adventures With Noah

Noah's Logbook

If Noah had kept a logbook during his adventure in the flood, it might have looked something like this one. The first entry has been made. Fill in the rest, as though you were Noah.

Scripture	Month	Day	Entry
Genesis 7:11	2nd	17th	The rain began to fall! The fountains of the deep have broken up, and the windows of heaven were opened!
Genesis 8:4			
Genesis 8:5			
Genesis 8:13			
Genesis 8:14-18			

God Keeps His Promises

Find eight things that God promised Noah would never cease (stop) while the earth remained. Read Genesis 8:22. Place the eight words in the puzzle squares.

Memory Verse: James 1:22

People and Places

Across:

1. Abraham's wife (Genesis 18:10).
4. Abraham's daughter-in-law (Genesis 24:61).
6. Rebekah's home (Genesis 11:31).
7. Abraham's son (Genesis 21:3).
8. Abraham's early home (Genesis 11:31).
9. Abraham's nephew (Genesis 19:23).

Down:

2. Terah's son (Genesis 18:18).
3. Abraham's new home (Genesis 17:8).
5. Abraham's grandson (Genesis 25:27).
7. New name given to Jacob (Genesis 32:28).

Abraham's Diary

The first event has been filled in. Complete the rest.

Genesis 12:1, 2 Today the Lord told me to go to a new land. He will bless me and my family.

Genesis 12:6, 7 ____________________

Genesis 12:10 ____________________

Genesis 17:5, 15 ____________________

Genesis 21:1-3 ____________________

Memory Verse: Hebrews 11:6

Joseph's Journal

(Complete the rest of the events as though you were Joseph.)

Important Events in My Life:

Genesis 37:1-4: In Canaan I received a special coat from my father.

Genesis 37:12-28: In Shechem ______________________

Genesis 39:1-4: In Potiphar's house ______________________

Genesis 39:20-23: In prison ______________________

Genesis 41:39-46: In the palace ______________________

Work the Puzzle

The letters in the heavy squares will spell the name of the main character in our lesson.

1. The father of twelve sons (Genesis 49:1).
2. The ruler in the land of Egypt (Genesis 47:2).
3. The name of Joseph's wife (Genesis 41:45).
4. The youngest of the twelve brothers (Genesis 44:12).
5. Joseph was sold as a slave to this man, who was one of Pharaoh's officers (Genesis 39:1).
6. The brother who offered to become a slave in the place of Benjamin (Genesis 44:18, 33).

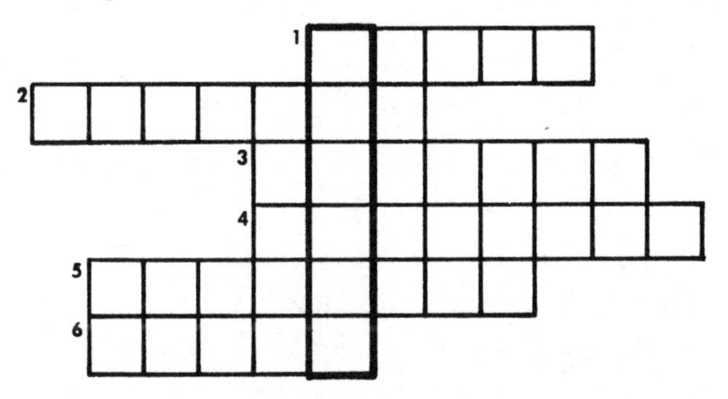

Memory Verse: Romans 8:28

Lesson 4
Adventures With Moses

Moses' Memoirs

If Moses had chosen his greatest adventure, which one might it have been? Pretend that you are Moses writing your memoirs. Choose one of these and write it in your own words.

1. In the Desert (Exodus 3:1-6)

2. Crossing the Red Sea (Exodus 14:19-22)

3. On Mount Sinai (Exodus 19:16-20)

____

____

____

Matching Questions

1. The family of Jacob had
2. The children of Israel
3. Moses took the branch of a tree and
4. When the people became hungry, God gave them
5. On top of Mount Sinai, God wrote on tablets of stone
6. While Moses was up on the mountain talking with God,
7. Because of their lack of faith, the people had to
8. Joshua and Caleb were the only two who thought

a. manna from Heaven to eat.
b. lived in Egypt for many years.
c. the people made and worshiped a golden calf.
d. the people could take the land of Canaan.
e. put it in the bitter water to make it sweet.
f. crossed the Red Sea on dry land.
g. travel in the wilderness for forty years.
h. laws for the Israelites.

Memory Verse: Philippians 4:19

Lesson 5
Adventures With Joshua

Choose the Right Words

1. The new leader of the children of Israel was
   A. Gibeon C. Ai
   B. Joshua D. Achan
2. When the priests, carrying the ark of the covenant, touched the Jordan River, the water
   A. turned to blood
   B. parted to let them through
   C. became bitter
   D. became a raging torrent
3. To capture Jericho the Israelites marched around the city once each day for six days, and on the seventh day they
   A. shouted and blew trumpets
   B. rested
   C. decided they couldn't capture the city
   D. marched around the city seven times, blew trumpets, and shouted
4. Achan disobeyed God and
   A. took gold and clothing from the city of Jericho
   B. would not help the Israelites capture Jericho
   C. became the leader of the Israelites
   D. fought against Ai
5. Joshua made the sun stand still so he could
   A. have more time to relax
   B. march around Jericho one more time
   C. make friends with Achan
   D. rescue Gibeon and defeat five enemy kings

Joshua's Records

If Joshua had kept a journal to record his battles to conquer the promised land, it might have looked like this. Fill in the chart using the Scripture references.

Scripture	City	Scripture	Outcome of Battle
Joshua 6:1	____________	Joshua 6:24	____________
Joshua 7:2	____________	Joshua 7:5	____________
Joshua 8:3	____________	Joshua 8:28	____________
Joshua 10:31	____________	Joshua 10:32	____________
Joshua 10:34	____________	Joshua 10:35	____________
Joshua 10:36	____________	Joshua 10:37	____________

Memory Verse: 2 Timothy 2:3

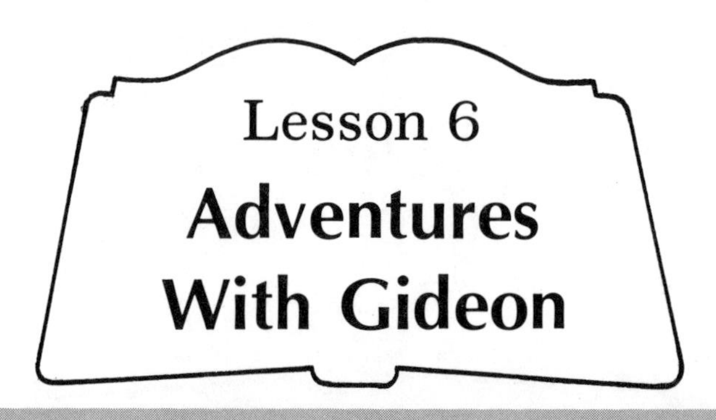

Gideon's Account

If Gideon had kept a personal diary of his talks with the Lord, he would have recorded times when he asked for special signs that the Lord was with him. Choose one of these times and write the account in your own words.

Judges 6:16-24 (The Fire That Appeared)
Judges 6:36-40 (The Fleece of Wool)

____

____

____

____

____

Acrostic Puzzle

The letters in the heavy lines will spell the name of the main character.

1. The people were led by these men who delivered them from their enemies (Judges 2:16).

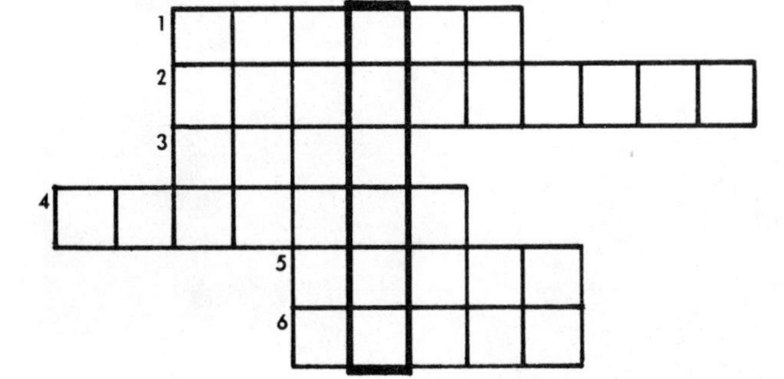

2. The name of one particular group of enemies of Israel (Judges 6:2).
3. Gideon told the men to shout, "The sword of the ____ and of Gideon" (Judges 7:18).
4. The army blew on this instrument (Judges 7:16).
5. Gideon's father (Judges 6:30).
6. Who appeared to Gideon and told him he was chosen by the Lord to lead the people? (Judges 6:12).

Memory Verse: Ephesians 6:10

Crossword Puzzle

Across:

2. The priest whom Samuel helped (1 Samuel 1:9).
3. The last judge of Israel (1 Samuel 3:7).
4. A town in the north of Israel (1 Samuel 3:20).
5. Samuel's mother (1 Samuel 1:19).
8. A town in the south of Israel (1 Samuel 3:20).
9. Enemies of the Israelites (1 Samuel 4:1).

Down:

1. Samuel's home (1 Samuel 7:17).
2. Samuel's father (1 Samuel 1:21).
6. The nation that Samuel judged (1 Samuel 4:1).
7. The idol worshiped by the Philistines (1 Samuel 5:2).

Samuel's Story

When people write stories about their lives, they often include events from their childhood. What important event could Samuel recall from his childhood? Write it here in your own words.

1 Samuel 3:1-10

____

____

____

____

____

Memory Verse: 2 Peter 1:21

Lesson 8
Adventures With Saul

Saul's Family History

Careful records of kings' families are kept. If you were in charge of recording the history of King Saul's family, you would have made a list similar to the following:

Saul's tribe: ________________________________ (1 Samuel 9:1)
Saul's father: ________________________________ (1 Samuel 9:3)
Saul's wife: ________________________________ (1 Samuel 14:50)

Saul's sons: ________________________________ (1 Samuel 14:49)
____
____

Saul's daughters: ________________________ (1 Samuel 14:49)
____

(Usually the oldest son of the king becomes the next king. What king followed King Saul? Why?)

Find the MiSSing Letters
1 Samuel 15

1. S _ _ _ _ _
2. S _ _ _
3. S _ _ _ _
4. S _ _ _ _ _
5. S _ _ _ _
6. S _ _ _ _
7. S _ _ _ _ _ _ _ _ _
8. S _ _ _ _ _

He spoke to Saul (v. 1).
He disobeyed God (v. 4).
Weapon (v. 8).
Saul said the people did this (v. 15).
What Saul said the people took (v. 21).
What Samuel could hear (v. 14).
Samuel said to obey is better than this (v. 22).
What Saul told Samuel he had done (v. 24).

Memory Verse: 1 Peter 5:6

Lesson 9
Adventures With David

Choose the Names

(Some of these names will be used more than once.)

DAVID JESSE SAUL
JONATHAN SOLOMON

1. My youngest son became the king of Israel (1 Samuel 16:1). ____________

2. My father disliked David and tried to kill him (1 Samuel 19:1). ____________

3. I became king after my father died, and I built a beautiful temple at Jerusalem (1 Kings 6:2). ____________

4. I was wounded in battle so I fell on my own sword (1 Samuel 31:4). ____________

5. I wrote many beautiful songs and played the harp (1 Samuel 16:23; Psalm 23). ____________

6. I had to flee for my life because the king wanted to kill me (1 Samuel 19:10). ____________

7. A shepherd boy played the harp to make me feel better (1 Samuel 16:23). ____________

8. I could have taken the king's life, but I would not harm one the Lord anointed (1 Samuel 24:6, 7). ____________

David's Psalms

King David wrote many psalms. One of them, Psalm 23, reminds us that David was once a shepherd. He thought of the Lord as his shepherd.

Read Psalm 23 in two or three different translations of the Bible. Then write the meaning of it in your own words.

____

____

____

____

____

____

Memory Verse: 1 John 1:9

Elijah's Problem

Elijah felt that he was all alone, that no one else in the whole kingdom was obeying the Lord's commands.

Read Elijah's problem: 1 Kings 19:9, 10.

Read the Lord's answer: 1 Kings 19:18.

Write this account in your own words, as though you were Elijah.

____

____

____

____

Fill in the Blanks

1. Read 1 Kings 17:1-7.

E_____ the prophet told King A_____ that God would not send any R_____. Then the prophet was told to hide by the brook C_____. There the R_____ would feed him.

2. Read 1 Kings 17:8-16.

God sent the prophet to the home of a W_____ and her son. She made a C_____ out of what she thought was the last of the M_____ and O_____ she had. Because she fed the prophet of God first, the B_____ where she kept the meal, and the C_____ where she kept the oil, were never empty during the famine.

3. Read 1 Kings 18:18-39.

E_____ asked the prophets of B_____ to gather on Mount C_____. Two altars were built, one for B_____ and one for G_____. The false prophets could not get F_____ to come down to burn up their S_____. When E_____ called to God, He immediately sent down fire to burn His sacrifice, even though it had been drenched in W_____.

4. Read 2 Kings 2:11.

When it was time for Elijah to leave the earth, God sent a C_____ of fire, and H_____ of fire, and Elijah was taken by a W_____ to Heaven.

Memory Verse: James 5:16

Find the Answers

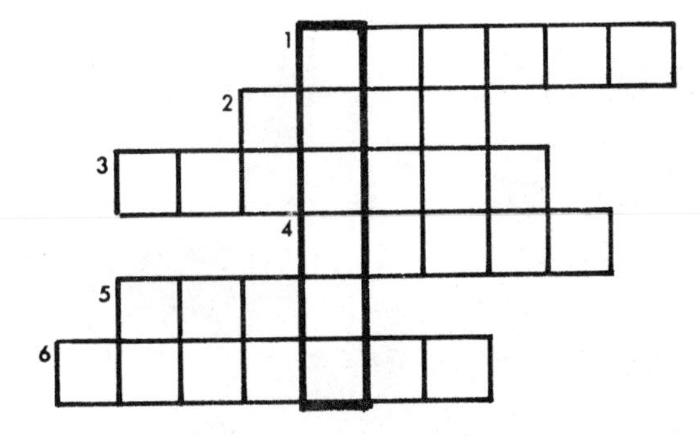

1. The name of the king who had Daniel thrown in the lions' den (Daniel 6:1).
2. Fingers of a man's ____ wrote on the wall (Daniel 5:5).
3. The thing Daniel's three friends were thrown into (Daniel 3:23).
4. Daniel's three friends would not worship this thing (Daniel 3:18).
5. The liquid drunk from the golden temple vessels (Daniel 5:4).
6. Daniel was taken to this country as a captive (Daniel 1:1).

(The word reading down in the heavy squares is the main character of this lesson.)

Daniel's Prayer Diary

Some people keep prayer diaries. They write out their prayer requests on one side of a page, and the answers God gives on the other side. Using the Scriptures listed below, write prayer requests and answers as though you were Daniel.

Scriptures	Requests	Answers
Daniel 1:8-15	____________	____________
Daniel 2:16-23	____________	____________
Daniel 6:6-12, 23	____________	____________

Memory Verse: 1 Peter 3:12

Lesson 12
Adventures With Jesus

Jesus: The Gospel Accounts

The life of Jesus fills the first four books of the New Testament. We call these books the Gospels. Choose one of the events that is recorded in all four books, and tell about it in your own words.

Event	Matthew	Mark	Luke	John
Jesus Feeds the Five Thousand	14:13-21	6:30-44	9:10-17	6:1-14
Jesus Enters Jerusalem	21:1-11	11:1-11	19:29-44	12:12-19
Jesus Is Crucified	27:31-50	15:20-37	23:26-46	19:16-30
Jesus Is Risen	28:1-8	16:1-8	24:1-12	20:1-8

Matching Quiz: The Words of Jesus

(All verses are in Matthew.)

1. Jesus to Satan: Thou shalt worship the Lord thy God . . .
2. Jesus to crowd: Repent . . .
3. Jesus to Peter and Andrew: Follow me . . .
4. Jesus to the multitude: Ask, and it shall be given you; seek . . .
5. Jesus to the disciples: Take, eat . . .
6. Jesus to Peter, James, and John: Watch and pray . . .
7. Jesus to the disciples: Go ye therefore, and teach all nations . . .

a . . . baptizing them in the name of the Father, and of the Son, and of the Holy Ghost (28:19).

b . . . and I will make you fishers of men (4:19).

c . . . and him only shalt thou serve (4:10).

d . . . and ye shall find; knock, and it shall be opened unto you (7:7).

e . . . for the kingdom of heaven is at hand (4:17).

f . . . that ye enter not into temptation (26:41).

g . . . this is my body (26:26).

Memory Verse: Hebrews 13:8

Lesson 13
Adventures With Paul

Paul's Voyage

Record Paul's voyage when he was taken to Rome as a prisoner. (All Scriptures are from Acts 27.)

1. "It was determined that we should sail into ____" (v. 1).
2. "The next day we touched at ____" (v. 3).
3. "We sailed under ____" (v. 4).
4. "We came to ____" (v. 5).
5. "We sailed under ____, over against ____" (v. 7).
6. "And . . . came unto . . . the Fair ____" (v. 8).
7. "They sailed close by ____" (v. 13).
8. "There arose . . . a tempestuous wind . . . the ship was caught . . . running under a certain island which is called ____" (vv. 14-16).

(After a shipwreck, Paul and the others wintered on the island of Melita, and then went on to Rome.)

Paul's Letters

Find the names of the letters Paul wrote to groups.

1. To the Christians in Ephesus.
2. To the Christians in Colosse.
3. To the Christians in Rome.
4. To the Christians in Corinth.
5. To the Christians in Philippi.
6. To the Christians in Galatia.
7. To the Christians in Thessalonica.

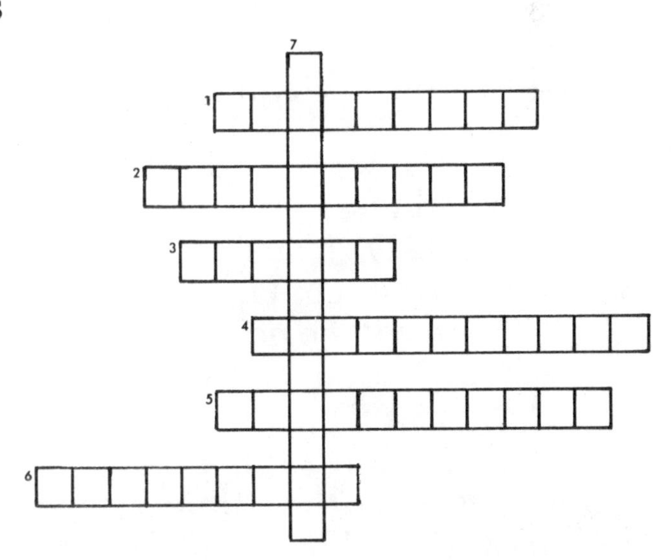

Memory Verse: Philippians 4:13

Part Two: Adventures in Christian Living

After studying "Adventures With Bible People," you are ready for "Adventures in Christian Living."

You may be surprised to learn that there is one more adventure to come, one that every Christian should be awaiting eagerly: the second coming of Christ!

How will Christ come? Why is He coming? What will happen when He comes? What will Heaven be like? These are some of the questions that are answered in God's Word.

Christ is coming on the clouds of Heaven (Matthew 24:30). Everyone will see Him (Matthew 24:27). Those who die before Christ comes will be raised from the dead at Jesus' coming (1 Thessalonians 4:14-16). Those who are alive when Jesus comes will be taken by Him into Heaven (1 Thessalonians 4:17).

In Heaven there will be no pain, no sadness, and no death (Revelation 21). Jesus' followers will live forever (Revelation 22:5). There will be no sin (Revelation 21:27). God will be there (Revelation 21:3). Christ will be there (Revelation 22:3, 4).

One question the Bible does not answer is: When will Jesus come? He will come when He is least expected (Luke 12:40). Only God knows when Jesus will come (Matthew 24:36).

The important thing to remember is to live every day as Jesus wants us to live. Then we shall be ready for His coming, no matter when it is.

Let's continue our adventures for Christ here on earth, and look forward to that last great adventure when Christ will come and take us to Heaven!

Projects for You!

Make a large scroll from a sheet of white or tan paper. Roll the sides and fasten with tape, or glue the edges. At the top, letter with black felt-tipped pen this heading: My Memory Verse Scroll.

Each memory verse that you learn during these lessons on "Adventures in Christian Living" may be added to the scroll.

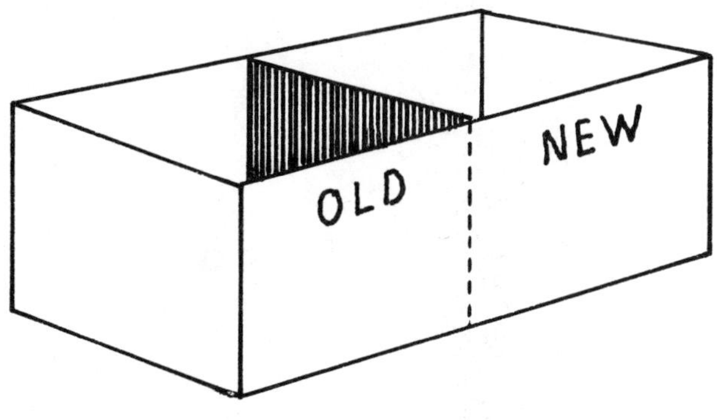

"Old and New" Game

Find a shoe box and stand a piece of cardboard in the center to make two sections in the box. (Use the lid for the cardboard divider.)

Label one end of the shoebox "Old" for Old Testament, and the other end "New" for New Testament.

On slips of paper or strips of lightweight poster board, letter the names of all the Bible characters you study during this series of lessons.

On the back of each paper containing a name, add "Old" if that person lived during Old Testament times, add "New" if the person lived during New.

Test yourself. Without looking on the backs of the papers, divide the names between the two sections of the box. Then check your own answers by turning over the cards.

Start a Spiritual Notebook

Buy a loose-leaf notebook or make your own by fastening sheets of paper together with metal rings or cord. Think of a title such as "Following Jesus" or "Way to Grow." Decorate the cover.

As you learn more about the Christian life, and what Jesus expects of you, write what you learn in your notebook.

If you have accepted Jesus as your Savior, put in the date of your "Spiritual Birthday."

Check up on yourself to see if you are growing as a Christian should in all the ways mentioned in the lessons you'll be studying.

Lesson 1

Understanding the Rules

Bible Verse Crossword

All answers are found in the book of Matthew.

Across:

4. "Love your _____" (5:44).
6. "Lay up for yourselves treasures in _____" (6:20).
8. "Lay up for yourselves _____ in heaven" (6:20).
10. "Love thy _____" (5:43).
12. "Your heavenly Father will also _____ you" (6:14).

Down:

1. "_____ your enemies" (5:44).
2. "Whosoever is _____ with his brother" (5:22).
3. "No man can _____ two masters" (6:24).
5. "Two _____" (6:24).
7. "_____ not" (7:1).
9. "But _____ ye first the kingdom of God" (6:33).
11. "The kingdom of _____" (6:33).

Memory Verse: John 14:15

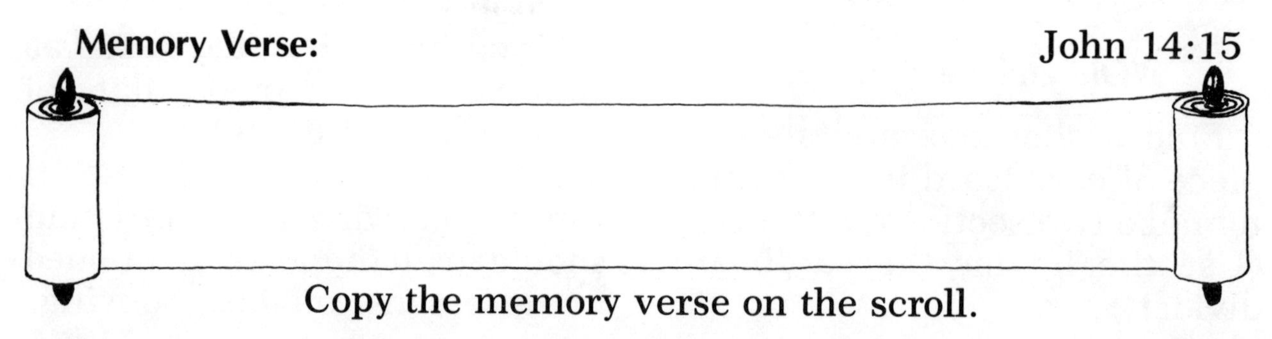

Copy the memory verse on the scroll.

Lesson 2

Following Jesus' Example

Scripture Crossword

The words to fill the squares are from six verses used in the lesson: 1 Corinthians 6:19; Luke 2:52; Matthew 5:8; Matthew 19:19; 1 John 3:22; James 1:5.

Across:

1. "In favor with God and _____."
4. "The pure in _____."
6. "Your _____ is the temple of the Holy Ghost."
7. "Blessed are the _____ in heart."
9. "Your body is the _____."
11. "We keep his _____."
12. "If any of you lack _____, let him ask of God."
13. "For they shall see _____."

Down:

2. "Thou shalt love thy _____."
3. "Jesus increased in wisdom and _____."
4. "The temple of the _____ Ghost."
5. "Thou shalt _____ thy neighbor as thyself."
8. "In _____ with God and man."
10. "Do those things that are _____ in his sight."

Matching Quiz

1. "Grow in wisdom"
2. "Grow in stature"
3. "Grow in favor with God"
4. "Grow in favor with man"

a. Matthew 19:19
b. James 1:5
c. 1 Corinthians 6:19
d. 1 John 3:22

Memory Verse: Luke 2:52

Lesson 3

Worshiping God

Places of Worship

Identify these places of worship mentioned in the Bible by drawing a line from the word to the picture.

SYNAGOGUE
TEMPLE
ALTAR
TABERNACLE

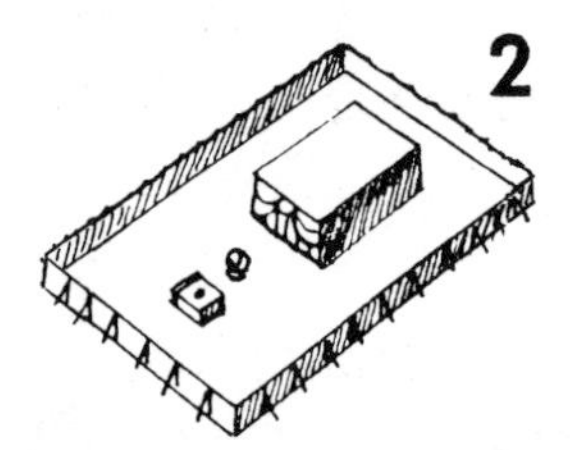

Draw a picture of the building in which your church meets. (Or paste a photo of your church building in this space.)

Circle the Scriptures

Look up these Scriptures and circle the ones that tell of worshiping God.

1. Revelation 22:9
2. Ephesians 4:32
3. Matthew 4:10
4. Luke 4:8
5. Revelation 14:7
6. Acts 2:22
7. John 4:23
8. Psalm 66:4
9. Mark 1:14
10. Acts 16:25
11. Isaiah 27:13
12. Psalm 95:6
13. John 3:16
14. Mark 2:12
15. Philippians 3:3

Memory Verse: John 4:24

Lesson 4

Sharing in the Lord's Work

Finish the Story
(Mark 12:41-44)

See how well you know this story by putting the right words in the blank spaces.

One day Jesus sat in the temple near the _____. He saw the people giving their offerings. He saw the _____ people put in _____ money. He saw a poor _____ put in _____ mites. He said to His _____, "This poor _____ has given more than all the rest because she has given _____ she had."

Can You Picture This?
Acts 4:32-37

Complete this story by drawing the right picture in each space. Choose from the pictures that are shown. One word of warning: several pictures are included that don't belong in this story. Look up the Scripture verses to make sure you get the right pictures!

The multitude of believers were of one

and soul. No one lacked anything because those who owned lands or

sold them and gave the money to the apostles. Barnabas sold his land and laid the

at the

of the apostles. Distribution was then made to every

according to his need.

Memory Verse: 2 Corinthians 9:7

Lesson 5

Praying Every Day

When Jesus Prayed

Look up these Scriptures and find where Jesus was when He prayed. Write the place below each reference.

1. Mark 1:35
2. Mark 14:15, 22, 23
3. Matthew 3:13; Luke 3:21, 22
4. Luke 5:16
5. Luke 9:10, 18
6. Luke 9:28, 29
7. Luke 22:39-41
8. John 11:38-43

Two Men Prayed

Draw lines through all sentences that are wrong in this parable about two men who prayed. (See Luke 18:10-14.)

Two men went to the temple to pray. The temple was in Jericho. They met John the Baptist there. One of the men was a Pharisee, the other a publican. A Pharisee was a tax collector. The people liked publicans. The Pharisee prayed, "I thank thee, that I am not as other men." The publican prayed, "God be merciful to me a sinner." And he jumped up and down on the floor. God heard the prayer of the publican.

The Prayer That Jesus Taught

Can you find these parts of prayer in the prayer Jesus taught (Matthew 6:9-13)?

1. Praising God:

____

____

2. Asking for help:

____

____

3. Asking forgiveness:

____

____

Memory Verse: 1 Thessalonians 5:17

Lesson 6

Reading God's Word

What Paul Said

Paul wrote these words about his pupil Timothy. Fill the blanks by looking up the references (Philippians 2:19-21).

"For this cause have I sent unto you Timothy, who is my ________________ son, and ________________ in the Lord, who shall bring you into ________________ of my ________________ which be in ________________, as I ________________ every where in every ________________" (1 Corinthians 4:17).

"But I trust in the Lord Jesus to ________________ Timothy shortly unto you, that I also may be of good ________________, when I know your ________________. For I have no ________________ likeminded, who will naturally ________________ for your state. For all seek their ________________, not the ________________ which are Jesus Christ's."

Scripture Acrostic

	1		S											
	2		C											
	3		R											
		4	I											
	5		P											
6			T											
		7	U											
		8	R											
		9	E											

(2 Timothy 3:16, 17)

1. Given by . . .
2. Profitable for . . .
3. For . . .
4. Instruction in . . .
5. For . . .
6. . . . in righteousness.
7. Thoroughly . . .
8. . . . for doctrine
9. Man of God may be . . .

Memory Verse: 2 Timothy 3:16

Lesson 7

Learning Obedience

Acrostic: People and Places

1. Mary's husband (Matthew 1:18).
2. King David's son (2 Samuel 15:13).
3. Queen of Persia, cousin of Mordecai (Esther 2:7).
4. King of Israel (2 Samuel 16:6).
5. Country ruled by King Ahasuerus (Esther 1:3).
6. Son of God (Matthew 2:1).
7. Evil man who plotted against the Jews (Esther 7:6).
8. Cousin of Esther (Esther 4:13).
9. Capital city of Israel (2 Samuel 15:14).

O
B
E
D
I
E
N
C
E

Are You Obedient?

_____ Do you obey your parents or guardians?
_____ Do you obey your teachers at school?
_____ Do you obey the laws of your town?
_____ Do you obey God willingly?

Unscramble the Sentence

Find what Jesus said about being obedient to His heavenly Father (John 8:29).

ALWAYS FOR I THINGS
DO PLEASE THOSE
HIM THAT

____

____

____

Memory Verse: John 13:17

Lesson 8

Choosing Friends

Make the Right Choices

1. Lot chose to live in
   a. a very wicked city.
   b. a place where people worshiped God.
   c. a place where some people were good and some evil.
2. Because Lot chose to live in Sodom,
   a. he was not troubled by the wickedness in the city.
   b. great troubles came to him.
   c. he was able to get many people to believe in God.
3. When Lot warned his sons-in-law that the city would be destroyed,
   a. they said they might decide to leave later.
   b. they refused to leave.
   c. they left with him immediately.
4. When the city was destroyed, Lot
   a. and all his family were saved from death.
   b. and his wife and two daughters were saved.
   c. and his two daughters were saved.
5. Lot could have avoided many sorrows if he had
   a. chosen not to associate with evil people.
   b. decided to go along with the evil people.
   c. moved to Gomorrah.

Match These Scriptures About Friends

(Proverbs 18:24; 22:24; 17:17; 17:9; 27:6; 16:28)

1. A friend	a. sticketh closer than a brother.
2. A man that hath friends	b. with an angry man.
3. There is a friend that	c. loveth at all times.
4. Make no friendship	d. must show himself friendly.
5. A whisperer separateth	e. separateth very friends.
6. He that repeateth a matter	f. of a friend.
7. Faithful are the wounds	g. chief friends.

Memory Verse: John 15:13

Lesson 9

Getting Along With Others

Unscramble and Match

1. M A R T I N A A S
2. C A D O R S
3. D D V I A
4. B A I G I L A
5. E T R E P
6. I S H L E A

a. one who was shown kindness by a husband and wife.

b. one who showed kindness to the man who was beaten and robbed.

c. one who was given power from God to raise Dorcas from death.

d. one who asked for food from a wealthy man and was refused.

e. one who made clothing for needy people.

f. one who was a peacemaker, and gave a generous gift of food to a group of soldiers.

Golden Rule

Jesus gave us a rule from God that will help us to get along with people. Find it in Matthew 7:12 and fill in the blanks.

Therefore _____ _____ whatsoever _____ would that _____ should do to _____, _____ ye even so _____ _____.

Another Rule

The apostle Paul, inspired by the Holy Spirit, gave us another rule that will help us get along with others. Find it in Ephesians 4:32 and fill in the blanks.

Be ye _____ one to _____, _____-_____, forgiving one another, even as _____ for _____ sake hath _____ you.

Memory Verse: Romans 12:18

Lesson 10

Learning Self-Control

Find Out

If you find the right answers, the first letters will spell something you should be careful not to lose.

1. _ _ _ _ _
2. _ _ _ _ _ _ _ _
3. _ _ _ _ _
4. _ _ _ _ _ _ _ _ _ _
5. _ _ _ _ _
6. _ _ _ _ _ _ _

"Thou shalt not ____ the Lord thy God" (Matthew 4:7).

"He spied an ____ smiting a Hebrew, one of his brethren" (Exodus 2:11).

"But ____ fled from the face of Pharaoh" (Exodus 2:15).

"Man shall not live by bread alone, but by every word that ____ out of the mouth of God" (Matthew 4:4).

"I shall be a fugitive and a vagabond in the ____" (Genesis 4:14).

"They did not ____ him" (Luke 9:53).

Look Up These Scriptures

Proverbs 15:1
Proverbs 14:17
Proverbs 22:24
Proverbs 29:22
Ecclesiastes 7:9
Matthew 5:22

The Printer's Mistake

Draw lines in the right places and read the Scripture:

B L E S S E D I S T H E M A N T H A T E N D U R E T H T E M P T A T
I O N: F O R W H E N H E I S T R I E D, H E S H A L L R E C E I V E T
H E C R O W N O F L I F E, W H I C H T H E L O R D H A T H P R O M
I S E D T O T H E M T H A T L O V E H I M.

Memory Verse: Ephesians 4:26

Lesson 11

Telling the Truth

"Words of Truth" Crossword

Across:

2. "I speak the truth in _____" (1 Timothy 2:7).
5. "_____ not against the truth" (James 3:14).
8. "_____ and truth came by Jesus Christ" (John 1:17).
10. "In _____ and in truth" (1 John 3:18).
11. "Ye shall _____ the truth" (John 8:32).

Down:

1. "I am the way, the truth, and the _____" (John 14:6).
3. "The _____ is not in us" (1 John 1:8).
4. "_____ the truth of God into a lie" (Romans 1:25).
5. "Speaking the truth in _____" (Ephesians 4:15).
6. "_____ unto the truth" (John 5:33).
7. "_____ in truth" (3 John 4).
9. "They shall turn _____ their ears" (2 Timothy 4:4).

Who Am I?

1. I am a prophet.
   I would not lie to the king.
   I was put in prison.
   I am _____________________.

2. I am the servant of a prophet.
   I told a lie about my master.
   I was punished with leprosy.
   I am _____________________.

3. I am a messenger from God.
   I told Herod the truth.
   I was beheaded.

   I am _____________________.

Memory Verse: Ephesians 4:25

Lesson 12

Learning to Forgive

Find These Words

The first letters, reading down, spell a word to remember:

_ _ _ _ _ _

_ _ _ _

_ _ _ _ _

_ _ _

_ _ _ _

_ _ _ _ _ _

_ _ _ _ _ _ _ _ _ _ _

"Your heavenly ____ will also forgive you" (Matthew 6:14).
"He gave his ____ begotten Son" (John 3:16).
"For thou, Lord, art good, and ____ to forgive" (Psalm 86:5).
"I see . . . the Son of man standing on the right hand of ____" (Acts 7:56).
"He . . . looked up steadfastly ____ heaven" (Acts 7:55).
"We are ____ guilty concerning our brother" (Genesis 42:21).
"Should not perish, but have ____ life" (John 3:16).

Choose the Right Words

1. Joseph (forgave, got even with) his brothers for what they did to him.

2. Jesus forgave those who crucified Him because (they asked Him to, He loved them).

3. As Stephen's enemies stoned him, he asked the Lord to (punish, forgive) them.

4. Jesus died on the cross that we might be (reminded, forgiven) of our sins.

Memory Verse: Matthew 6:14

Lesson 13

Telling Others About Jesus

Right Choices (Acts 8:26-40)

1. The road the angel told Philip to take led across the
   a. desert.
   b. mountains.
2. The Ethiopian whom Philip met there worked for
   a. the queen of Sheba.
   b. Queen Candace.
3. He had come to Jerusalem
   a. to buy supplies.
   b. to worship.
4. The Ethiopian was reading
   a. the prophet Isaiah.
   b. the Ten Commandments.
5. Philip asked him if he
   a. understood what he was reading.
   b. liked what he read.
6. Philip got into the chariot with the Ethiopian and
   a. drove to Jerusalem.
   b. preached about Jesus.
7. When they came to a pool of water, Philip
   a. stopped to rest.
   b. baptized the Ethiopian.

Word Search

The words listed below are from Acts 16:5-40. You will find the words going up, down, across, backward, and diagonally. Circle each word.

Lydia	Prison
Paul	Believe
Silas	Jesus
Philippi	Christ
Troas	Prayed
Macedonia	Sang
Baptized	Jailer
Spirit	Midnight

T	R	O	P	A	S	T	M	M	A	C	S
E	D	O	H	P	N	R	I	A	A	U	B
L	Y	D	I	A	A	O	P	C	S	T	I
S	Z	E	L	U	D	A	P	E	H	M	I
P	L	S	I	L	A	S	J	D	I	I	D
I	P	E	P	P	I	P	R	O	I	D	E
R	S	V	P	R	I	S	O	N	O	N	Z
I	N	E	I	O	P	R	A	I	Y	I	I
T	E	I	D	L	S	A	S	A	N	G	T
N	G	L	L	I	T	D	I	A	P	H	P
A	D	E	Y	A	R	P	U	L	S	T	A
I	L	B	A	J	C	H	R	I	S	T	B

Memory Verse: Mark 16:15

Part Three: Adventures With Peter

Class Projects

Felt Pennants

When you think of Peter, you think of a man of faith. You will enjoy making a pennant of felt to help you remember this. You will need these materials: a piece of felt eighteen inches long, some yarn in a contrasting color, a stick eighteen inches long, glue, and scissors.

The felt should be cut to a center point at one end. Letters may be cut from yarn and glued to the pennant. (You may wish to cut letters from felt scraps of other colors.) The stick is glued to the wide end of the pennant.

Other Scripture mottoes, in addition to "Keep the Faith," could be used. Here are two from Peter's writings:
"He careth for you" (1 Peter 5:7);
"Grow in grace" (2 Peter 3:18).

A Shoe-box Movie

You may draw pictures of the various events in Peter's life.

Use 8½ x 11″ sheets of paper, cut in half lengthwise (4¼ x 11″). The sheets may be pasted or taped together to form a long roll.

A shoe box or box of similar size may be prepared for showing the "movie." Cut a rectangular-shaped section from the bottom of the box to form the "screen." The ends of the strip of paper containing the pictures may be pasted or taped to sticks, and rolled up as a scroll.

Cut holes in the bottom and top of the sides of the box and insert the sticks. You may hold the bottom parts of the sticks as you show your movie to an audience, rolling the pictures from one stick to the other.

You may prepare a script to go along with the pictures, or take turns with other students explaining the scenes.

Perhaps you will want to present this "movie of Peter's life" to a group of younger children. For a presentation to a large group, you may wish to use a bigger box, such as a grocery carton, and larger paper, such as a roll of shelf paper.

If you wish, you may make your own shoe-box movie as a reminder of the lessons.

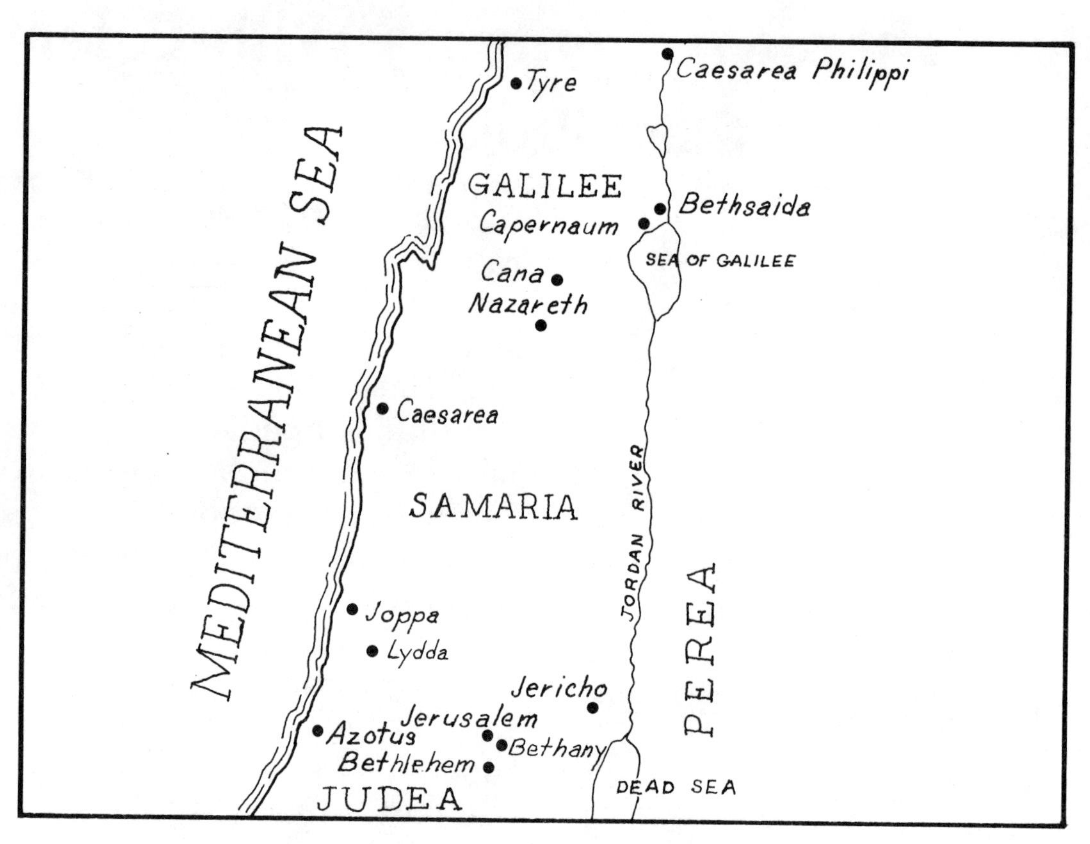

Map of Peter's Travels

You are beginning a study of "Adventures With Peter." He was a fisherman who had lived in BETHSAIDA, but then went to CAPERNAUM.

Peter became a follower of Jesus. He was chosen as one of the twelve apostles. One night the apostles were in a boat on the SEA OF GALILEE when a sudden wind came up. Jesus appeared, walking on the water. Peter tried to walk to Jesus, but he began to sink and Jesus saved him.

At CAESAREA PHILIPPI, Peter confessed that Jesus is Christ, the Son of the living God.

In JERUSALEM, Jesus ate the Passover meal with Peter and the other apostles; then He was arrested, put on trial and, crucified. Peter saw Jesus after He arose from the tomb. In that same city Peter preached the first gospel sermon, and later healed a man who had been lame from birth.

In SAMARIA Peter encountered a man named Simon who had been a sorcerer, or magician.

In LYDDA, Peter healed a man named Aeneas. He went then to JOPPA, where he raised Dorcas from the dead. From there, Peter traveled up the coast to CAESAREA to preach to Cornelius.

These are some of the places where Peter, the apostle, traveled to do the work that Jesus wanted him to do.

Who Do Men Say That I Am?

Words to Remember

All of the memory verses in this study about Peter are taken from Jesus' words to Peter, Peter's words to Jesus, Peter's messages to others, or Peter's letters to Christians. You'll want to learn all of these verses.

The song on this page, "Who Do Men Say That I Am?" contains these Bible verses: Matthew 16:13-16. Part of the song (verses 3 and 4) will be found in "Words to Remember," the memory verses for Lesson 2. You can sing as well as say this Scripture passage.

Lesson 1

Peter Becomes a "Fisher of Men"

Peter's Occupation

Answers are found in Matthew 4:18-20.

If your answers are correct, Peter's occupation will appear in the heavy squares.

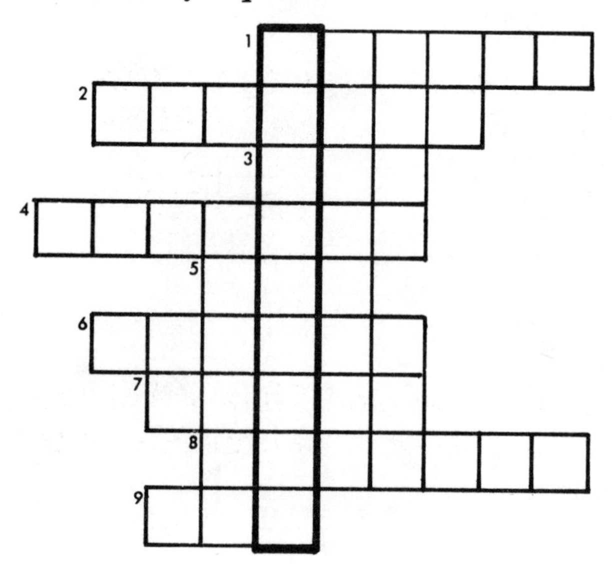

1. What did Jesus tell Peter and Andrew to do?
2. By what sea did Jesus find them?
3. Into what were they casting a net?
4. What relation was Andrew to Peter?
5. What were they using to catch fish?
6. What was the name of Peter's brother?
7. What was Peter's other name?
8. What was Jesus doing beside the sea?
9. What did Jesus say they would catch?

Scrambled Names

Write the right names on the blank lines.

1. Peter is known also as M I N O S and as P E C A H S.

_______________ _______________

2. Peter once lived in T H E B D A I A S.

____

3. Peter's brother was named E R A N W D.

____

4. Peter's fishing partners were M A J S E and H O J N.

_______________ _______________

Words to Remember: Mark 1:17

Jesus said, "______________________________

______________________________."

Lesson 2

Peter's Faith in Jesus

Word Maze

J	O	H	N	W	S	P	A
G	A	L	I	L	E	E	L
P	P	S	R	E	A	T	M
R	O	M	C	F	D	E	O
O	S	W	A	T	E	R	T
P	T	I	E	S	X	T	S
H	L	N	S	L	S	E	I
E	E	D	A	I	U	L	T
T	S	U	R	H	S	I	P
S	J	H	E	P	E	A	A
O	C	R	A	T	J	S	B
J	E	R	E	M	I	A	S

In this maze are fourteen words from the two stories about Peter's faith. The words may be found across, up, down, and diagonally.

GALILEE	CAESAREA
PETER	JEREMIAS
APOSTLES	ELIAS
SEA	PROPHETS
WIND	CHRIST
WATER	JOHN
JESUS	BAPTIST

(Jeremias and Elias are different ways of spelling Jeremiah and Elijah.)

Faith . . .

1. "Faith ______________________________" (James 2:20).
2. "Faith is ______________________________ ______________________________" (Hebrews 11:1).
3. "Faith cometh ______________________________ ______________________________" (Romans 10:17).

Words to Remember: Matthew 16:15, 16

Jesus said to Peter, "______________________________ ______________________________."

Peter replied, "______________________________ ______________________________."

Lesson 3

Peter Learns Some Lessons

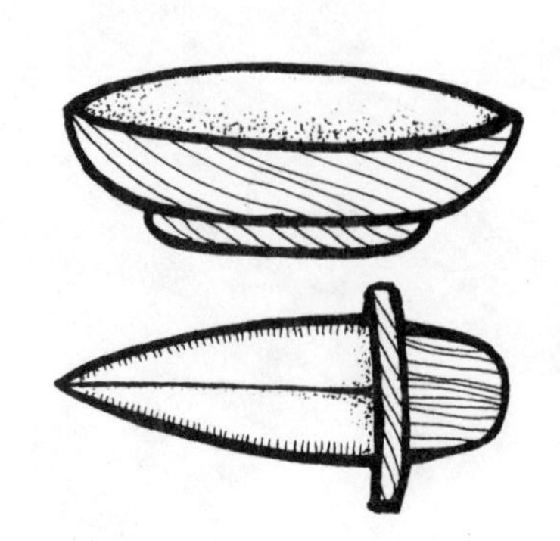

Put These Events in Order

These are the stories about Peter that we have studied. Number the events in the order they occured.

_____Peter sees Jesus, Moses, and Elijah on the mount.
_____Peter tries to walk on the water.
_____Peter becomes a fisher of men.
_____Peter eats the last supper with Jesus.
_____Peter makes the "good confession."
_____Peter tries to defend Jesus with his sword.

Fill in the Blanks

PETER	DISCIPLES
JESUS	SERVANT

1. The disciples and Jesus came together for the Passover the night before _______________ was to be crucified.
2. Jesus took a basin and a towel and washed the feet of His _______________.
3. _______________ said he would not let Jesus wash his feet.
4. It was the task of a _________ to wash the feet of a guest.
5. The followers of __________ had to be ready to do anything for Him.

What Peter Learned

Write one of these statements on each line below: Love is the only weapon. Listen only to Jesus. Be willing to serve others.

1. What did Peter learn at the transfiguration of Jesus?
____
2. What did Peter learn when Jesus washed the disciples' feet?
____
3. What did Peter learn in the Garden of Gethsemane?
____

Words to Remember: Matthew 26:41

Jesus said to Peter, "_______________
____
_______________________________."

Lesson 4

Peter Denies Christ

Crossword Review (Luke 22:54-62)

Across:

2. Peter ____ by the fire (v. 56).
5. They had kindled a ____ (v. 55).
6. The ____ crowed (v. 60).
8. Jesus was led into the ____ priest's house (v. 54).
10. "Of a ____ this fellow also was with him" (v. 59).
13. The fire was in the ____ (v. 55).
14. Peter wept ____ (v. 62).
17. Peter ____ (v. 62).
19. A certain ____ said of Peter, "This man was also with him" (v. 56).
20. Peter ____ Him, saying, "Woman, I know him not" (v. 57).

Down:

1. Peter followed afar off when Jesus was led to the high ____ house (v. 54).
3. They ____ Jesus and led Him (v. 54).
4. "This man was also ____ him" (v. 56).
7. Peter went ____ (v. 62).
9. "He is a ____" (v. 59).
11. Another person accused Peter about one ____ later (v. 59).
12. Jesus had said that Peter would ____ Him three times (v. 61).
13. He denied ____ (v. 57).
15. While he spoke ____ cock crowed (v. 60).
16. The ____ turned and looked at Peter (v. 61).
18. Peter said, "____, I am not" (v. 58).

Words to Remember: Luke 22:32

Jesus said to Peter, "________________________
____
________________________________."

Lesson 5

Peter's Love for Jesus

Memory Verse Match-up

1. "Come ye after me . . .
2. "Thou art the Christ . . .
3. "Watch and pray . . .
4. "But I have prayed for thee . . .
5. "Thou knowest all things . . .

A . . . that ye enter not into temptation."
B . . . that thy faith fail not."
C . . . the Son of the living God."
D . . . and I will make you fishers of men."
E . . . thou knowest that I love thee."

Peter Goes Fishing

Read John 21:3-12. Close your Bible and see if you can fill the squares in the puzzle. If your work is correct, the letters in the heavy lines, reading down, will spell the name of some of the people in the story.

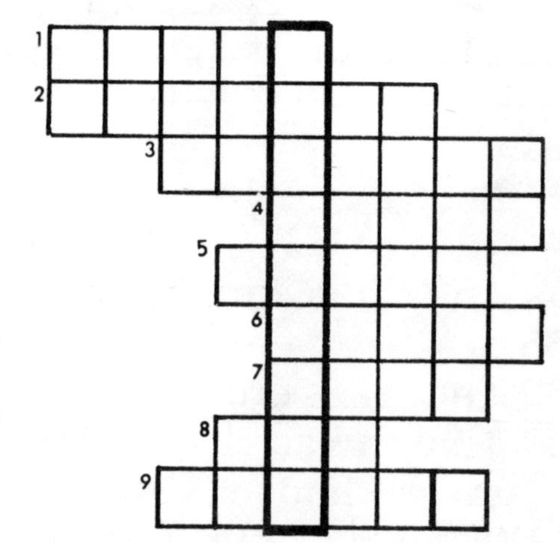

1. What was to be eaten with the fish? (v. 9)
2. What time of day was it? (v. 4)
3. Where was Peter going? (v. 3)
4. What was being used for the fire? (v. 9).
5. When had the fishermen caught nothing? (v. 3)
6. Who jumped into the sea? (v. 7)
7. What did John call Jesus? (v. 7)
8. With what did the fishermen fish? (v. 8)
9. What did they finally catch? (v. 11)

Words to Remember: John 21:17

Jesus said to Peter, "__________________?"
Peter replied, "__________________."
Jesus said, "__________________."

Lesson 6

Peter Preaches to the Jews

Acrostic Clues

The words reading across can be found in Acts 2.

1. Where the church began.
2. What Peter told the people to do first.
3. Who guided the apostles in their teaching?
4. What fiery things appeared?
5. When did the church begin?

The letters inside the heavy lines, reading down, spell the name of the One whose church was established.

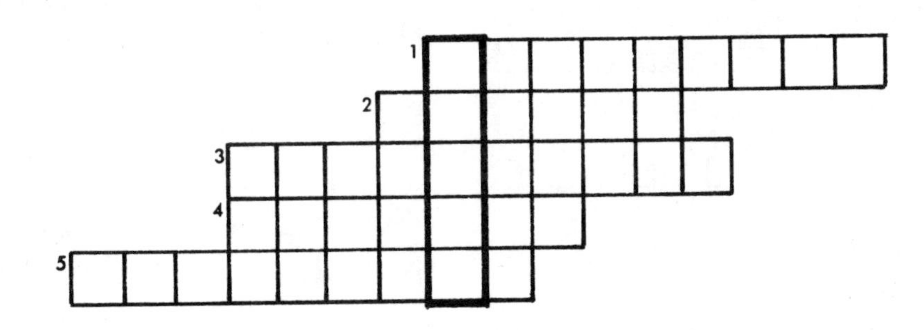

Match the Meanings

Acts 2:42

1. Continued	a. Talking to God
2. Steadfastly	b. Communion
3. Apostles' doctrine	c. Sharing
4. Fellowship	d. Teachings
5. Breaking of bread	e. Faithfully
6. Prayers	f. Kept doing

Words to Remember: Acts 2:38

Peter said, "______________________________

____

____

_____________________________________."

Lesson 7

A Lame Man Is Healed

Find the Missing Words (Acts 3, 4)

1. "They saw the ____ of Peter and John" (4:13).
2. "Which before was ____ unto you" (3:20).
3. "He leaping up stood, and ____" (3:8).
4. "Ye ____ of the people" (4:8).
5. "Then ____ said, Silver and gold have I none" (3:6).
6. "A notable ____ hath been done" (4:16).
7. "Immediately his ____ and ankle bones received strength" (3:7).
8. They "commanded them not to speak at all nor teach in the name of ____" (4:18).
9. "The ____ man which was healed" (3:11).

The word in the heavy lines, reading down, is the name of the temple gate where the man sat.

Three-way Match-ups

Draw lines to connect the sentences:

1. Peter and John	A. asked for alms	a. at the hour of prayer
2. The people	B. took him by the hand	b. at the temple gate
3. The lame man	C. went to the temple	c. and lifted him up
4. Peter	D. ran to Peter and John	d. in Solomon's porch

Words to Remember: Acts 3:6

Peter said, "________________________________

____

________________________________."

Lesson 8

A Lesson About Honesty

Make It Right

In a way this quiz is like the man and woman in our Bible story. There are some statements in this story that are not true. Read the story and cross out all the wrong information.

Ananias and Sapphira lived in Jerusalem. They were tentmakers. They had some land and decided to sell it and give the money to the apostles. They could take it off their tax to the Roman government. But they decided to keep part of the money for themselves. They would buy a new chariot with it.

When the land had been sold, Ananias brought some of the money to the apostles. Peter said, "Satan has caused you to lie to God." And Ananias fell dead. The apostles took him out and buried him.

About four hours later, Saphira, his sister, came to the apostles. She did not know that Ananias was dead. Peter asked her if the land had been sold for so much, and she said, "Yes." Peter knew she had lied, too.

"Your husband was killed with a sword," Peter told her, "and you shall die, too." She fell dead at his feet, and was taken out and buried in a different place. Great fear came upon the Christians because of what had happened to Ananias and Sapphira.

What Does God's Word Say About Telling Lies?

Colossians 3:9: ______________________

Revelation 21:27: ______________________

Revelation 22:15: ______________________

Words to Remember: 1 Peter 3:10

Peter wrote, " ______________________

____

______________________."

Lesson 9

Peter Encounters Simon the Sorcerer

Crossword Quiz

(Acts 8:1-25)

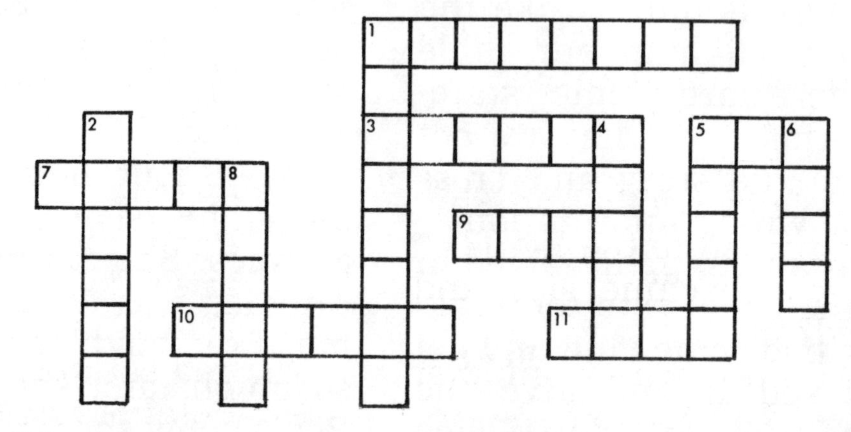

Across:

1. What did the people do when they heard Philip's message? (v. 12)
2. Who first went to preach in Samaria? (v. 5)
5. Who, with the women, were baptized? (v. 12)
7. In whose name were the people baptized? (v. 16)
9. What could not be purchased with money? (v. 20)
10. What did Peter and John preach in Samaria? (v. 25)
11. What did Simon ask Peter to do? (v. 24)

Down:

1. What did the men and women do when they believed? (v. 12)
2. What did Peter tell Simon to do? (v. 22)
4. Who went with John to Samaria? (v. 14)
5. What did Simon offer to give Peter? (v. 18)
6. Philip preached about the kingdom of God, and the _____ of Jesus Christ. (v. 12)
8. Who was called a sorcerer? (v. 9)

Words to Remember: 2 Peter 2:9

Peter wrote, " ______________________________
____
______________________________________."

Lesson 10

More Miracles

Which Verse?

Read Acts 9:32-43. Which verse tells that . . .

__ 1. Peter visited the saints (Christians) at Lydda?
__ 2. Aeneas had been sick for eight years?
__ 3. People in Lydda and Sharon turned to the Lord?
__ 4. Dorcas became sick and died?
__ 5. Tabitha was another name for Dorcas?
__ 6. Peter was in Lydda?
__ 7. Peter was asked to come to Joppa?
__ 8. Peter was taken to the "upper chamber" where Dorcas was laid?
__ 9. Dorcas had done many good works?
__10. Lydda was near the town of Joppa?
__11. Peter said, "Tabitha, arise"?
__12. Dorcas opened her eyes, and sat up?
__13. Peter saw the clothing that Dorcas had made?
__14. Peter stayed in Joppa for many days?
__15. Many in Joppa believed in the Lord?

Talents and Abilities That I Can Use for the Lord

________________________ ________________________

________________________ ________________________

________________________ ________________________

________________________ ________________________

Words to Remember: 1 Peter 4:8

Peter wrote, "________________________

____

________________________."

Lesson 11

Peter Preaches to the Gentiles

Choose the Right Word

(Acts 10)

1. Cornelius was a centurion of the (Italian, Syrian) band.
2. He prayed to God and gave (clothes, alms) to the people.
3. God told him to send for Peter who was in (Jericho, Joppa).
4. Peter was staying with Simon the (fisherman, tanner).
5. In Peter's vision he saw (clean, unclean) animals.
6. While Peter was thinking about his vision, he was told by God that (three, two) men were seeking him.
7. Peter talked to Cornelius and his family about (John, Jesus).
8. Afterward Cornelius and his family were (persecuted, baptized).
9. Peter learned that God loves (certain people, all people).

Peter's Report (Acts 11:15-18)

Across:

1. "Granted _____" (v. 18).
4. "Ye shall _____ baptized" (v. 16).
7. "The like _____" (v. 17).
8. "I began to _____" (v. 15).
9. "Baptized with _____" (v. 16).

Down:

2. "They held their _____" (v. 18).
3. "The Lord Jesus _____" (v. 17).
4. "_____ ye shall be baptized" (v. 16).
5. "Lord _____" (v. 17).
6. "The _____ gift" (v. 17).
10. "_____ he did unto us" (v. 17).

Words to Remember: Acts 10:34

Peter said, "_______________________________

____

_______________________________."

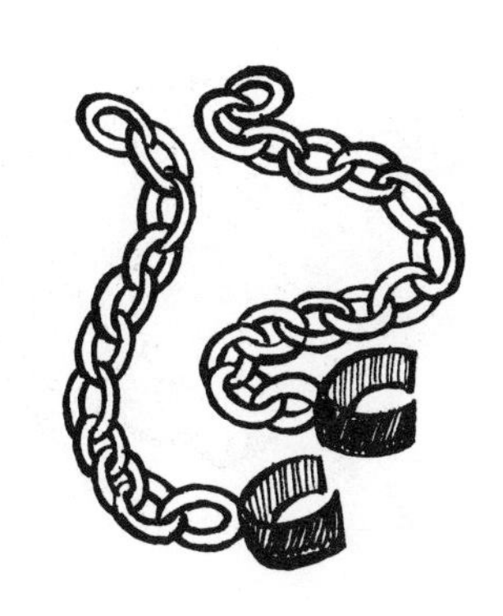

Lesson 12

Peter Is Put in Prison

First and Last (Acts 12)

_ _ _ _ _ _
_ _ _ _ _
_ _ _ _ _
_ _ _ _
_ _ _ _
_ _ _ _ _

If you get the right answers to the questions, the first letters of the first three words and the last letters of the last three words will spell something that helped Peter.

1. Where Peter was put by King Herod.
2. The name of the girl who came to the door.
3. Someone who came to Peter in prison.
4. The name of John Mark's mother.
5. Peter stood at the door of this.
6. The name of the one who was led out of prison.

Match Symbols and Stories

1. Fish in a net
2. Waves
3. Lamb
4. Tongues of fire
5. Rooster
6. Crutches
7. Clothes
8. Sheet with animals
9. Chains
10. Coins (money)

a. Peter denies Christ.
b. Jesus asks if he loves Him.
c. Peter is led out of prison.
d. Peter becomes a "fisher of men."
e. Peter tries to walk on water.
f. Peter raises Dorcas.
g. Peter preaches to Cornelius.
h. Peter meets Simon the sorcerer.
i. Peter preaches on Pentecost.
j. A lame man is healed.

Words to Remember: 1 Peter 4:16

Peter wrote, "______________________________
____
______________________________."

Lesson 13

Peter Writes Some Letters

Fill in the Blanks

Read 2 Peter 1:5-7 and fill in the blank spaces:

"Giving all diligence, add to your ________ ________; and to ________, ________; and to ________, ________; and to ________, ________; and to ________, ________; and to ________, ________ ________; and to ________ ________, ________."

Scrambled Letters

Peter was not only a leader among the apostles, a powerful preacher, and a courageous Christian, he also was a letter writer. You will find a few verses from his letters below. Some of the words have been scrambled. Find out what Peter wrote.

Gird up the S N O I L of your mind, be R O B E S, and hope to the end for the C R A G E that is to be brought unto you at the T R A V E L O N I E of Jesus Christ (1 Peter 1:13).

The D R O W of the Lord endureth for V E E R (1 Peter 1:25).

If ye F U S E R F for righteousness' sake, P H A P Y are ye (1 Peter 3:14).

H E L M U B yourselves therefore under the mighty N A D H of God (1 Peter 5:6).

Words to Remember: 2 Peter 3:18

Peter wrote, "____
____
____."

Part Four: Adventures in Bible Lands

Make a Relief Map of Palestine

Materials Needed

Pressed board or plywood, shellac or enamel paint, water colors, brushes, small dish of water, table knife, carbon paper, pencil, box large enough to enclose map, two balls of cotton, clay.

Recipe for Clay

1½ cups salt
¾ cup cornstarch
1 cup + 2 tablespoons water

Mix salt and cornstarch in a double boiler and add water. (Do not cook directly over a flame.) Stir constantly until the mixture thickens. Cool the mixture, then knead it on a platter until smooth.

Directions for Making Map

Coat the pressed board or plywood with shellac or enamel paint. Allow to dry completely.

Using carbon paper and pencil, trace the map onto board.

Flatten a lump of clay to a thickness of about one-eighth inch and to a size that covers the Mediterranean Sea. Form another lump of clay the same thickness to cover the Jordan Valley. Press these pieces of clay firmly into place on the map. Dip fingers into water if the clay becomes too sticky.

Roll a lump of clay into a thickness of one-fourth inch and lay it along the coast of the Mediterranean Sea (shaded area). Flatten another lump of clay (same thickness) and cover the remaining shaded area.

Roll a lump of clay into a thickness one-half to three-fourths of an inch thick to fit the area between the Jordan Valley and the coastal area. Form the last of the clay into a long roll to fit the eastern side of the map.

These are the suggested heights of the mountains:

Gilboa: ¼″	Gerizim: ½″
Carmel: ¼″	Ebal: ⅝″
Olivet: ⅜″	Lebanon: 1″
Tabor: ⅜″	Hermon: 1⅛″

Scrape the table knife along the outside edges of the board to make the map's edges smooth.

Place the map and two balls of wet cotton in the box and cover with a lid. Keep the map in the box for at least two days, to allow it to dry slowly and keep the clay from cracking. When the map is dry, color it with water colors. Outline the seas and color in the rivers with dark blue. Fill in the seas with a lighter shade of blue. Color the area below the Dead Sea yellow-brown to represent a desert area. Color the coastal area and the Jordan Valley light green. Color the mountains light brown. (The tops of Lebanon and Hermon are white to indicate that they are snowcapped.)

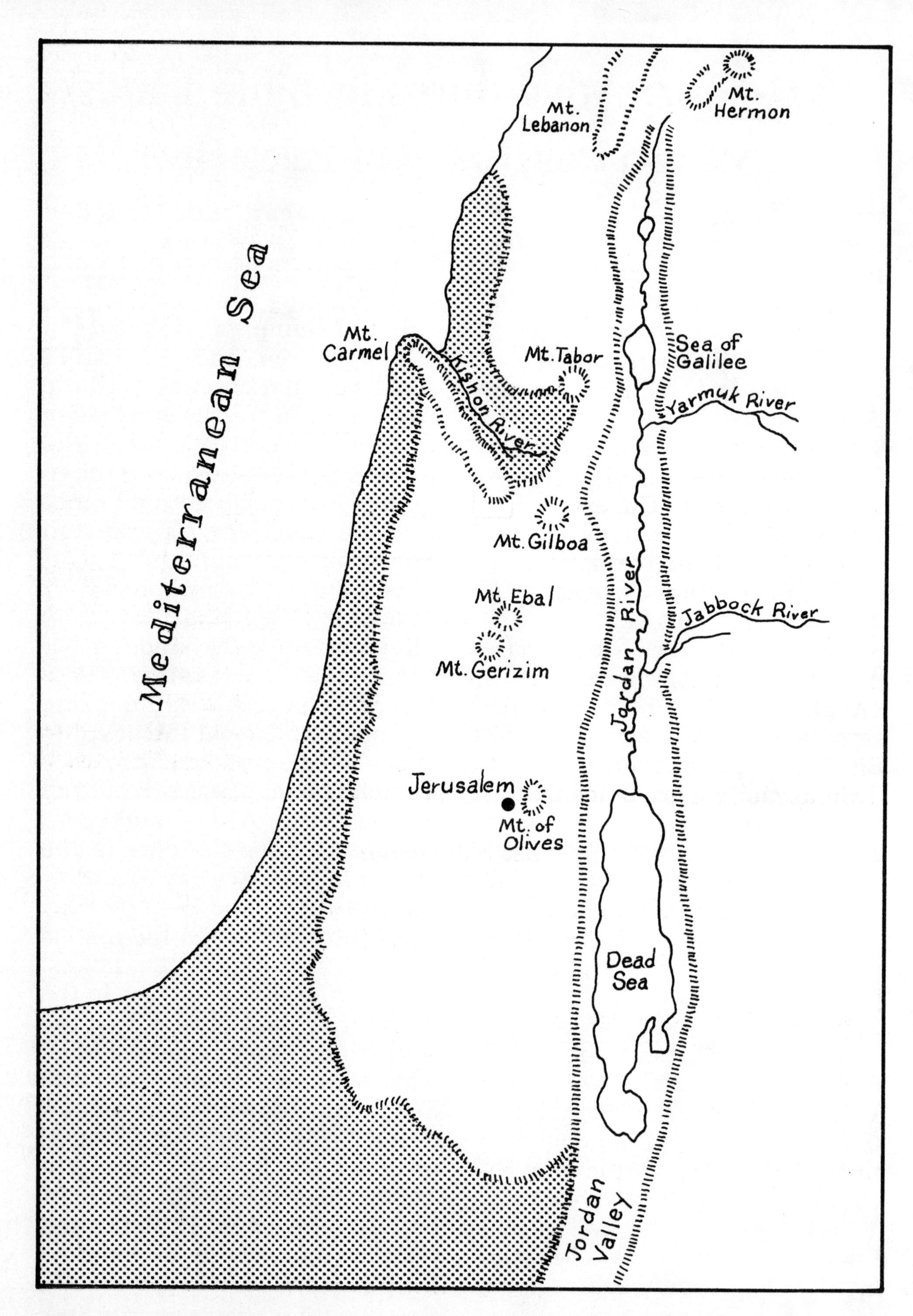
Mt.
Hermon
Mt.
Lebanon
Mediterranean Sea
Mt.
Carmel
Kishon River
Mt. Tabor
Sea of
Galilee
Yarmuk River
Mt. Gilboa
Mt. Ebal
Mt. Gerizim
Jabbock River
Jordan River
Jerusalem
Mt. of
Olives
Dead
Sea
Jordan
Valley

Lesson 1

Damascus

Find Out

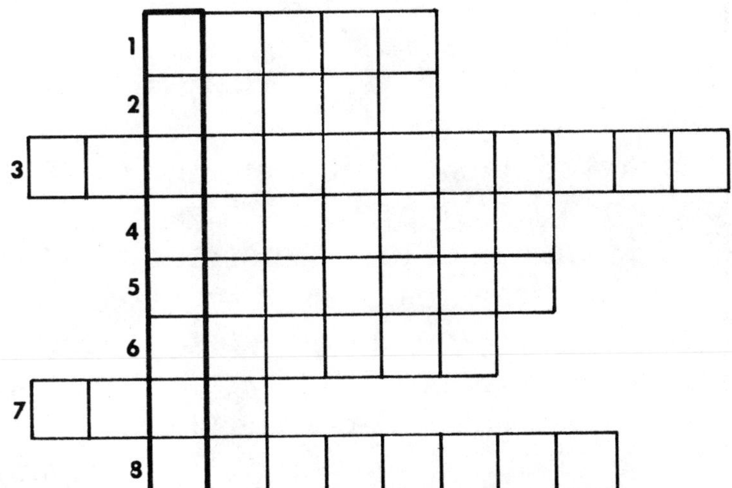

The letters in the heavy lines will tell you the name of a city.

1. A king who captured Damascus (2 Samuel 8:6).
2. A man who rescued his nephew from a place near Damascus (Genesis 14:14, 15).
3. What King Joash and the people disobeyed (2 Chronicles 24:20).
4. The man who was sent to give Saul a message from Jesus (Acts 9:10, 11).
5. The people who captured the Israelites and took them to Damascus (2 Chronicles 24:24).
6. What Saul preached in the synagogue (Acts 9:20).
7. Paul's name before it was changed (Acts 9:22).
8. The name of the street where Paul stayed in Damascus (Acts 9:11).

Match the Verses

2 Chronicles 24:20
2 Samuel 8:6

Genesis 15:1
Acts 9:22

1. "Fear not, Abram: . . .
2. "And the Lord preserved David . . .
3. "Because ye have forsaken the Lord, . . .
4. "But Saul increased the more in strength, . . .

A . . . whithersoever he went."
B . . . he hath also forsaken you."
C . . . and confounded the Jews which dwelt at Damascus, proving that this is very Christ."
D . . . I am thy shield, and thy exceeding great reward."

Memory Verse: 1 Corinthians 15:57

Lesson 2

The Sea of Galilee

What Happened Here?

Below is a list of Bible events. Cross out the ones that did not happen on or by the Sea of Galilee.

1. Jesus called four fishermen to follow Him (Matthew 4:18-22).
2. The Israelites crossed on dry land (Joshua 2:10).
3. Jesus preached to the people from a boat (Luke 5:1-3).
4. Jesus was baptized by John the Baptist (Mark 1:9-11).
5. Jesus visited Zaccheus (Luke 19:1, 2).
6. Jesus stilled a storm (Luke 8:22-25).
7. Jesus walked on the water (John 6:1, 18-21).
8. Jesus asked His disciples who people thought He was (Mark 8:27).
9. Naaman dipped in the water seven times (2 Kings 5:14).
10. Jesus crossed the water to get to Capernaum (Matthew 9:1; 4:13).

A Puzzle

Find a sea when you put the right words in the squares.

1. Jesus and His disciples preached the _____ (Mark 1:14, 15).
2. Jesus _____ on the waters of Galilee (John 6:19).
3. Jesus _____ to four fishermen (Matthew 4:18-22).
4. Jesus said to the stormy waters, "Peace, be _____" (Mark 4:39).
5. What did Jesus come to show and teach? (John 13:34).
6. Four of Jesus' disciples were _____ (Matthew 4:18-22).
7. What was the name of the Son of God? (Mark 1:1).

1
2
3
4
5
6
7

Memory Verse: Matthew 8:27

Lesson 3

Capernaum

What's the Word?

1	2	3	4	5	6	7	8	9
__	__	__	__	__	__	__	__	__

1. If Jesus went to the centurion's house, put X under 4; if He did not, put R under 5.
2. If Jairus' daughter died, put U under 8; if she was only sick, put A under 9.
3. If Matthew was a fisherman, put P under 7; if he was a publican, put M under 9.
4. If Peter's mother-in-law had the palsy, put A under 1; if she was sick with a fever, put A under 2.
5. If the centurion loved his servant, put P under 3; if he did not, put K under 8.
6. If the tax collectors were not popular with the people, put N under 6; if they were well-liked, put L under 3.
7. If the man Jesus healed in the synagogue at Capernaum had an unclean spirit, put E under 4; if he had palsy, put S under 5.
8. If a sick man was let down through a roof, put A under 7; if he was brought through a door, put K under 5.
9. If Jesus was disappointed in the centurion's faith, put S under 1; if He marveled at the man's faith, put C under 1.

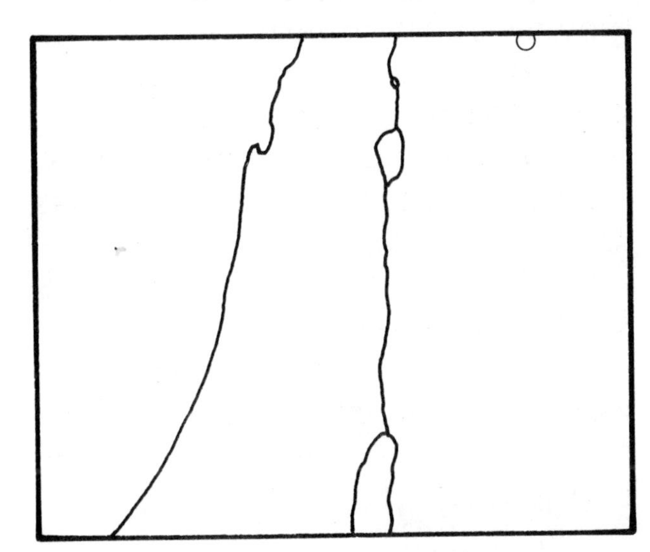

Map Study

Check up on your map knowledge! Add these places that you have studied: Damascus
Sea of Galilee Capernaum

Ways I Can Show My Faith in Jesus

____

____

____

Memory Verses: John 20:30, 31

Lesson 4
Nazareth

Crossword Review

All these Scripture verses are from the book of Luke.

Across:

1. City Jesus visited when He was twelve years old (2:42).
5. City where Jesus, Mary, and Joseph lived (2:51).
6. Mary's husband (2:43).
7. Where Jesus went on the Sabbath Day in Nazareth (4:16).
9. The angel who was sent to Mary (1:26).
11. The angel told Mary that the _____ Ghost would come upon her (1:35).
13. Jesus increased in wisdom and _____ (2:52).
14. Jesus returned in the _____ of the Spirit into Galilee (4:14).
16. "He shall reign over the house of _____ for ever" (1:33).
18. Jesus said, "This day is this Scripture fulfilled in your _____" (4:21).
19. "Of his _____ there shall be no end" (1:33).

Down:

2. Mary's cousin (1:36).
3. The mother of Jesus (1:27).
4. Elisabeth's son (1:60).
6. The Son of God (2:43).
8. "Jesus returned in the power of the Spirit into _____" (4:14).
10. Another way of spelling the name of the prophet Esaias.
12. "The _____ of God was upon him" (2:40).
15. Jesus was "filled with _____" (2:40).
17. "And he closed the _____" (4:20).

Can you add "Nazareth" to the map on page 51?

Memory Verse: Acts 10:38

Lesson 5

The Jordan River

Crossword Clues

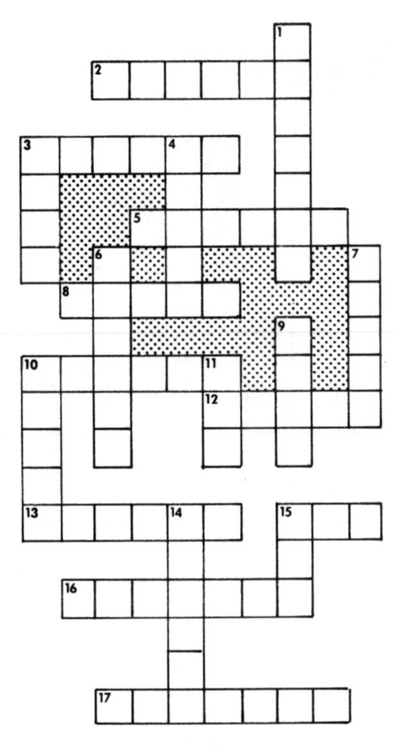

The words used in this puzzle are found in these Scriptures:

Joshua 3 2 Kings 5
2 Kings 2 Matthew 3

Across:

2. The prophet who struck the waters of the Jordan with his cloak and walked across on dry ground.
3. The river in which Jesus was baptized.
5. The army captain who had leprosy.
8. When Naaman dipped in the Jordan, his skin became ____.
10. The leader who brought God's people across the Jordan.
12. John was baptizing people in the Jordan ____.
13. The ____ of God came in the form of a dove and rested upon Jesus after His baptism.
15. What Naaman was told to do in the Jordan River.
16. Disease that Naaman had.
17. God said, "This is my ____ Son."

Down:

1. One of the rivers in Naaman's country.
3. The one who baptized Jesus.
4. Another river in Naaman's country.
6. The prophet who told Naaman how to be cured.
7. The priests were to carry the ark of the covenant and step into the ____.
9. The Spirit of God came in this form.
10. The Son of God.
11. What the priests carried into the Jordan River.
14. The land where the Jordan River flows.
15. The Israelites walked across on ____ ground.

Memory Verses: Matthew 3:16, 17

Lesson 6

Jericho

Find the Word

The first letters of the words, reading down, will spell the name of a city.

— — — — —
— — — — —
— — — — — — — —
— — — — — — — — — — — —
— — — — — —
— — — — —
— — — — — —

1. The name of the one who healed the blind men (Matthew 20:34).
2. The land from which Moses led the Israelites (Joshua 5:6).
3. Zaccheus said, "I _____ him fourfold" (Luke 19:8).
4. Jesus touched their eyes and _____ their eyes received sight (Matthew 20:34).
5. The promised land (Joshua 5:12).
6. Jesus said, "This day is salvation come to this _____" (Luke 19:9).
7. The blind men said to Jesus, "Lord, that our eyes may be _____" (Matthew 20:33).

Four-way Matching

Joshua	sitting	wayside	in Jericho
Zaccheus	marching	city wall	outside of Jericho
Blind men	climbing	sycamore tree	around Jericho

Match the right names, places, and actions and write them on these lines.

____

____

____

Read More Scriptures About Salvation

Romans 1:16
Ephesians 6:17
Acts 4:12
2 Corinthians 6:2
1 Peter 1:5
2 Timothy 2:10
Philippians 2:12
1 Thessalonians 5:8

Memory Verse: Luke 19:10

Lesson 7

Jerusalem

Fill the Blanks (Acts 2:38-42)

1. Peter told the people to ______________________________
____

2. Three thousand people were ______________________________

3. They continued steadfastly ______________________________
____
____
____

The "New Jerusalem" Word Search

Circle the words to fill these blanks. Words are found going up, down, forward, and backward.

1. "And I saw a new heaven and a new _ _ _ _ _" (v. 1).

2. "I _ _ _ _ saw the _ _ _ _ _ _ _ _, new _ _ _ _ _ _ _ _ _" (v. 2).

3. "God shall wipe away all _ _ _ _ _ from their eyes; and there shall be no more _ _ _ _ _, neither _ _ _ _ _ _, nor _ _ _ _ _ _, neither shall there be any more _ _ _ _" (v. 4).

4. "And he said unto me, _ _ _ _ _: for these words are true and faithful" (v. 5).

5. "Her _ _ _ _ _ was like unto a stone most precious" (v. 11).

6. "A _ _ _ _ great and high, and had _ _ _ _ _ _ _ _ _ _ _" (v. 12).

7. "He that talked with me had a golden _ _ _ _ to measure the city" (v. 15).

8. "The first foundation was jasper; the second; _ _ _ _ _ _ _ _; . . . the fourth, an _ _ _ _ _ _ _; . . . the ninth, a _ _ _ _ _" (vv. 19, 20).

9. "The twelve gates were twelve _ _ _ _ _ _ . . . and the street of the city was pure _ _ _ _" (v. 21).

10. "They which are written in the Lamb's _ _ _ _ _ _ _ _ _ _" (v. 27).

T S Q B C R T R E E D
W A G O L D E A V M J
E F A O Q E T I E E E
R L T K P A I N R R R
I I E O N T R B C A U
H G S F S H W O R L S
P H O L Y C I T Y D A
P T P I T E W K I T L
A E R F W J O H N O E
S T T E A R S T G P M
P E A R L S A R Z A V
C T W E L V E A G Z D
P W O R R O S E O L S

Memory Verse: Revelation 22:14

Lesson 8

Bethlehem

Guess My Name!

_ _ _ _ _ _ _ _ _
1 2 3 4 5 6 7 8 9

My first is in bake,
but not in cake.
My second's in pet,
but not in pat.
My third is in try,
but not in fry.
My fourth is in hat,
but not in cat.
My fifth is in help,
but not in heap.

My sixth is in beat,
but not in boat.
My seventh is in hair,
but not in pair.
My eighth is in meat,
but not in moat.
My ninth is in mow,
but not in row—
Together they spell a place
you know!

Match the Families

All of these people lived for a time in Bethlehem.

Wives	*Husbands*	*Children*
1. Ruth	A. Elimelech	a. Joseph
2. Rachel	B. Joseph	b. Obed
3. Naomi	C. Boaz	c. Mahlon
4. Mary	D. Jacob	d. Jesus

Family History

Joseph and Mary traveled to Bethlehem to be taxed. Joseph was descended from the family of King David, who came from Bethlehem. In Matthew 1:1-17, you will find the names of Joseph's ancestors. Can you unscramble the names?

First try to unscramble without looking in your Bible.

1. M A H A R B A (v. 1)
2. C A I S A (v. 2)
3. B O J A C (v. 2)
4. Z A B O (v. 5)
5. D E O B (v. 5)
6. E J S E S (v. 6)
7. D I V A D (v. 6)
8. N O M O L O S (v. 7)
9. B O A M O E H R (v. 7)
10. S A A (v. 8)

Memory Verse: John 3:16

Lesson 9

The Dead Sea

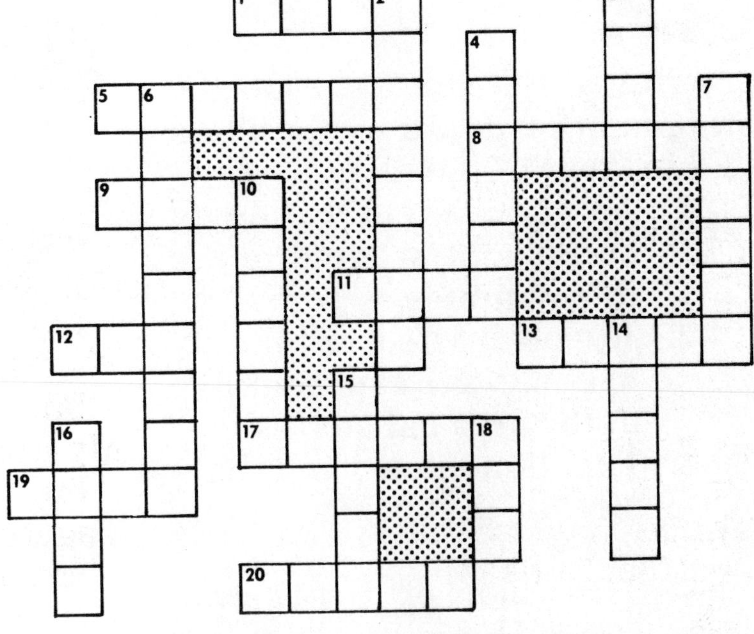

Crossword Quiz

The answers to the questions are found in these Scriptures:

Genesis 18:20-33; 19:1-29
Numbers 33:50-56; 34:1-16
1 Samuel 24

Across:

1. What was David chosen to be?
5. Who asked the Lord to spare Sodom if at least ten good people could be found?
8. Which tribe bordered the Dead Sea, just above the land of Moab?
9. What did the Lord rain upon Sodom and Gomorrah?
11. What king was jealous of David?
12. Who was Abraham's nephew?
13. Who gave the people God's instructions on dividing the promised land?
17. What were the Israelites to destroy in the promised land?
19. Where was David hiding from Saul?
20. What tribe bordered the Dead Sea across from the tribe of Reuben?

Down:

2. What other wicked city was to be destroyed with Sodom?
3. What country was just below the tribe of Reuben?
4. What nation was to possess the promised land?
6. What else did God rain from Heaven on the wicked cities?
7. Who were sent into Sodom to bring Lot and his family out?
10. In what wilderness was David hiding?
14. In what city did Lot live?
15. Who had an opportunity to do evil, but did good instead?
16 and 18. What is another name for the Dead Sea?

Memory Verse: Romans 12:21

Lesson 10

The Land of Egypt

True or False?

Write a "T" in front of the statements that are true, and an "F" in front of the false.

__ 1. Abraham went to Egypt because he wanted to see the pyramids.

__ 2. Joseph invited his family to come to Egypt and live in the area called Goshen.

__ 3. The Israelites lived happily in Egypt for many years.

__ 4. The ruler of Egypt was called Herod.

__ 5. After Joseph died, the new ruler of Egypt made slaves of the Israelites.

__ 6. The Israelites were forced to work in the salt mines.

__ 7. The Israelites prayed to God for help.

__ 8. God sent Moses to lead His people out of Egypt.

__ 9. Moses led the Israelites across the Dead Sea.

__10. The Egyptians who followed after them were drowned in the sea.

__11. Joseph took Mary and the baby Jesus to Egypt.

__12. They stayed in Egypt until Jesus was twelve years old.

Map Problem

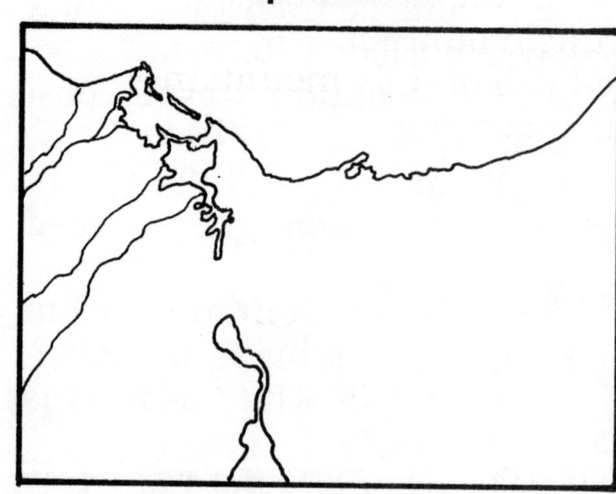

These places have been left off the map. Can you add them?

1. The country of Egypt
2. The land of Goshen
3. The Red Sea
4. The Mediterranean Sea

(Look at the map on page 61, and find this section.)

What Does God's Word Say About Jealousy and Envy?

Proverbs 6:34
Romans 1:29, 32
Galatians 5:21
Romans 13:13
Galatians 5:26
James 3:16

Memory Verse: James 3:16

Lesson 11

Bible Mountains—Part 1

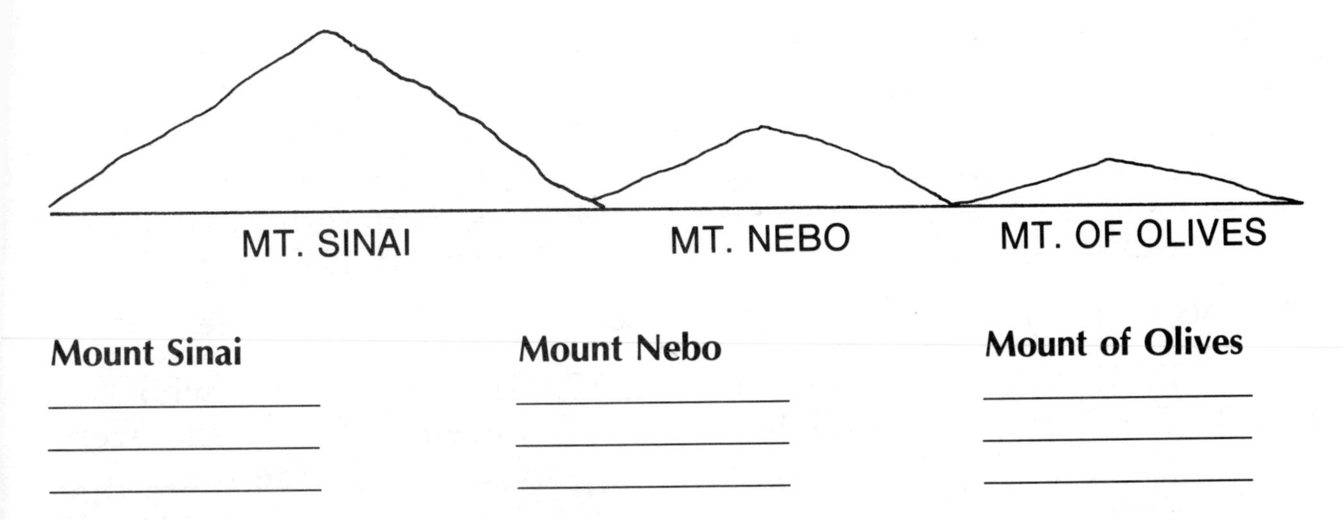

Mount Sinai	Mount Nebo	Mount of Olives
______________	______________	______________
______________	______________	______________
______________	______________	______________

Under each mountain, place the letters that tell of events that took place on that mountain, or facts about the mountain.

A. Jesus rode down this mountain into Jerusalem.
B. Moses went up into this mountain for the Ten Commandments.
C. Jesus prayed in a garden on this mountain.
D. Moses viewed the promised land from this mountain.
E. Jesus went back to Heaven from this mountain.
F. Moses may have seen the burning bush on this mountain.
G. Moses died and was buried on this mountain.
H. This mountain is between Egypt and the land of Canaan.
I. This mountain was in the land of Moab.

Fill the Blanks

Psalm 121:1, 2

"I will lift up mine _____ unto the _____, from whence cometh my _____. My help cometh from the _____, which made _____ and _____."

Psalm 125:2

"As the _____ are round about _____, so the _____ is round about his _____ from henceforth even for _____."

Memory Verse: Hebrews 13:6

Lesson 12

Bible Mountains—Part 2

MT. GERIZIM   MT. EBAL   MT. CARMEL   MT. HERMON

Mounts Gerizim and Ebal	Mount Carmel	Mount Hermon
____________	____________	____________
____________	____________	____________
____________	____________	____________

Under each mountain place the letters showing the events that took place on that mountain or facts about the mountain.

A. Elijah challenged the false prophets of Baal to a contest.
B. Jesus took three of His disciples here to pray.
C. The people stood to listen to God's laws.
D. God's voice said, "This is my beloved Son: hear him."
E. The people shouted, "The Lord, He is God!"
F. Moses and Elijah appeared and talked to Jesus.
G. God sent fire down from Heaven to burn the sacrifice.
H. Moses told the people to read God's law at this place.
I. Joshua put up a stone and wrote God's laws on it.

Climb the Mountains

Can you name these mountains?

1. The mountain where Jesus talked with Moses and Elijah was _____.
2. The mountain where God gave Moses the Ten Commandments was _____.
3. The mountain from which Jesus ascended into Heaven was _____.
4. The mountain from which Moses viewed the promised land was _____.
5. The mountains where the "blessings" and "cursings" were read were _____ and _____.
6. The mountain where Elijah built an altar to the true God was _____.

Memory Verse: Romans 10:17

Lesson 13

"Adventures in Bible Lands" Review

Finish the Map

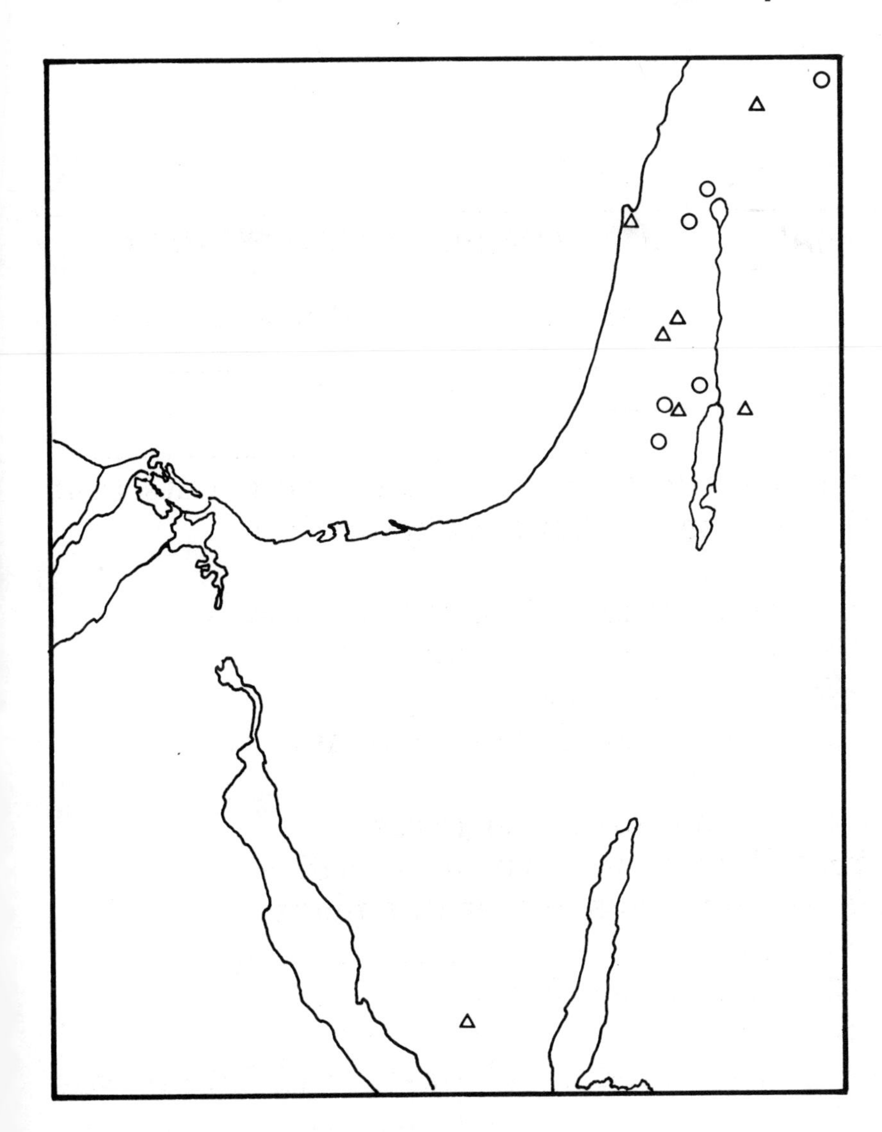

Towns:
Bethlehem
Capernaum
Damascus
Jericho
Jerusalem
Nazareth
Bodies of water:
Dead Sea
Jordan River
Red Sea
Sea of Galilee
Mediterranean Sea
(Great Sea)
Mountains:
Carmel
Ebal
Gerizim
Hermon
Olivet
Nebo
Sinai
Lands:
Egypt
Goshen

Jesus was born in ____, then taken to ____. He grew up in ____. He was baptized in the ____ ____, and spent much time teaching and preaching around the ____ ____ ____. He was crucified, buried, and raised again just outside of ____. He ascended to Heaven from the ____ ____ ____.

Jesus spent His life in a very small part of the world, but He commanded His followers to take the gospel into all the world!

Memory Verses: Matthew 28:19, 20

Answers to Puzzles

Part One: Adventures With Bible People

Lesson 1: **Noah's Logbook:** Genesis 8:4, seventh month, seventeenth day, Ark rests on Mount Ararat. Genesis 8:5, tenth month, first day, Tops of mountains seen. Genesis 8:13, first month, first day, Ground is dry. Genesis 8:14-18, second month, twenty-seventh day, God told me to take my family and leave the ark.

God Keeps His Promises:

Lesson 2: **People and Places: Across:** 1. Sarah. 4. Rebekah. 6. Haran. 7. Isaac. 8. Ur. 9. Lot. **Down:** 2. Abraham. 3. Canaan. 5. Jacob. 7. Israel. **Abraham's Diary:** Genesis 12:6, 7, The Lord promised me the land, and I built an altar. Genesis 12:10, There was a famine and I went to Egypt. Genesis 17:5, 15, God changed my name from Abram to Abraham, and Sarai's to Sarah. Genesis 21:1-3, My son, Isaac, was born.

Lesson 3: **Joseph's Journal.** In Shechem I was sold as a slave and went to Egypt. In Potiphar's house I was made overseer. In prison I was put over all the prisoners. In the palace I was made ruler over Egypt, second to Pharaoh. **Work the Puzzle:** 1. Jacob. 2. Pharaoh. 3. Asenath. 4. Benjamin. 5. Potiphar. 6. Judah. Down: JOSEPH.

Lesson 4: **Moses' Memoirs** (Pupils are to write the Scripture in their own words.) **Matching Questions:** 1. b. 2. f. 3. e. 4. a. 5. h. 6. c. 7. g. 8. d.

Lesson 5: **Choose the Right Words:** 1. B. 2. B. 3. D. 4. A. 5. D. **Joshua's Records:** Jericho, Burned the city. Ai, Lost the battle. Ai, Burned the city. Lachish, Took the city. Eglon, Took the city. Hebron, Took the city.

Lesson 6: **Gideon's Account:** (Pupils are to write the Scripture in their own words.) **Acrostic Puzzle:** 1. Judges. 2. Midianites. 3. Lord. 4. Trumpet. 5. Joash. 6. Angel. **Down:** GIDEON.

Lesson 7: **Crossword Puzzle: Across:** 2. Eli. 3. Samuel. 4. Dan. 5. Hannah. 8. Beer-sheba. 9. Philistines. **Down:** 1. Ramah. 2. Elkanah. 6. Israel. 7. Dagon. **Samuel's Story:** (Pupils are to write the Scripture in their own words.)

Lesson 8: **Saul's Family History:** Benjamin, Kish, Ahinoam, Jonathan, Ishui, Melchi-shua, Merab, Michal. (King David followed Saul. Saul's sin caused God to take the kingdom from Saul's family.) **Find the Missing Letters:** 1. Samuel. 2. Saul. 3. Sword. 4. Spared. 5. Spoil. 6. Sheep. 7. Sacrifice. 8. Sinned.

Lesson 9: **Choose the Names:** 1. Jesse. 2. Jonathan. 3. Solomon. 4. Saul. 5. David. 6. David. 7. Saul. 8. David. **David's Psalms:** (Pupils are to write the Scripture in their own words.)

Lesson 10: **Elijah's Problem:** (Pupils are to write the Scripture in their own words.) **Fill in the Blanks:** 1. Elijah, Ahab, Rain, Cherith, Ravens. 2. Widow, Cake, Meal, Oil, Barrel, Cruse. 3. Elijah, Baal, Carmel, Baal, God, Fire, Sacrifice, Elijah, Water. 4. Chariot, Horses, Whirlwind.

Lesson 11: **Find the Answers:** 1. Darius. 2. Hand. 3. Furnace. 4. Image. 5. Wine. 6. Babylon. **Down:** DANIEL. **Daniel's Prayer Diary:** (Pupils are to write the Scriptures in their own words.)

Lesson 12: **Jesus: The Gospel Accounts:** (Pupils are to choose one of the topics and tell about it in their own words.) **Matching Quiz: The Words of Jesus:** 1. c. 2. e. 3. b. 4. d. 5. g. 6. f. 7. a.

Lesson 13: **Paul's Voyage:** 1. Italy. 2. Sidon. 3. Cyprus. 4. Myra. 5. Crete, Salmone. 6. Havens. 7. Crete. 8. Clauda. **Paul's Letters:** 1. Ephesians. 2. Colossians. 3. Romans. 4. Corinthians. 5. Philippians. 6. Galatians. 7. Thessalonians.

Part Two: Adventures in Christian Living

Lesson 1: **Bible Verse Crossword: Across:** 4. Enemies. 6. Heaven. 8. Treasure. 10. Neighbor. 12. Forgive. **Down:** 1. Love. 2. Angry. 3. Serve. 5. Masters. 7. Judge. 9. Seek. 11. God.

Lesson 2: **Scripture Crossword: Across:** 1. Man. 4. Heart. 6. Body. 7. Pure. 9. Temple. 11. Commandments. 12. Wisdom. 13. God. **Down:** 2. Neighbor. 3. Stature. 4. Holy. 5. Love. 8. Favor. 10. Pleasing. *Matching Quiz:* 1. b. 2. c. 3. d. 4. a.

Lesson 3: **Places of Worship:** 1. Altar. 2. Tabernacle. 3. Temple. 4. Synagogue. **Circle the Scriptures:** 1, 3, 4, 5, 7, 8, 11, 12, 15.

Lesson 4: **Finish the Story:** Treasury, rich, much, widow, two, disciples, widow, all. **Can You Picture This?:** Heart, one, houses, money, feet, man.

Lesson 5: **When Jesus Prayed:** 1. Solitary place. 2. Upper room. 3. Jordan River. 4. Wilderness. 5. Desert place. 6. Mountain. 7. Mount of Olives. 8. Tomb of Lazarus. **Two Men Prayed:** The temple was in Jericho. They met John the Baptist there. A

Pharisee was a tax collector. The people liked publicans. And he jumped up and down on the floor. **The Prayer That Jesus Taught:** 1. "Hallowed be thy name." 2. "Give us this day our daily bread;" "Lead us not into temptation;" "Deliver us from evil." 3. "Forgive us our debts."

Lesson 6: **What Paul Said:** Beloved, faithful, remembrance, ways, Christ, teach, church, send, comfort, state, man, care, own, things. **Scripture Acrostic:** 1. Inspiration. 2. Doctrine. 3. Correction. 4. Righteousness. 5. Reproof. 6. Instruction. 7. Furnished. 8. Profitable. 9. Perfect.

Lesson 7: **Acrostic: People and Places:** 1. Joseph. 2. Absalom. 3. Esther. 4. David. 5. Persia. 6. Jesus. 7. Haman. 8. Mordecai. 9. Jerusalem. **Unscramble the Sentence:** "For I do always those things that please him."

Lesson 8: **Make the Right Choices:** 1. a. 2. b. 3. b. 4. c. 5. a. **Match These Scriptures About Friends:** 1. c. 2. d. 3. a. 4. b. 5. g. 6. e. 7. f.

Lesson 9: **Unscramble and Match:** 1. Samaritan, b. 2. Dorcas, e. 3. David, d. 4. Abigail, f. 5. Peter, c. 6. Elisha, a. **Golden Rule:** See Matthew 7:12. **Another Rule:** See Ephesians 4:32.

Lesson 10: **Find Out:** 1. Tempt. 2. Egyptian. 3. Moses. 4. Proceedeth. 5. Earth. 6. Receive. Word reading down: Temper. **The Printer's Mistake:** See James 1:12.

Lesson 11: **"Words of Truth" Crossword: Across:** 1. Christ. 5. Lie. 8. Grace. 10. Deed. 11. Know. **Down:** 1. Life. 3. Truth. 4. Changed. 5. Love. 6. Witness. 7. Walk. 9. Away. **Who Am I?:** 1. Micaiah. 2. Gehazi. 3. John the Baptist.

Lesson 12: **Find These Words:** 1. Father. 2. Only. 3. Ready. 4. God. 5. Into. 6. Verily. 7. Everlasting. Word reading down: Forgive. **Choose the Right Words:** 1. Forgave. 2. He loved them. 3. Forgive. 4. Forgiven.

Lesson 13: **Right Choices:** 1. a. 2. b. 3. b. 4. a. 5. a. 6. b. 7. b. **Word Search:**

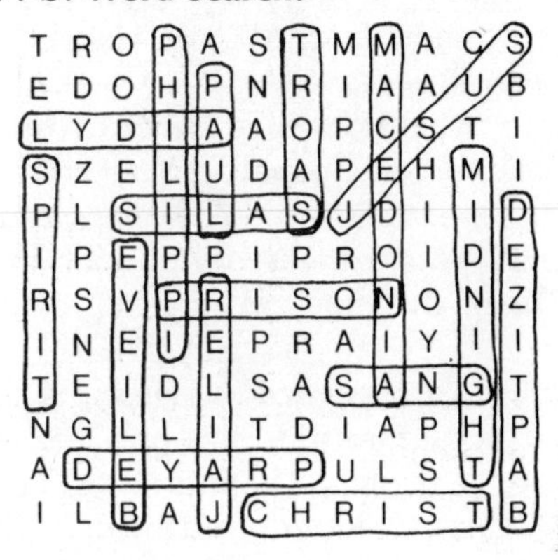

Part Three: Adventures With Peter

Lesson 1: **Peter's Occupation: Across:** 1. Follow. 2. Galilee. 3. Sea. 4. Brother. 5. Net. 6. Andrew. 7. Simon. 8. Walking. 9. Men. **Down:** FISHERMAN. **Scrambled Names:** 1. Simon, Cephas. 2. Bethsaida. 3. Andrew. 4. James, John.

Lesson 2: **Word Maze**

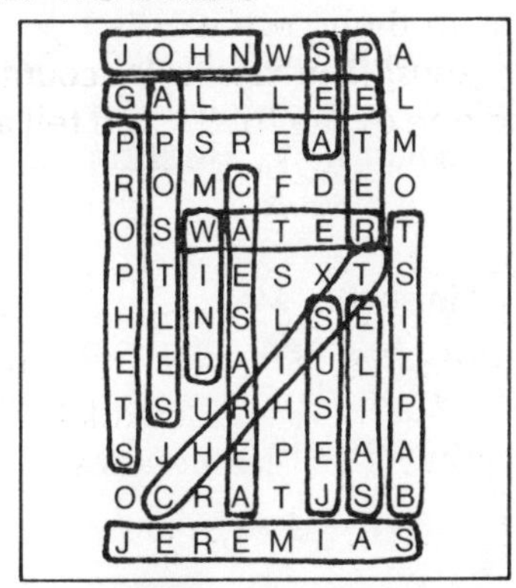

Faith . . . : (Students are to look up Scriptures.)

Lesson 3: **Put These Events in Order:** 4, 2, 1, 5, 3, 6. **Fill in the Blanks:** 1. Jesus. 2. Disciples. 3. Peter. 4. Servant. 5. Jesus. **What Peter Learned:** 1. Listen only to Jesus. 2. Be willing to serve others. 3. Love is the only weapon.

Lesson 4: **Crossword Review: Across:** 2. Sat. 5. Fire. 6. Cock. 8. High. 10. Truth. 13. Hall. 14. Bitterly. 17. Wept. 19. Maid. 20. Denied. **Down:** 1. Priest's. 3. Took. 4. With. 7. Out. 9. Galilean. 11. Hour. 12. Deny. 13. Him. 15. The. 16. Lord. 18. Man.

Lesson 5: **Memory Verse Match-up:** 1. D. 2. C. 3. A. 4. B. 5. E. **Peter Goes Fishing:** 1. Bread. 2. Morning. 3. Fishing. 4. Coals. 5. Night. 6. Peter. 7. Lord. 8. Net. 9. Fishes. **Down:** DISCIPLES.

Lesson 6: **Acrostic Clues:** 1. Jerusalem. 2. Repent. 3. Holy Spirit. 4. Tongues. 5. Pentecost. **Down:** JESUS. **Match the Meanings:** 1. f. 2. e. 3. d. 4. c. 5. b. 6. a.

Lesson 7: **Find the Missing Words:** 1. Boldness. 2. Preached. 3. Walked. 4. Rulers. 5. Peter. 6. Miracle. 7. Feet. 8. Jesus. 9. Lame. **Down:** BEAUTIFUL. **Three-way Match-up:** 1. C, a. 2. D, d. 3. A, b. 4. B, c.

Lesson 8: **Make It Right:** Cross out these statements: They were tentmakers. They could take it off their tax to the Roman government. They would buy a new chariot with it. The apostles took him out and buried him. About four hours later, Sapphira, his sister, came to the apostles. "Your husband was killed with a sword." In a different place. **What Does God's Word Say About Telling Lies?:** (Pupils are to look up the Scriptures.)

Lesson 9: **Crossword Quiz: Across:** 1. Believed. 3. Philip. 5. Men. 7. Jesus. 9. Gift. 10. Gospel. 11. Pray. **Down:** 1. (Were) Baptized. 2. Repent. 4. Peter. 5. Money. 6. Name. 8. Simon.

Lesson 10: **Which Verse?:** 1. v. 32. 2. v. 33. 3. v.

35. 4. v. 37. 5. v. 36. 6. v. 38. 7. v. 38. 8. v. 39. 9. v. 36. 10. v. 38. 11. v. 40. 12. v. 40. 13. v. 39. 14. v. 43. 15. v. 42.

Lesson 11: **Choose the Right Word:** 1. Italian. 2. Alms. 3. Joppa. 4. Tanner. 5. Unclean. 6. Three. 7. Jesus. 8. Baptized. 9. All people. **Peter's Report: Across:** 1. Repentance. 4. Be. 7. Gift. 8. Speak. 9. Water. **Down:** 2. Peace. 3. Christ. 4. But. 5. Jesus. 6. Like. 10. As.

Lesson 12: **First and Last:** 1. Prison. 2. Rhoda. 3. Angel. 4. Mary. 5. Gate. 6. Peter. **Down:** PRAYER. **Match Symbols and Stories:** 1. d. 2. e. 3. b. 4. i. 5. a. 6. j. 7. f. 8. g. 9. c. 10. h.

Lesson 13: **Fill in the Blanks:** (See 2 Peter 1:5-7.) **Scrambled Letters:** LOINS, SOBER, GRACE, REVELATION, WORD, EVER, SUFFER, HAPPY, HUMBLE, HAND.

Part Four: Adventures in Bible Lands

Lesson 1: **Find Out:** 1. David. 2. Abram. 3. Commandments. 4. Ananias. 5. Syrians. 6. Christ. 7. Saul. 8. Straight. DAMASCUS. **Match the Verses:** 1. D. 2. A. 3. B. 4. C.

Lesson 2: **What Happened Here?** Cross out 2, 4, 5, 8, 9. **A Puzzle:** 1. Gospel. 2. Walked. 3. Called. 4. Still. 5. Love. 6. Fishers. 7. Jesus. GALILEE.

Lesson 3: **What's the Word?** Capernaum. **Map Study:** Check the map on page 87 of teacher's manual.

Lesson 4: **Crossword Review: Across:** 1. Jerusalem. 5. Nazareth. 6. Joseph. 7. Synagogue. 9. Gabriel. 11. Holy. 13. Stature. 14. Power. 16. Jacob. 18. Ears. 19. Kingdom. **Down:** 2. Elisabeth. 3. Mary. 4. John. 6. Jesus. 8. Galilee. 10. Isaiah. 12. Grace. 15. Wisdom. 17. Book.

Lesson 5: **Crossword Clues: Across:** 2. Elijah. 3. Jordan. 5. Naaman. 8. Clean. 10. Joshua. 12. River. 13. Spirit. 15. Dip. 16. Leprosy. 17. Beloved. **Down:** 1. Pharpar. 3. John. 4. Abana. 6. Elisha. 7. Water. 9. Dove. 10. Jesus. 11. Ark. 14. Israel. 15. Dry.

Lesson 6: **Find the Word:** 1. Jesus. 2. Egypt. 3. Restore. 4. Immediately. 5. Canaan. 6. House. 7. Opened. JERICHO. **Four-way Matching:** Joshua, marching, city wall, around Jericho; Zaccheus, climbing, sycamore tree, in Jericho; Blind men, sitting, wayside, outside Jericho.

Lesson 7: **Fill the Blanks:** 1. Repent, be baptized. 2. Baptized. 3. In the apostles' doctrine, fellowship, breaking of bread, prayers. **The "New Jerusalem":** 1. Earth. 2. John, holy city, Jerusalem. 3. Tears, death, sorrow, crying, pain. 4. Write. 5. Light. 6. Wall, twelve gates. 7. Reed. 8. Sapphire, emerald, topaz. 9. Pearls, gold. 10. Book of life.

Lesson 8: **Guess My Name:** Bethlehem. **Match the Families:** 1. C, b. 2. D, a. 3. A, c. 4. B, d. **Family History:** 1. Abraham. 2. Isaac. 3. Jacob. 4. Booz (Boaz). 5. Obed. 6. Jesse. 7. David. 8. Solomon. 9. Rehoboam. 10. Asa.

Lesson 9: **Crossword Quiz: Across:** 1. King. 5. Abraham. 8. Reuben. 9. Fire. 11. Saul. 12. Lot. 13. Moses. 17. Images. 19. Cave. 20. Judah. **Down:** 2. Gomorrah. 3. Moab. 4. Israel. 6. Brimstone. 7. Angels. 10. Engedi. 14. Sodom. 15. David. 16 and 18. Salt Sea.

Lesson 10: **True or False?** 1. F. 2. T. 3. T. 4. F. 5. T. 6. F. 7. T. 8. T. 9. F. 10. T. 11. T. 12. F. **Map Problem:** Check the map on page 87 of the teacher's manual.

Lesson 11: **Mount Sinai:** B, F, H. **Mount Nebo:** D, G, I. **Mount of Olives:** A, C, E. **Fill the Blanks:** Psalm 121:1, 2: Eyes, hills, help, Lord, heaven, earth. Psalm 125:2: Mountains, Jerusalem, Lord, people, ever.

Lesson 12: **Mounts Gerizim and Ebal:** C, H, I. **Mount Carmel:** A, E, G. **Mount Hermon:** B, D, F. **Climb the Mountains:** 1. Hermon. 2. Sinai. 3. Mount of Olives. 4. Nebo. 5. Gerizim and Ebal. 6. Carmel.

Lesson 13: **Finish the Map:** Check the map on page 87 of the teacher's manual. Bethlehem, Egypt, Nazareth, Jordan River, Sea of Galilee, Jerusalem, Mount of Olives.

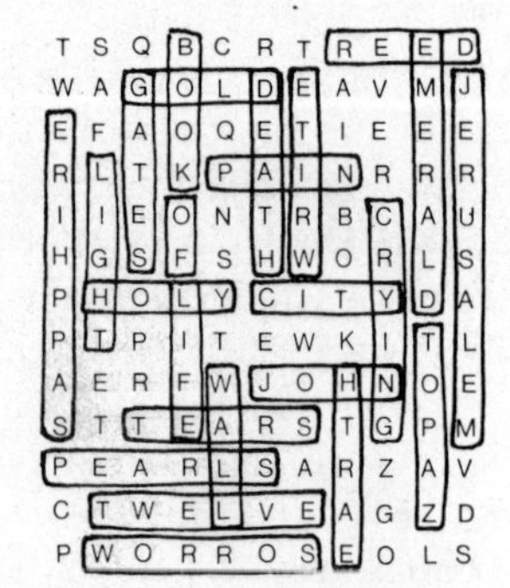